SEP -- 2013

W9-CKH-220

WITHDRAWN
Woodridge Public Library

THE WAR ON
FOOTBALL

THE WAR ON
FOOTBALL

SAVING AMERICA'S GAME

DANIEL J. FLYNN

Author of *Blue Collar Intellectuals*

WOODRIDGE PUBLIC LIBRARY
3 PLAZA DRIVE
WOODRIDGE, IL 60517-5014
(630) 964-7899

REGNERY
Publishing, Inc.

An Eagle Publishing Company • Washington, DC

Copyright © 2013 by Daniel J. Flynn

All rights reserved. No part of this publication may be reproduced or trans-
mitted in any form or by any means electronic or mechanical, including
photocopy, recording, or any information storage and retrieval system now
known or to be invented, without permission in writing from the publisher,
except by a reviewer who wishes to quote brief passages in connection with
a review written for inclusion in a magazine, newspaper, broadcast, or on a
website.

Cataloging-in-Publication data on file with the Library of Congress
ISBN 978-1-62157-155-1

Published in the United States by
Regnery Publishing, Inc.
One Massachusetts Avenue NW
Washington, DC 20001
www.Regnery.com

Manufactured in the United States of America

10 9 8 7 6 5 4 3 2 1

Books are available in quantity for promotional or premium use. Write to
Director of Special Sales, Regnery Publishing, Inc., One Massachusetts
Avenue NW, Washington, DC 20001, for information on discounts and terms
or call (202) 216-0600.

Distributed to the trade by
Perseus Distribution
250 West 57th Street
New York, NY 10107

To Tim Donovan,
the kind of kid they invented football for

CONTENTS

INTRODUCTION

Concussions mess with our brains.

Anyone within shouting distance from a television might absorb by osmosis that football increases a man's susceptibility to suicide; that its bruised and bulky players die decades earlier than their non-playing counterparts; that recalcitrant rule makers stubbornly refuse to adapt yesterday's game to today; that it results in more catastrophic head injuries than any other youthful recreation; that NFL retirees find themselves broke and broken-hearted after the cheers subside; that football solons have only recently wrapped their brains around brain injuries; and that bigger, faster, stronger competitors make the game deadlier than ever.

"The first casualty when war comes is truth," Hiram Johnson observed.[1] The War on Football affirms this aphorism. Conventional wisdom, as readers of this book will soon discover, clashes with reality in each of the aforementioned examples. But the oft-repeated falsehoods buttress the interests of lawyers seeking billion-dollar settlements from the National Football League and doctors rolling in hundreds of millions of dollars in concussion grants. The fibs make dollars, so they make sense. They also propel a tired media narrative that accentuates the negative and ignores the positive. The *news* about football may be uniformly negative, but the *facts* are overwhelmingly positive, if well hidden. Football plays safer than ever.

But the cultural tic masquerading as a public health crusade runs on emotion, not reason—even for highbrains who imagine themselves purely rational creatures. "When people die of a dumb and violent nineteenth-century game that serves no educational function, I think the obvious thing to do is to stop playing the dumb and violent nineteenth-century game," Malcolm Gladwell told an Ivy League audience in 2013. The popular *New Yorker* scribe maintains that whenever we watch football, there's a good chance that someone on the field will eventually die a terrible death as a result of playing. He candidly admits to lacking evidence for many of his beliefs. Nevertheless, he implored his student listeners to picket football games and demand that administrators ban the sport. "If they ask for proof, tell them you don't need proof. Sometimes proof is just another word for letting people suffer."[2]

The game finds itself running against cultural currents, the intellectual's aversion to "dumb" physical combat being one such headwind. Increasingly, we show ourselves cowardly in the face of danger, litigious in response to injury, lazy when the situation demands exertion, and offended if pushed, disciplined, or assigned grunt work without any glory. With school districts banning Nerf-ball dodgeball and schoolyard tag for the havoc they inflict upon young psyches, and parental wardens locking their children indoors lest the monsters of suburban neighborhoods gobble them up, nobody can say that the War on Football started by way of a Pearl Harbor sneak attack.[3] We have seen the future, and it is bubble wrapped.

Football has become a political football. "I'm a big football fan, but I have to tell you if I had a son, I'd have to think long and hard before I let him play football," President Barack Obama told the *New Republic* in January 2013. "And I think that those of us who love the sport are going to have to wrestle with the fact that it will probably change gradually to try to reduce some of the violence. In some cases, that may make it a little bit less exciting, but it will be a whole lot better for the players, and those of us who are fans maybe won't have to examine our consciences quite as much."[4]

The truth about football is a lot less scary than an unblocked Haloti Ngata closing in from your blindside. Football is good for you. Video game anesthetization, iPods blasted to eleven, and gummy bears for lunch aren't. Surely the president, who spent his teenage years in a light-hearted and light-headed marijuana-themed "Choom Gang," knows better than most that teenage boys face greater threats to brain cells than sports.[5]

American boys are overfed, overmedicated, and, to coin a term, underfathered. The adolescent obesity rate has more than tripled in the last three decades, rising from afflicting 5 percent of twelve- to nineteen-year-olds around the time the fit commander in chief graduated from high school to 18 percent today.[6] A third of the military's pool of seventeen- to twenty-four-year-old potential recruits is too physically decrepit to serve.[7] Rather than force recruits to adapt to their program, branches have diminished standards to adapt to the times. "What we were finding was that the soldiers we're getting in today's Army are not in as good shape as they used to be," Lieutenant General Mark Hertling explains. "This is not just an Army issue. This is a national issue."[8] Four in ten boys now enter the world with a father unmarried to his mother.[9] Divorce, death, and other factors ensure that too many boys grow up without a father showing them how to be men. The Centers for Disease Control and Prevention reports that one in five high school–age boys has been diagnosed with attention-deficit/hyperactivity disorder (ADHD), with doctors medicating two-thirds of those diagnosed. ADHD cases have risen by 41 percent during the last decade.[10]

Boyhood isn't a disease to be medicated away. Boyhood is the age that makes men. Boys need activity and exercise, not Ritalin and Adderall. They need competition and camaraderie. They need direction and discipline. They need male role models. They need fun. They find all this on a football field.

CHAPTER ONE

FOOTBALL IS THE
NEW SMOKING

"My gosh, I loved football," reminisces Paul Butler. "I absolutely adored playing it. For one thing, it gave me a sense of myself as a fourteen-, fifteen-, sixteen-year-old kid. It helped me to understand that if you put in hard work, you can make things happen. I learned teamwork. I learned cooperation. I learned sacrifice. I learned sportsmanship. I learned camaraderie, bonding. I learned a lot from football."

One would be hard-pressed to articulate a more forceful endorsement of football than Paul Butler's. What Butler has learned in the half century since he played at Amherst College makes him committed to banning the game.

The former end makes a strange football prohibitionist. Approaching seventy, he still skates for a no-check adult hockey club. He skis but does so wearing a helmet. "Football uses the head as a battering ram as an intrinsic part of the game," Butler reasons. "These other sports can cause deaths. There's no question about that. Even though you can have a concussion or a brain injury from them, that's not the intent of the sport. You don't use your head to bump another person's head." Butler's opposition to the game he once played isn't so dogmatic that he opposes watching it. In the fall, when his family isn't in his living room, the New England Patriots are.[1]

Before he retired a few years back, Butler fixed spleens, gallbladders, and hernias as a general surgeon at Wentworth-Douglass Hospital in Dover, New Hampshire. Like any number of small-town Yankee doctors, he comes across as intelligent, measured, and prudent, qualities that surely endeared him to voters in Dover when they elected him to their school board. Nine months into Butler's term, many of his constituents began experiencing voter's remorse.

It started on October 1, 2012, during a typically tedious Dover school board meeting. The members heard a brief on schoolhouse flu vaccines. The student representative reported that "Spirit Week and the pep rally were most enjoyable for all involved." Then, more than an hour after the Pledge of Allegiance, Butler, in a deceptively monotonous tone, livened up the proceedings.

"I think it's the moral thing to do, the ethical thing to do, to try to stop football at Dover High School and throughout all of Dover," he said. "I think the lawyers will probably stop it for us if we don't do it soon." Recommending books on concussions by former professional wrestler Chris Nowinski and forensic pathologist Dr. Bennet Omalu, Butler told his fellow overseers that they "have a moral imperative to at least begin the process of ending this game in Dover."[2]

The board responded by not responding. Following a polite but awkward pause, elderly member Doris Grady abruptly transitioned into a discussion of grammar school class sizes: "Note that Woodman Park's total numbers are climbing rapidly."[3] The school board meeting droned on, but the media recognized that something important had happened, with *Good Morning America*, the *New York Times*, and NBC News eagerly clamoring for time with Dr. Butler.

The reception in Dover wasn't so warm. The high school's athletic director noted that girls' basketball outpaced football in concussions the previous school year.[4] Fellow board member Rocky D'Andrea told the local paper, regarding concussions, "I know it's an issue, and I'm not trying to belittle it. But getting rid of a sport? If you get rid of football, you might as well get rid of all sports."[5] Butler's hometown paper editorialized against the proposed ban, portraying "athletics as an integral part of the educational process. It helps in building character, fights the obesity epidemic and encourages many to remain in school who otherwise might drop out."[6] No football—then no cheerleaders, no band, no majorettes, no pep rallies, no Spirit Week. Affection for the pigskin runs deep in Dover.

Butler confessed: "I did not expect the reaction, I must admit, that happened. If the school board somehow had sponsored smoking in the high school, it was almost as if I was saying, 'We should not sponsor smoking.'"[7]

The smoking analogy is a peculiar but popular one. Tobacco "does nothing constructive," Notre Dame coach Knute Rockne wrote to a schoolboy in 1931. "Athletes who smoke are the careless type and any advertisement to the effect that smoking cigarettes helps an athlete is a falsehood."[8] Early twentieth-century Harvard coach Bill Reid, who hatched a plan to ban coaches from smoking on the field, castigated a player through the mail: "Every time I have seen you you have been smoking and in company with a number of fellows who didn't seem any more serious than you."[9] More than a century ago, Tulane University President Edwin Alderman noted that he would prefer to see a "boy of mine on the rush line fighting for his team than on the sideline smoking a cigarette."[10]

Translation? Football and smoking go together like mayonnaise and ice cream. Sports build young bodies. Cigarettes corrode them. It's generally not the guys in varsity jackets who habituate themselves to cigarettes in high school. Nevertheless, anxious to cast a crusade against public health as one *for* public health, activists repeatedly parallel football with smoking.

- "A growing mound of research makes it clear that football is too dangerous for the human brain," Ken Reed, a Ralph Nader acolyte, explains in the *Chicago Tribune*. "It's hazardous to one's health, just like smoking. Once the evidence on smoking was clear we banned it from our high school campuses. The same fate should now happen to football."[11]

- Syndicated columnist John Kass laments that "still kids are signed up to play a game designed to punish the human body, and the brain. So why not make it simple and just give the kids packs of cigarettes instead?"[12]

- "The NFL's negative response gives the impression that it has always been aware of this but has hidden it from the public, just like the cigarette manufacturers," contends Dr. Bennet Omalu.[13]

- "Hey, why don't we let tobacco companies determine whether smoking is bad for your health or not?" Linda Sanchez, a California congresswoman, rhetorically asked about the NFL's research on the safety of its sport. "It's a very appropriate metaphor."[14]

- "I am not so sure football is not the next tobacco," Fox Sports' Jen Floyd Engel opines. A surgeon general–style mock-up graphic—"Warning: Playing Football Causes Brain Damage"—precedes the text of her article. She writes, "Dirty players do not kill players. Bounties do not kill players. Football kills players. There is no entirely safe way to play the game—not on the level we watch on Sundays—just like there is no safe amount of cigarette smoking."[15]

- "We are, however, rapidly reaching the point where playing football is like smoking cigarettes: The risks are well-known," writes Pulitzer Prize–winning columnist George Will.[16]

Smoking, according to the Centers for Disease Control and Prevention, kills five million people every year across the globe.[17] How many does football kill? The comparisons, though largely unchallenged, demand the invention of a word beyond "hyperbole."

In one crucial, unintended way, the smoking analogy holds. In 1965, a year after the surgeon general released his warning on tobacco, more than half of all Americans smoked.[18] It's hard to get a majority of Americans to do anything in unison. Greater than six in ten Americans now watch football.[19] Banning football would seem about as popular as banning ice cream. It seems preposterous—perhaps as preposterous as cigarette bans might have seemed in the mid-1960s.

Already, scattered legislators have initiated bills to restrict and even ban the game. "Pop Warner football would get blitzed out of New York if a Bronx lawmaker gets his way," explains the lead of a February 2013 *New York Daily News* story on an assemblyman's ambitions to ban tackle football for kids under eleven. "I want to protect the children," the bill's author reasons.[20] In January 2013, a state legislator in football-crazy Texas filed a bill seeking to limit tackling to one practice a week in the state's middle and high schools.[21] The same month an Illinois lawmaker introduced legislation prohibiting tackling in all but one practice per week in the state's high schools.[22]

Is the ending starting?

For the moment at least, Americans can't kick their autumn habit. The National Football League—not *The Voice*, not *NCIS*, not *60 Minutes*—boasts the highest ratings on television. The late Sunday game so dominates Nielsen's ratings that its pregame and postgame shows regularly invade the top five programs of the week, too.[23] A 2012 Harris poll on the favorite sport of American adults showed football nearly a four-to-one favorite over baseball, the second most popular sport. Thirty-six percent of respondents chose professional football, thirteen percent chose college football, and 13 percent chose baseball. In 1985, Americans were evenly split between professional baseball and professional football as their favorite sport.[24] In the 1980s, a thirty-second Super Bowl ad cost $370,000. For the 2013 Super Bowl, CBS charged upwards of $3.8 million for thirty seconds of ad time.[25] Fox's ratings for their featured late games during the regular season eclipsed Fox's ratings for Major League Baseball's World Series games.[26]

The national pastime is a thing of the nation's past time. Football is America's game. But for how long? Tastes—for cigarettes, for dueling, for premarital chastity, for books, for enslaving other humans—change. Americans once drank Schlitz, worked in factories, and listened to AM radio. They probably thought that would be the American way forever. Some players fatalistically assume that football's critics will win. NFL MVP Adrian Peterson quipped, "Sooner or later we're going to be playing touch football."[27] Heavy-hitting safety Bernard Pollard lamented before the 2013 Super Bowl, "Thirty years from now, I don't think [the NFL] will be in existence."[28]

For fans, there has been plenty of bad news. On March 2, 2012, NFL commissioner Roger Goodell suspended New Orleans Saints coach Sean Payton and linebacker Jonathan Vilma for a year, and former defensive coordinator Gregg Williams indefinitely. The commissioner found that Saints players and coaches pooled money for a slush fund that rewarded hits that sent opponents to the sidelines.[29] Two months later, retired San Diego Charger linebacker Junior Seau committed suicide, shooting himself in the chest; researchers later found that he suffered from chronic traumatic encephalopathy, a degenerative brain disease linked to blows to the head.[30] At the same time, the league defended more than 200 concussion-related lawsuits brought by more than 4,000 former players.

Football's enemies want to relegate the sport to the barbaric past. To a growing number of parents, including, apparently, the president, boys crashing into boys at full speed is just so twentieth century. In a world of parent-surveilled play dates, Xbox companionship, and monkey-bar abolitionists, football doesn't conform. It's too outdoor, too dirty, and too beyond the control of control-freak parents. Who would risk their only son to the gridiron? Play *Madden 14* instead. Video games don't injure your child's brain, right?

"Kids haven't changed. Parents have. I've never met a bad kid. I've met a lot of bad parents."[31]

Scott Lazo's observation results from eighteen years of coaching Pop Warner in Southbridge, Massachusetts, where, more than a half century ago, he played on the town's youth teams that he now leads. Like Paul Butler, former football player Lazo also serves on his city's school board. He works in the concrete business when he isn't on the football field. He also owns Lazo's Café, an unmarked bar at the end of a street of boarded up homes and old mill buildings. The anachronistic real estate reminds one of the grizzled barkeep. Can they transition into the twenty-first century? We meet at the near-empty bar on a Sunday afternoon in December before CBS televises the San Diego Chargers-Pittsburgh Steelers game to his patrons. The denizens of Southbridge know Lazo as a local politician and community character. Nationally, people know him as the coach who led his pee-wee division players to a headline-grabbing 52 to 0 thrashing over neighboring Tantasqua. That September 15, 2012, matchup left five players on the opposing team with concussions, the two head coaches suspended, and the referees banned from officiating in the league.[32]

It started seconds after the game did. The Southbridge-Tantasqua contest effectively ended on its first play. The Southbridge Pioneers took the opening kickoff for a touchdown. On the following kickoff, the Tantasqua Braves fumbled and Southbridge recovered. After just one offensive down from scrimmage, Southbridge led 16 to 0. Six minutes into the first quarter, when Southbridge held a four-touchdown lead, mercy rules kicked in.

"I tried to do everything in my power not to score again," Lazo contends. "But they were doing everything in their power to help us to score." Southbridge abandoned passes and sweeps, attempted an unlikely field goal from thirty yards, and once punted on first down. The coach inserted a lineman at tailback, but his plan backfired when the heavyset, inexperienced runner willed himself to a touchdown. In the fourth quarter, a defender intercepted a pass for a pick-six to bring Southbridge's point total above fifty.

The score hurt Tantasqua's pride. The hits hurt their heads. "In that game, the EMT never went on the field," Lazo maintains. "No kids ever fell or stayed down. I didn't see any injuries outside of a shoulder injury." He maintains he first heard of the opposition's concussions three weeks later through the grapevine.[33] His opponents contest his account. "Southbridge had an obligation to abide by the Pop Warner national mercy rules," a Tantasqua Pop Warner statement read. "These rules were not followed and were not enforced by the 3 paid referees."[34] They also charged that Southbridge gave a pass to overweight players at the pre-game weigh-in. "Nobody gets refused to play football in Southbridge," the official at the scale allegedly said.[35] "In Pop Warner," Lazo asks, "if a kid is one pound overweight, do you want to bump that kid?" Whereas Lazo dismisses the scale dispute as getting hung up on technicalities, he becomes pedantic when highlighting Tantasqua's failure to forfeit once they dropped below the minimum number of available players. Games between parents and coaches can get chippy, too.

Despite the age of most of his pee-wee players, Lazo occasionally scouts opposing teams. "We're a very small town. My team plays Boston, Springfield, Worcester—I request all the biggest and baddest towns." He beats them too. Lazo's teams have been undefeated and unscored upon the last two regular seasons. That record—and the nearly two decades he has remained in a transient position normally reserved for fathers with sons on a team—serves as proof for some that he's obsessed, too much the brusque drill sergeant and not enough the avuncular guidance counselor. "Shame on them," Lazo responds. "It's the further pussification of America. Look at the table over there. It says, 'Are you tough enough?' That's our mantra for Pop Warner football. That started probably fifty, sixty years ago. You know what the old timers used to say, 'Are you tough enough to play?'"

The motto, the blowouts, the scouting, and the intensity cause some to look at Lazo as a little too dedicated to his hobby. But perhaps his players, some of whom come from single-parent homes with fathers who are a little too out of it, benefit from a coach who is a little too into it. Aside from springing for pizza after key victories, Lazo helped pay for registration fees and team photos for players who couldn't afford it.

He and four fellow coaches chipped in $1,800 to buy new cleats for his entire team at $80 a pair.[36] He cares. Too much?

Just as the Southbridge-Tantasqua contest generated headlines, I embedded with another Massachusetts pee-wee Pop Warner team fifty miles to the northeast: the Arlington Spy Ponders.[37] The Spy Ponders practice for a crucial contest with playoff implications against the neighboring Winchester Sachems. The team that wins gets in.

Thirty years ago, when I was an eight-year-old trying to make the eleven-year-old team in Arlington, I was cut. They had more players than uniforms. Now the team struggles to field the minimum number of players. "Most of my friends, they don't play football because they don't want to, they think they'll get hurt, or they can't because they have a bunch of other sports," informs Jared, a tackle who tells me he likes "tackling people" and shows me by sacking the quarterback in the day's game. "This kid I know, he's really good but he just doesn't play because he thinks he'll get hurt."[38] His teammates echo his sentiments. "Their mothers are overprotective," Cam tells me. "Some kids don't want to get hurt. They just don't want to get hit."[39]

Many strangers don't want them to get hit, either. "It's no longer appropriate for public institutions to fund gladiators," declared Patty Sexton, a school board member in suburban Philadelphia. Like Paul Butler, she wants to abolish football. "We wouldn't dream of putting our kids in a vehicle without a seat belt, but we put them out on the field and cheer for them," Sexton said. "Our mission is to grow brains, not destroy them."[40]

"I love football," wrote Dr. Larry Robbins at RealClearSports.com, "but as a neurologist and headache specialist I have seen how football can harm a youngster's brain and life. Many of the millions of young players will live to ripe old ages, and we must protect their only brain. And one way to do that is to eliminate tackle football before age 18."[41] Neurosurgeon Robert Cantu is a little more lenient, thinking tackle football shouldn't be allowed until a boy is fourteen.[42] A retired Bay State teacher blogged, "It is time for the Commonwealth of Massachusetts to act and make tackle football illegal for young children."[43]

Whether one speaks of making tackle football illegal for kids or limiting participation to adults, the result is a de facto ban on the game. Football enigmatically remains at once the manliest team sport and the epitome of a kids' game. Whereas we exclusively watch adults playing football on our television sets, those playing the game outside of the notice of the network camera's eye are almost exclusively kids. Paul Butler still remarkably plays in a hockey league as he approaches seventy, and he could find an over-fifty baseball or basketball league if he looked hard enough. But football for the senior circuit doesn't exist. The game demands too much from aging bodies able to give very little. Kids high-school age or younger constitute about nineteen out of every twenty tackle-football participants in the United States.[44] The proposals by Dr. Butler and Dr. Robbins, if embraced on a national level, would prevent almost everyone who currently plays football from playing football. To say you don't want kids to play football is to say you don't want football played.

The hard hitting that worries adults appeals to boys. "It's a mental and physical sport," Brendan, a Spy Ponder lineman, explains. "There are things in football that you can do on the field. You can get your anger out on the field."[45] "Say there's this one kid that's making you really mad," Jack stipulates. "You can just hit him."[46] Cam, who also plays basketball, baseball, golf, and hockey, notes that he likes football best because you "get your anger out" and "get to hit hard and run fast." To get a sense of his interests beyond athletics, I ask his favorite subject in school. He tells me "physical education." I ask his favorite activity when he's not playing on a team. He says, "I like to go out and jump on my trampoline."[47]

Kids just possess a lot of energy. When you're young, you don't need coffee, Red Bull, or anything else to get you jumping off the walls. It comes naturally. Football, which Coach Lazo bluntly calls "legalized violence," serves as a conduit for all that moxie.[48] The game provides boys a structured outdoor environment to run, jump, tackle, and roughhouse—activities that boys would partake in otherwise in an unstructured environment. Classrooms often fail to contain the vigor of preteen boys, but fields funnel that energy in a positive direction.

More than a century ago, football's founding father had a bead on boys such as Cam. "Every boy who is to become a real man in the light in which we now have learned to view the real man has bred in the very marrow of his bones the desire for personal physical combat with boys of his own age on the athletic field," Yale coach Walter Camp observed, "and no game so simulates the features of such personal combat as does the sport of football."[49]

Society has changed greatly from Camp's time to Cam's time. Boys haven't.

As several of the young athletes explained to me, they love football because it serves as an outlet for their aggression. In a nation where obesity, not head injuries, remains the primary children's health concern, talk of banning youth football lacks perspective. Try as we might to repeal biological laws, boys reaffirm them by fighting, wrestling, and tackling. If football didn't exist, Cam would have invented it.

The Arlington and Winchester game is a three-yards-and-a-cloud-of-dust affair. Plays for negative yardage are common. The offenses, to their detriment, remain primitive. The defenses, to their credit, do too. The players relish putting solid hits on opponents. The squads finish regulation tied at six. It takes four overtimes for Winchester to end the stalemate.

Unlike the concussion-causing contest to the southwest, the hard-fought struggle ends without injury. "It's all coaching," maintains Winchester coach Brandon Bergstrom, a fit, fortyish father. "Most of the hitting the kids see is in practice. It's not games. You can manage practice. What it means is you teach more, prepare more, and stress fundamentals. Most of these injuries, especially at the youth level where the kids are small and the physics are a little different, most of these come from poor technique—kids leading with their heads. It's very coachable."[50]

The science meshes with Coach Bergstrom's observations. Virginia Tech researchers monitored head impacts for seven youth players. The boys experienced an average of 107 helmet impacts resulting in no concussions over the course of a season, with the most forceful and greatest number of jolts occurring not in a game but during a practice.[51] Coaching matters.

The techniques Bergstrom employs during practice, which include hitting drills atop padded mats and "form freeze" tackling that enable a coach to critique player technique in stop motion, may not be very old-school. But his team, which struggled to sustain an offensive drive, excels at tackling.

Arlington, on the other hand, runs an old-school football practice. Bull-in-the-ring, that brutal drill in which an encircled player clashes with randomly called incoming teammates, has long since been prohibited. But pretty much everything else remains from when I made the Arlington team a few years after getting cut. Drills in which ball carrier and tackler lie on the ground, helmet-to-helmet, before the whistle prompts the confrontation, and drills that task the blocker with driving the defender— "Stay low and pump your feet!"—make Arlington's practice a throwback.[52]

Their preparations differ. But on game day Winchester and Arlington compete as defensive-minded teams that put more licks on the opposition than points on the scoreboard. Had Arlington switched its maroon-and-gray for Winchester's black-and-red, nobody's mom would have been the wiser for it. Boys will be boys will be boys.

Football, as Cam and his friends remind, is cathartic. The game enables players to leave on the field what they shouldn't carry around off the field.

One hundred years prior to the controversial Southbridge-Tantasqua contest and the pedestrian Winchester-Arlington game, West Point faced off with the Carlisle Indian School in the most anticipated game of the 1912 season. As recently as two decades earlier, soldiers and Indians killed one another on the Western plains. The symbolism of the soon-to-be soldiers warring on the gridiron with Indians plucked off the reservation appeared obvious to all, particularly to Carlisle coach Glenn "Pop" Warner. "On every play I want all of you to remember one thing," Warner told his Carlisle Indians before they took the field to defeat West Point. "Remember that it was the fathers and grandfathers of these Army players who fought your fathers and grandfathers in the Indian Wars. Remember it was their fathers and grandfathers who killed your fathers and grandfathers. Remember it was their fathers and grandfathers who destroyed your way of life. Remember Wounded Knee. Remember all of this on every play. Let's go!"[53]

One imagines Scott Lazo giving a similar pep talk to his players prior to their game against Tantasqua. "They always look down on us," Coach Lazo tells me of his opponents. "They're a predominantly affluent community, predominantly white. We have a tremendous amount of Hispanics and blacks. We're a multicultural community. When it comes time and we go in, we always hear snickers and the hoots at us, and we steamroll them. We look at 'em, point to the scoreboard, and say, 'It's time to go home.'"[54]

Football, once dubbed "the Boston Game," a violent diversion for super-wealthy college boys, now attracts the bruise collar class. There's a parallel between the condescension Lazo perceives from his neighbors and the way the chattering classes are starting to talk about football. There are parallels between Lazo and Pop Warner, too—but only to a point.

Pop Warner leaked fake injury information to the press. He bankrolled his players' high living through gate receipts. He recruited athletes of dubious academic, and amateur, standing.[55] He gambled on teams he coached.[56] He pushed rules to (and past) limits by employing a hunchback hidden-ball trick, sewing to-scale football patches on jerseys to confuse opponents, and replacing an injured player with an assistant coach.[57] A century after he won through means fair and foul, the coach's name has become so synonymous with youth football that players don't even know that Pop Warner lived as a person before it did as an organization.

Like Pop Warner, Scott Lazo doesn't spare expense to win. He purchases cleats for players. He scouts other teams of eleven-year-olds. He takes great pride in preventing opposing squads of sixth graders from scoring on his defense.

Perhaps for being too much like the league's namesake, Lazo found himself suspended for the remainder of the season. A league bearing Pop Warner's name upholds standards that Pop Warner never lived up to. It's ironic. It's also progress.

It's a shame whenever coaches pile on the score in a kids' game. The worse bullying occurs when adults pile on a kids' sport.

Pop Warner played a more dangerous, and more corrupt, game than Pop Warner players do today. Football, particularly when it involves grammar school kids, plays more safely than it did a century, or even a generation, ago.

Still, as Winchester coach Bergstrom concedes, "It's a rough game. It's not for everyone."[58]

It's also not obligatory. It might soon be forbidden.

CHAPTER TWO

CONCUSSIONS, INC.

"I always wanted to play when I was younger," explains Briannah Gallo, a twenty-eight-year-old manager at Dick's Sporting Goods. "My mom never let me. She signed me up for cheerleading."

When Briannah grew up, she signed herself up for football. When she tells people that she plays in a women's professional tackle football league, "They don't believe me at all." Bubbly Briannah still looks more the part of the cheerleader, confounding stereotypes twice over—as a woman playing football and as a woman prettier than Tom Brady playing football. Briannah not only plays, she excels. An all-star defensive player, the five-foot-six cornerback has won two Super Bowl rings with the Boston Militia. Feminine athletes playing a masculine game defy society's expectations on numerous levels. In one crucial, controversial way, they conform to them: concussions.

Four years ago in a late-season game against the New York Nemesis, Briannah blitzed and got blindsided by the fullback. "I don't remember

the hit," she explains. "I don't remember anything. I just remember falling down, getting up. I didn't know at that point in time that I had a
concussion. I got up. I stayed in the game. My adrenaline was just rushing. It was the fourth quarter. I was upset that they just scored." Teammates discovered Briannah's condition only on the ensuing kickoff. "I
was on the kick return team, and I went to go line up on kickoff. I had
no idea what was going on."

Briannah received a CT scan and sat out three weeks before returning
for the playoffs. She sat out her profession—the one that enables her to
afford the $510 fee to play women's professional football—for a period,
too. "I was out of work for a few days," she notes. "It was a different
feeling. You're just groggy. You feel that everything you do is very slow
motion. It gets frustrating. You try to formulate a sentence and try to
communicate with people, and it just seems like you're not at your normal
pace. You're sitting there and you see people's reaction, 'C'mon. Spit it
out. Spit it out. Spit it out.'"[1]

Women's football, unfortunately, conjures up a perfect storm for head
injuries. A recent academic article cited football as the cause for nearly
half of all concussions in high school athletics. The findings could hardly
shock anyone following the increasingly heated debate surrounding the
sport. But the rest of the list offered surprises. Girls' soccer placed second
among the concussion-causing contests. Girls' basketball appeared in
fourth, immediately behind wrestling. The sheer number of students
participating in these popular sports helps explain their high number of
injuries. When calculating the concussion *rate*, football, the high school
sport attracting the most participants, still places first. But less mainstream sports—ice hockey and boys' lacrosse—follow closely behind.[2]

"Historically, authors of sports-related concussion studies have examined symptoms in males and focused on football because of the increased
risk of concussion in that sport," a 2011 study noted. "However, both
the risk of injury and the incidence rate of sport-related concussions are

higher among female athletes."[3] Women's football remains too much an eccentricity to attract scientific attention. But one need only put two and two together to deduce that the sex with the greater propensity for concussions playing the major team sport featuring the highest concussion rate combines for a riskier game. Sports that field teams for both sexes generally show higher concussion rates for women. Girls' soccer outranks boys' soccer, softball beats baseball, and girls' basketball places higher than boys' basketball.[4] Why would football be any different?

Chauvinists mock the notion of ladies on the field. But Briannah and her fellow competitors in the Women's Football Alliance may actually play a more dangerous game than those in the National Football League. The physics say no. The physiology says yes.

Psychology suggests that women may be more likely to report concussions than men. Physiology offers an alternative explanation for the male-female disparity. Women's heads rest on slighter necks.[5]

"We don't have as much force as men because we're not as heavy," notes Jen Pirog, "but we still hit pretty hard for our body weight." Pirog, in her first year with the Militia, knows this firsthand. Playing both linebacker and running back for an undermanned (underwomanned?) New Hampshire Freedom the previous season, Jen suffered a concussion—at which position, she still doesn't know. She remained on the field. "After the games, we go out and do a little partying," she explained. "I thought, 'Geez, I didn't drink that much. Why do I still have a hangover?' And I'm cloudy and fuzzy. Then it occurred to me when I couldn't sleep." The "hangover" lasted about four days.[6]

At forty-four, Jen Pirog is the oldest player on the roster. At twenty, Danielle Resha is the youngest. "My first day [with the team] I was petrified," Resha recalls. "I had never heard of it before. And I literally just showed up to tryouts. And I knew I was the youngest. And people were saying, 'You're still in high school?'" Like Pirog, Resha revolves her life around fitness. She works at two Boston health clubs, plays soccer in college, and interns at CrossFit. "I'm really getting into CrossFit, which is like my next big thing. I'm training with their team to hopefully participate in the games with them." In her two previous seasons with the Militia, Resha, a kicker/receiver who describes herself as a "finesse" player, avoided concussions. The collisions with soccer goalposts haven't been as forgiving as those with football players. The goalie concedes, "I've had a couple of concussions from soccer, so [football was] kind of scary at first." Despite this, she dubs the sport, in the New England vernacular, "wicked fun."[7]

Jessica Cabrera was pretty much present at the creation of women's professional football. "When people think about women in sports, they think we don't belong out there," Cabrera reflects. "I have been an athlete all my life. I like the competition. I like to prove people wrong. People say, 'Women don't belong on the football field.' Really?" Her avocation isn't as rough as her corrections officer vocation. "I get a stress reliever for work," the defensive end says. "I get the aggravation out on the field. The line of work I do sometimes you have to get physical but you have to be careful about how you get physical." That holds for the game she plays, too. When the Militia brawled with the D.C. Divas, Jessica found herself in the familiar role of peacemaker. An impromptu battle royal isn't the most dangerous part of the game; the game itself is. "I think I suffered one concussion in my thirteen years playing football. It was against the New York Sharks. I went in for a tackle and pretty much collided helmets. I'm not sure if it was with a New York player or one of my teammates. All I remember was being out"—as in *knocked out cold*. Her concussion—symptoms included headaches, blurry vision, and dizziness—"took a good two weeks" to overcome.[8]

The most-proposed way of preventing concussions in sports is to ban football. A never-proposed but nevertheless effective way of preventing concussions would be to ban girls' sports. Why sack the sport with the most concussions? Why not block the sex more prone to concussions from playing sports?

No concussion crusader dares propose anything so unfashionable. The *New Yorker* isn't going to commission Malcolm Gladwell to pen a long-form piece on the dangers of women's athletics. Their readers would rebel. And George Will won't embark anytime soon on a crusade against girls' soccer in the manner of his crusade against boys' football. A writer's reputation wouldn't survive the skirmish—and a good thing, too. Girls' soccer, like boys' football, offers exercise, life lessons, camaraderie, and a thousand other blessings that outweigh the few curses. Hang around the Boston Militia, and the profound benefits of athletics become personified.

Women's professional football exudes an infectious exuberance the likes of which could only emanate from amateurs. Observers can't help but experience a vicarious thrill. The players sense something groundbreaking about their heterodox hobby. The Boston Militia players take pride in their team, their championships, and, especially, their participation in something new and different. These women dare to stand out rather than fit in, which, in addition to remaining feminine while playing a masculine sport, means staying fit in a fat culture. If football presents so many hazards to our health, why does it attract, and produce, so many healthy people?

Somehow, banning women's football because of female concussion rates seems reactionary; banning men's football because of the sport's concussion rates seems progressive. One man's barbarism is another woman's liberation. The double standard reflects cultural attitudes toward both female athletes (self-possessed, liberated, and well-rounded) and male athletes (arrogant, stupid, and possibly criminal). Culturally, football players rub some people the wrong way, and it's hard not to read many of the anti-football screeds as inspired more by old injuries to the ego than new injuries to the head. Some people, apparently, never got over high school. They still remember the prom rejection decades later; they still resent the popularity of the girls who were cheerleaders and the guys who were jocks; the high school nose guard they would never have taken a swing at in the hallway they can now safely assault in print.

But if you were to make a list of what's wrong with America, there's no way that sports should rank . . . anywhere. Briannah, Jen, Danielle, and Jessica exemplify what out-of-shape America should strive for instead of crusade against.

"None," Danielle Resha, the work-at-two-gyms, CrossFit-competing, soccer-football player tells me of her interests beyond school and sports. "It's my life."[9] Jen Pirog barely contains a sneer when speaking about the public's confusion between women's professional football and the

Lingerie League.[10] But if the forty-four-going-on-twenty-four fitness fanatic mistakenly ambled into Lingerie League tryouts, one senses she wouldn't get cut. Briannah Gallo eschews partying for surfing, snowboarding, football, and the gym. Her leisure pursuits and sporting-goods store occupation give her jock identity away even as her outgoing personality exposes her inner-cheerleader.[11]

Sports enhance their lives. They saved Jessica Cabrera's. "I grew up in Brooklyn, New York," the former college basketball player explains. "I didn't grow up with my mom or my dad. I got moved around. It wasn't a stable lifestyle. If there weren't sports—I see where the people I hung out with ended up—I could see myself going down a negative path."[12] The corrections officer needn't return to Brooklyn to think what might have been. She need only go to work.

Sports ruin a few lives. They save many.

Paternalistically forbidding women from athletic participation because their physiology puts them at greater risk for concussions would be shortsighted. Banning football on the same grounds for the Cams and Jacks of the world similarly misses the big picture. Physicians, who exclusively see the bumps, bruises, and breaks, necessarily glean a small-picture impression. But football, the good, the bad, and the ugly, isn't just about the bad and the ugly. The game transforms weak bodies into strong ones. Better still, it shapes character and stirs souls. That's exciting. One can feel the passion by spending a fall Sunday afternoon at Arrowhead Stadium. One would feel it more by spending a few hours with the Boston Militia.

The experiences of the Militia players demonstrate why concussions vex the medical profession. Jessica, in at least one sense, lucked out when she lost consciousness. Few concussions open eyes like the ones that turn out the lights. Everybody watching and playing sensed a medical emergency because Jessica lay prostrate and unresponsive on the field. She had no say in whether she would continue to play. The medical staff determined that a hospital was a better place for her than off tackle, on the sidelines, or in the locker room. If only every concussion were as cut-and-dried as Jessica's, then diagnosis would not prove so problematic.

Concussions generally don't announce themselves so clamorously clear. They occur quietly on the outskirts of innocuous plays that escape the notice of spectators, trainers, and teammates. Think Briannah's concussion against the New York Nemesis. Not until she lined up as the twelfth player on a kick return team did anyone notice something amiss. In such circumstances, the patient must play doctor. A groggy athlete, whose training came in the weight room rather than the emergency room, issues the diagnosis. The circumstances demand a lot from a brain in command of a little.

The athlete's best trait then works toward the worst result. Hyper-competitiveness generally characterizes those who perform at a high-level. Adrenaline and gut compel them to truck on. Voluntarily taking themselves out of the game goes against their nature. So, like Jen Pirog, they fight through the pain and remain in the game, a default decision coming from a brain on autopilot.

Instinct impairs judgment. The same never-quit spirit that fuels fourth-quarter comebacks can cruelly squash an athlete's attempts to come back from the results of staying on the field too long with a concussion. It's extremely important that athletes cease to compete upon receipt of a concussion. It's also extremely unlikely that, on their own, they will all remember to act against their nature at a time when they may not remember the score, the quarter, or the date.

Time travelers from a century ago might be astonished at email, Xboxes, and iPhones, but they would immediately recognize the way we identify and treat concussions, a condition well known to them. "The term concussion, in the modern sense, was first used by one of the great-est Muslim physicians, Rhazes (AD 850–923?)," Paul McCrory and Samuel Berkovic explain in the journal *Neurology*. "This fundamental distinction between concussion as an abnormal physiologic state rather than a severe brain injury is the critical turning point in the history of the understanding of this condition." The authors write that Rhazes "taught that symptoms after a concussive injury could rapidly disappear and were the result of a transient paralysis of cerebral function caused by the brain being shaken."[13] The understanding may be old, but it's not particularly antiquated.

A lack of significant advancement in the understanding of concussions frustrates. So, too, does the primitive manner of identifying and treating the mild brain injury. No technological device diagnoses concussions; no pill cures them. Doctors manage them essentially the same way today as they did a hundred years ago: giving the brain time and rest to heal. The world turns. Concussion care stays mired in much the same spot it stood for our fathers' fathers' fathers.

A company in Pittsburgh hopes to modernize an outmoded medical field. ImPACT, Immediate Post-Concussion Assessment and Cognitive Testing, gauges a player's post-concussion test scores against a baseline established in the preseason. They do this through computerized assessment. The twenty-minute test helps decide whether a player is cleared to participate or needs to sit out. The NHL, MLB, and three-fourths of the teams in the NFL rely on the product. So do Vince McMahon's professional wrestling outfit, Formula 1 racing, and Sweden's World Cup soccer team.[14] When science speaks, the world, and World Wrestling Entertainment, listens.

Mark Lovell, the founding director of the University of Pittsburgh Medical Center's Sports Medicine Concussion Program, concentrates much of his scholarly work on ImPACT. It's a niche. But the specialized world of academia often recognizes expertise by way of total knowledge of slivers. One scholar becomes the go-to guy on a subject, and other scholars enrich their broad understanding of an overarching topic through reliance on such specialists. For academics interested in the wider subject of sports concussions, Lovell established himself as the authority on computerized neuropsychological testing and, specifically, the emerging field's leader, ImPACT.

In a 2003 *Journal of Neurosurgery* article, Lovell showed that concussed athletes whose other symptoms have disappeared may still perform poorly relative to their baseline scores on neuropsychological tests.

"This finding is of concern given that most high schools do not use neuropsychological testing and athlete self-report is often the primary determinant in return to play," Lovell and co-authors observed. "This study suggests that neuropsychological test results provide unique information to the sports medicine practitioner." In other words, a kid who feels okay may not be. High schools need such testing to protect their student-athletes. "Currently, formal neuropsychological baseline evaluations are routinely implemented at the professional and major college levels," Lovell informed. "Our results suggest that administration of baseline/postinjury neuropsychological testing procedures should be considered at the high school level and that neuropsychological test results, in conjunction with other diagnostic information, can provide valuable information regarding return to play." The article repeatedly references one such test, ImPACT, whose symptoms scale, the authors point out, is "used throughout both amateur and professional sports."[15]

In a 2004 *Current Opinion in Orthopedics* article, Lovell reports with coauthors that "new research using the ImPACT computerized test battery demonstrates that athletes who are asymptomatic after a concussive injury have impairments in visual memory, verbal memory, processing speed, and reaction time that tend to be less severe than those of symptomatic concussed athletes, but significantly more impaired than unconcussed controls."[16] Put another way, a physician may not recognize signs of a lingering concussion that this computer program can.

That same year, Lovell even offered an endorsement of sorts of ImPACT in *Clinics in Sports Medicine*. "We recommend formal neuropsychologic testing (e.g., ImPACT) the day after injury to assess initial neurocognitive status," wrote Lovell along with coauthors Micky Collins and James Bradley.[17] Even in articles ostensibly on other subjects, ImPACT made its way into Lovell's scholarly work. In a 2004 *American Journal of Sports Medicine* article coauthored with four others titled "Grade 1 or 'Ding' Concussions in High School Athletes," for instance, Lovell mentions ImPACT twenty-one times in eight pages.[18]

Readers glean a definite impression that the professor has established himself as the expert on all things ImPACT. But nowhere within the aforementioned studies would readers discover that Mark R. Lovell, the man who has authored scores of academic articles detailing the work of ImPACT, also owns ImPACT Applications, developed its software, and serves as its chairman and chief executive officer. Several of his coauthors are also co-owners.

This is science?

People magazine wouldn't dare allow a director to review his own film. Why do academic journals lack even the standards of supermarket checkout gossip sheets? Lovell's peers can judge the science of his scholarship on ImPACT. But one needn't be a scientist to judge the ethics of not disclosing ownership of a product under examination.

The text highlighted Mark Lovell's product. The endnotes highlighted his scholarship. In a 2009 article in the *Clinical Journal of Sports Medicine*, for instance, 17 of 37 source citations directed readers to Lovell's past work to vouch for this current work.[19] Going to the endnotes referred readers to still other studies by Lovell that cited still other studies by Lovell. The circular referencing assured readers that they can trust Mark Lovell's scholarship because Mark Lovell's scholarship says that they can.

Scholars initially ignored the ethics but eventually investigated the science. A *Journal of Athletic Training* article revealed "low to moderate test-retest reliability coefficients" in ImPACT and other computerized baseline tests.[20] "ImPACT does not meet the reliability and validity criteria desired in a test used for assisting return-to-play decisions," Lester Mayers and Thomas Redick write in the *Journal of Clinical and Experimental Neuropsychology*. "We therefore question the rationale of using ImPACT for clinical management of sport-related concussion and specifically for determining the time of return to play." The pair even wondered if, by taxing a brain requiring rest, ImPACT might prove "injurious" to athletes.[21] Loyola University Medical Center's Christopher Randolph pointed to the test's high rate of false positives and its insensitivity to concussions in clinically asymptomatic athletes. The unreliability of the five cognitive evaluations within ImPACT, Randolph concluded, "reduces the tool from the level of a clear-cut statistical algorithm to that of clinical guesswork in most cases."[22]

"Hmmm," intoned an article featured on the ImPACT website, "why would a Doctor who is the creator of one Neuro-Cognitive test write a

critical review of other providers including the most widely used competing product; ImPACT? Provocative question no doubt." The piece suggests a provocative answer: "Perhaps he has a better product that he
wants to bring to [the] fray being the developer of 'the most commonly-
used neurocognitive battery for the evaluation of dementia in North
America.'"[23] ImPACT's decision to highlight a piece suggesting *a critic's
conflict of interest*—particularly when his "competing product" dealt
primarily with the senile elderly and not concussed young athletes—
baffled.

Chutzpah? Projection? Obtuseness?

Lovell continued his barrage in peer-reviewed journals. By indis-
creetly promoting ImPACT, the pitchman professor subtly, and unwittingly, promoted the idea that his peers, the journals, and the entire field
lacked seriousness. When Lovell's articles disclosed his shareholder stake,
the boosterism appeared even less guarded. In a 2006 *Clinical Neuropsychology* article, Lovell with four coauthors, including ImPACT co-
owner Micky Collins, wrote that "ImPACT provides post-injury
cognitive and symptom data that can assist a practitioner in making safer
return to play decisions," "ImPACT can serve as an effective tool in the
concussion management process," and "ImPACT has been shown to be
an effective tool for concussion management, and is not subject to the
large practice effects sometimes seen on pencil and paper tests."[24]
ImPACT. ImPACT. ImPACT. All the namedropping surely had an
impact.

So did the *paid* advertising. "You wouldn't get on the field without
this," a helmet-toting Jerome Bettis explains in an ad for Dick's Sporting
Goods. "And you shouldn't get on the field without a baseline concussion
test, either." The former Pittsburgh Steeler, standing alongside ImPACT's
Joseph Maroon, explains that for each pair of sneakers purchased—from
Briannah if you're lucky—at Dick's, the sporting-goods giant will
"donate" $1 to ImPACT for testing up to a million student athletes.[25]

Since when does a corporation accept donations as though a charity?

Concussions are big business. ImPACT sells its software at $750 a
pop for 500 baseline tests and 150 post-injury follow-up tests. The price
isn't right for every program. The Boston Militia, for instance, sticks to

the pencil-and-paper tests criticized by Lovell and his coauthors.[26] But with a guilt-trip pitch casting a few bucks to preserve young brains as a bargain, ImPACT cajoles other programs to fork over the dough. As the company website boasts, "ImPACT is the most widely used computer-based testing program in the world and is implemented effectively across high school, collegiate, and professional levels of sport participation."[27]

Mark Lovell didn't respond to questions raised by this chapter regarding the intersection of his entrepreneurial and academic pursuits. The conflict between business and scholarship doesn't seem to have harmed Professor Lovell's academic reputation. And it certainly hasn't hurt his bottom line. Concussion specialist Dr. Robert Cantu writes, "The company has become so big and profitable that recently Lovell gave up his academic appointments at the University of Pittsburgh to become ImPACT's full-time president."[28] Who says the scholarly life doesn't pay?

Concussions make athletes' lives hell. They make the lives of a few quacks heaven. There's profit in pain. There's bigger profit in fear, a phenomenon that the medical profession traditionally fights to extinguish rather than stoke. The people who hype what athletes have to lose from concussions often have the most to gain from them.

American athletes, and their parents, spend millions of dollars purchasing false hope.

- *Might the concussion cure-all come in a can?* "If you participate in contact sports, you never know when you are going to take a blow to the head," Bioperforma warns. "And you never know the potential consequences of traumatic brain injury. Until now, there was little you could do to protect yourself." To mitigate such on-field dangers, the Salt Lake City–based nutritional company offers NeuroSafe, "a daily drink that should be taken in season by every person participating in sports with a moderate to high risk of head injury."[29]

- *Can headbands prevent headaches?* "This can come between you and a head injury," Force Field Headbands boasts of its product, which appears from a distance something that John McEnroe might have worn at Wimbledon. Primarily marketed toward soccer players, such headwear, testified a doctor before a U.S. Senate committee, has inspired patients he has treated to "become more aggressive" and hurt "themselves and others because they have the headband on."[30]

- *Take the red pill or buy the blue pill?* "Purchase a 30 day supply of Sports Brain Guard to help protect your brain from concussion injury and play your best," suggested an ad for this since-defunct pill product. Dr. Joseph Maroon, team doctor for the Pittsburgh Steelers and ImPACT co-creator who appeared in that Dick's Sporting Goods advertisement with Jerome Bettis, endorsed the concussion pills as "scientifically proven to help protect the brain before concussion and also enhance recovery following a brain injury."[31]

The internet has become the primary marketplace for concussion cure-alls. The snake-oil peddlers have exchanged a buckboard for a laptop. Desperation, the motivator for numerous nineteenth-century scams, again inspires buyers. Whereas yokels once handed over their daily bread for cures for blindness, Ponce-de-Leon fountains of youth, and chair-bound-walk-again elixirs, they now pay top dollar to preserve their brains. And they remarkably do so with the belief that modern medicine, and not modern quackery, gives its imprimatur. Dropping one's dollars at the health food store for peace of mind seems another way of losing one's mind.

Contact sports employ mouth pieces to protect the teeth from impact and everything else from the teeth's impact. Sports in which athletes have a propensity to lose teeth have a propensity to make athletes lose their heads, too, so perhaps a connection exists between the mouth and the brain above it. Briannah thought so after her concussion. "I do have a better mouth guard," she explains. "It might just be a mental thing. I upgraded since the concussion." At the Dick's Sporting Goods store where she works, the plastic inserts cost anywhere from $5 to $150. She coughed up about $30 for hers.[32]

Can the instrument designed to keep mouths from looking like *Deliverance*'s hillbilly debaucher keep brains from thinking like his, too?

- NO-KO boasts of "a mouth guard that is incomparable to all others." Featuring the visage of heavyweight mixed-martial artist Junior dos Santos, NO-KO's website claims "a 93.03% reduction in concussion with the use of this patented design"—not 93% or 93.2% but a precise 93.03%. The marketing boasts the added bonus of "a coincident increase in physical strength!"[33]
- Another sports equipment company makes a less elaborate if more straightforward case: "By wearing a Guardian Mouthguard, you are helping to protect yourself against concussions!"[34]
- A web promotion for Brain-Pad mouthpieces boasted, "Reduces Risk of Concussions!" The Federal Trade Commission then forced the company to remove the unsubstantiated claim. An updated Brain-Pad site warns: "Don't be FOOLED by PHONY IMITATORS or VAGUE CLAIMS!"[35]

The exclamation points may have made it all seem so scientific. But there isn't any scientific proof that mouth guards guard brains as they do mouths.[36] Though science doesn't affirm mouth pieces as protection against concussions, it doesn't quite negate them, either. Boxers swear the rubbery inserts prevent in-ring unconsciousness. But the scientists don't see it the way the pugilists do.

The gauche, unseemly hard sells make the infomercials masquerading as scholarly articles appear tame in comparison. So far-fetched have the marketing boasts become that the U.S. Senate Committee on Commerce, Science, and Transportation held hearings on them in October 2011. Professor of neurology Jeffrey Kutcher of the University of Michigan testified on the dangers of fast-and-loose marketing. "The potential harm that I see caused by products that claim to prevent concussion when they do not is far more than simply the financial harm of paying more for something that isn't likely to work as claimed," he told senators. "It is the harm that comes from having a false sense of security, from not understanding how the injury occurs, and what can actually be done to prevent it."[37]

Who has time for the truth with so many dollars up for grabs? It's only Jessica, Danielle, Jen, and Briannah's brains that we're talking about.

The huckster's secret weapon is guilt. What kind of a parent allows a child on the grass, the ice, or the court with an inferior piece of plastic in his mouth? Just fork over the $69.95—a pittance for a clean conscience. For the salesman, it's the mental health of the parent in the stands, not the child on the field, that counts. A one-sided transaction similarly characterizes the financial relationship between concussion researchers and the NFL. The former shames the latter. The latter pays the former and hopes for absolution.

Ginning up controversy goes against everything the detached man of science stands for. The researcher faces a dilemma: without fear, without grants; without crisis, without endowed chair; without hysteria, without research institute. Thus does doctor play carnival barker. The most esteemed medicine men often know more about public relations than concussions. The best doctors often toil in obscurity for want of media, fundraising, and networking savvy.

"Five years ago the National Football League was in a state of denial about head trauma in its game," writes Dr. Robert Cantu in his book

Concussions and Our Kids. "Today, it's a force for change. The difference between then and now is the current commissioner."[38] Roger Goodell, of course, has cracked down on helmet-to-helmet hits and largely negated the kickoff, safety measures no doubt pleasing to Cantu. But where he really differs most from his predecessors involves his lack of scruples in buying off the league's critics. Whereas Pete Rozelle famously forked over just $3 to the USFL in a court settlement he had refused to earlier settle, Roger Goodell awarded $1 million to Cantu's research outfit after the doctor's public hectoring.[39] Surely Cantu, a respected physician treating concussions long before it became fashionable, merits the assumption of noble motives. But one can't help but notice how positive words for the NFL corresponded with positive cash flow to its longtime critic. The *New York Times* described Cantu in 2007, for instance, as someone "who has repeatedly criticized the N.F.L.'s handling of concussions."[40] Nobody would say that today.

"The NFL has generously supported Boston University's Center for the Study of Traumatic Encephalopathy, of which I am a co-director," Cantu writes. "In 2010, the league donated $1 million to the center to support our work exploring links between repeated head trauma over many years and CTE. The money is given without strings."[41] Money changes everything.

In 2009, NFL Charities gave zero dollars to concussion research. This didn't please concussion researchers, who railed against the league, and the sport it plays. The following year the league, in addition to the $1 million it gave to Cantu's BU outfit, gave another $988,224 to hospitals and universities working on brain injuries.[42] It wasn't just the NFL. In 2009, helmet manufacturer Xenith pledged a million dollars (a dollar for each helmet Xenith sold) to the National Athletic Trainers' Association Foundation to support concussion research, the money ultimately going to the Cantu-Guskiewicz Endowment.[43] The NFL's charitable interests, not as overtly tethered to their business interests as Xenith's, nevertheless make one wonder where a cynical desire for profits stops and selfless giving begins.

Small gifts begat bigger gifts. In 2012, the NFL dropped $30 million on the Foundation for the National Institutes of Health to study concussions and Alzheimer's, Parkinson's, and other neurodegenerative conditions.[44] The NFL Players Association pledged $100 million to Harvard Medical School in 2013. The grant seeks to improve the lives of athletes through improvements in medicine, science, and technology.[45] We'll find out whether it benefits retired players. We already know that it has benefitted many a Harvard Medical School employee.

It didn't benefit Cantu. After his Boston University group received its million from the league, it missed out on the tens of millions. The senior advisor to the NFL's concussion committee, as well as his protégé Chris Nowinski, acted as a paid consultant to attorneys suing professional football's cash kingdom. Cantu, who asks $800 an hour for legal services, reportedly upset both the players' lawyers and the NFL for playing both sides. He later told reporters Steve Fainaru and Mark Fainaru-Wada that "if [the NFL] wanted to put me on their payroll, to defend their case, then I'm not gonna say boo about those issues [to the plaintiffs]."[46] Like players, doctors switch allegiances as free agents when bids from the competition entice.

Cantu, like the Harvard researchers, performs important work. It's not as though the grants he solicits—consulting fees are another matter—go straight into his pocket. They support crucial research. Cantu's Center for the Study of Traumatic Encephalopathy, unlike, say, Sports Brain Guard, isn't a for-profit venture. The grants support him, yes, but they also support the research in which he believes. And in a field overwrought by alarmism, Cantu's has been a voice of restraint. He cautions, for instance, that chronic traumatic encephalopathy (CTE), the mysterious degenerative brain condition discovered in the brains of deceased football players, may result from environmental, genetic, or other triggers in addition to resulting from brain trauma.[47] "Concussions generate buzz and get all the publicity," the doctor concedes. "For my patients who've had multiple concussions and fear that they are at risk for developing CTE later in life, I offer simple advice: Relax. The connection has been greatly overstated."[48] The prudence, dedication, and experience reassure. The field, and all the money flying around it, doesn't. The shameless shakedowns, knee-jerk alarmism, seedy commercialism, and brazen conflicts of interest by the bad doctors can't help but make outsiders wonder about the good doctors, too.

But one fact is clear. The prolonged PR campaign has worked. Finite grant dollars otherwise underwriting research into cancer, AIDS, paralysis, male pattern baldness, and myriad other maladies increasingly flow toward concussions. The squeaky wheel got the grease, which, of course, prompted it to squeak louder.

It's not as though scientists need to shout about sports brain injuries to attract ears. Athletes and their parents eagerly listen for every bit of new information on concussions emanating from the scientific community. But the layman doesn't always understand what he hears, and the scientist doesn't always permit eavesdroppers. Science speaks outside its house in a singular voice. Stick your ear close to the closed front door. Science speaks as a cacophony of conflicting voices within its own house. Thinking science and asserting "science" involve contrary understandings of the term. The *idea* of science evokes raising unsettling questions. The *word* science conveys a settled question. "This is science!" hits the ears as a conversation stopper, not a conversation starter. Science acts with a split personality.

Science appears to us as a process and a product. Watching the process of making science, like watching the process of making sausage, induces squeamishness over the final product. So the highbrains, in dryly written jargon laid out in obscure journals, partake in the process largely away from the public. If doctors appear as children bickering during the process, they appear as gods handing down divine edict when presenting the product. Questioning, the bedrock of the scientific process, becomes the taboo of the scientific product.

Concussion medicine fits this schizophrenic pattern. In the public spotlight, many scientists speak with all-knowing univocal authority. Even when they don't, the press often simplifies and exaggerates for them. Behind the curtain, researchers disagree with one another's theories, shift positions on key issues, and admit that our knowledge of the brain has a long way to go.

Concussions may be cutting-edge media copy. They don't make for cutting-edge medicine. There is no concussion test as there is an HIV test. Dr. Jeffrey Kutcher explains: "Concussions cannot be diagnosed by any test. That is extremely important to remember. It is a diagnosis that can only be made after a careful clinical evaluation performed by a healthcare professional, and preferably one with training and experience caring for brain injuries."[49] There is no magic pill to dissipate symptoms, no new miracle treatment that wasn't known to doctors a hundred years ago. One scholarly article bluntly notes that "the only treatment currently available for concussion is physical and cognitive rest."[50] Get that? Not expensive sports drinks or fish-oil tablets, but bed rest, which is free, cures concussions. Beyond clinical evaluation and rest therapy, respected scholars can't even agree on very basic issues.

The bigger, faster, stronger sex faces a greater risk of a concussion, right? One study discovered that concussions were "observed in girls' sports at rates similar to or higher than those of boys' sports."[51] Another reported a four to one male-female disparity in its concussed group, rationalizing the chasm by holding "that many sports traditionally played by males (especially football) have significantly higher rates of concussion per athletic exposure."[52] Certainly it's true that hockey and football witness more concussions than gymnastics and field hockey. But a concussed group skewing that heavily toward males, as readers surely have deduced from the discussion surrounding Briannah, Jessica, Jen, and Danielle, appears increasingly dated. The American Medical Society for Sports Medicine, for instance, points out that "in sports with similar rules females sustain more concussions than their male counterparts," taking longer to recover from symptoms that are more severe and greater in number.[53]

Academic articles agree that concussions appear in football more than in any other mainstream sport both as a total number and as a rate per athletic exposure. They occasionally make claims about the most concussed position in the most concussed sport. Those claims often conflict with other claims. NFL injury reports for the 2012 season, for instance, listed wide receiver and cornerback as the positions sustaining the greatest number of concussions.[54] But scholarly studies of high school and college teams place the most concussed position elsewhere on the field. A paper on high school athletes reported linebackers suffering 59 percent of defensive concussions and running backs suffering 46 percent of offensive concussions.[55] An earlier paper on university football players found that running backs reported the fewest prior concussions and quarterbacks reported the most.[56] Both studies, differing in size and, to a small extent, in subject (high school versus college players), no doubt found what the papers said that they found. But what they found isn't, given the inconsistencies, very helpful.

It turns out the most dangerous place at a football game isn't on the field but high above it—during halftime. "I think I had more injuries cheering than I've had in football," Briannah Gallo points out. "I was a flyer so I got dropped a lot."[57] The cheerleader-turned-cornerback's experience actually meshes with the statistics. "The activity of the flyer is many, many times more dangerous than a football play," Robert Cantu details. "The incidence of concussion in flyers in cheerleading is more than tenfold what it is in football players. The same is true of the incidence of catastrophic injuries."[58]

Science speaks with a forked tongue on whether translational (up-down) or rotational (right-left) head jolts are more likely to cause concussions. A study of NFL concussions in *Neurosurgery* reported "a strong correlation of concussion with translational acceleration, indicating that translational acceleration should be the primary measure for assessment of the performance of helmet protection systems."[59] A subsequent study of high school players rejected this thesis: "Our data do not support the use of linear acceleration as the prime variable of interest as rotational acceleration was the chief predictor within our classification tree."[60]

Scientists remain ignorant of the pervasiveness of sports concussions, issuing guesstimates that diverge wildly. "In the United States," a 2012 *American Journal of Sports Medicine* article asserts, "an estimated 300,000 sports-related concussions occur annually."[61] "More than 1.6 million sports-related concussions occur every year in the United States," reads a 2011 *Journal of Athletic Training* article.[62] A third study published in 2012 reports that "between 1.6 and 3.8 million sports related concussion[s] occur each year in the United States."[63] Scientists disagree on the numbers. So, apparently, does *a* scientist, whose name appears as an author on the first two articles.

One reason for the different numbers is the wide divergence on estimates for *undiagnosed* concussions. The position statement of the American Medical Society for Sports Medicine, for instance, claims that as many as half of all sports concussions go unreported.[64] An earlier study reported that nine out of ten sports concussions go undiagnosed.[65] Chris Nowinski theorizes that we overlook fifty-five out of fifty-six sports concussions.[66] Of course, when counting invisible concussions, the ouija board works as well as the abacus. The inclusion of uncounted concussions in concussion counts necessarily makes the counts worthless.

All this conflicting data doesn't inspire confidence, but in a strange way, it should. There's nothing wrong with conflict, disagreement, debate. It's part of the process. Trial and error involves, lest we forget, error. Finding truth involves uncovering falsehood. But it's important for both the public and the scientists to understand that a field of medicine that hasn't advanced much in our lifetimes speaks more as a student learning than as an authority decreeing. Neurology works currently to gain a better understanding of concussions. But brain scientists don't yet have brain science down to a science.

Some people like finding the truth. Others like thinking they already possess it. Science attracts both personalities.

CHAPTER THREE

SHOW ME THE MONEY!

T he starting quarterback for the New York Giants bagged groceries at $4 an hour before joining the team. The Washington Redskins signed a player on prison furlough. Another quarterback received a call from the Minnesota Vikings immediately after a flag football game.[1] In the strike-stricken 1987 season, Alphonso (Al) Williams may have been the only replacement player living a more glamorous life *before* he got the call to play in the NFL. The wide receiver matter-of-factly recounts, "I was hanging out at Neverland."

Williams had become friends with Janet Jackson, who compelled her reclusive brother to meet him. "He was taller than I thought," Williams says of the dancing-singing phenomenon, adding that Jackson's light complexion startled him. "His whole face was white." Standing 5'10" and weighing just 180 pounds, the football player's appearance may have alarmed the King of Pop, too. Surely Michael Jackson looked more the pop star than Al Williams looked the football player.

The graduate of Long Beach Polytechnic High School—alma mater of Snoop Dogg and Cameron Diaz—had close encounters with the rich and famous before. Greater Los Angeles overflows with celebrities, after all. It doesn't overflow with Michael Jacksons. In the mid-1980s, Michael Jackson was more famous than famous. The biggest star in the universe's orbit briefly captured Al Williams. With Al jonesing for Kentucky Fried Chicken drive-thru, he took the Jehovah's Witness–raised Janet for her first fast-food meal. Another evening, he craved candy. "We went night-clubbing one night and I said, 'Janet, I got a little sweet tooth.'" She directed him to a room in Neverland. "I opened this door and I went: 'holy crap!'" Michael Jackson had a gigantic room in his gigantic home converted into a gigantic candy store. "He had a bubble gum statue of him—his size."

Before Al Williams played in the NFL's *Twilight Zone* strike season, he lived a stranger-than-fiction life outside of the league. He had played two amazing seasons in the United States Football League, leading the Oklahoma Outlaws, and then the Arizona Outlaws, in receiving yardage. The Outlaws routed Donald Trump's New Jersey Generals despite Heisman Trophy winners Doug Flutie and Herschel Walker powering the Generals' offense. Al almost single-handedly defeated Jim Kelly and the Houston Gamblers by catching a 56-yard Hail Mary to tie the game as time expired and a 53-yard bomb to set up the game-winning field goal in overtime. Al could count consecutive 1,000-yard seasons after two years in the USFL. He could also count the fans, whose shrinking numbers doomed the upstart league.

The NFL, whose players had enjoyed a salary spike from the spring league's competition, came calling for Al Williams and for his quarterback, Doug Williams. Their proximity in the alphabet led to a proximity "on every plane, hotel, you name it." The atomic-armed passer expressed his frustrations over the NFL regarding him as a "black quarterback" rather than simply a quarterback. The speedy receiver hoped for an opportunity to showcase his talents in the marquee league that had overlooked him. The Washington Redskins wanted the dynamic duo, but only got the quarterback. Al had verbally agreed but backed out when the San

Diego Chargers, almost his hometown team, courted him. "Do me this big favor," Doug Williams prophetically told his former teammate. "Since the Super Bowl is going to be in San Diego this year, start looking for a hotel for my family."

Doug Williams went on to become that season's Super Bowl MVP. Al Williams went on to play three NFL games as a replacement player.

"I'll take it to my grave," Al confesses. Rebuffing the eventual Super Bowl champs for the Chargers proved a bad career move. So, in retrospect, did Al's decision to play during the league's 1987 strike. What then sounded like opportunity knocking now clearly strikes Al's ears as a door slamming shut. Men who had called Al "teammate" in training camp now called him other names. "It was really scary," Al recounted. "Nobody said, 'Hey, there's going to be people picketing here.'" The first bus ride to the team facility jarred. Al recalls that "guys were yelling and screaming obscenity words."[2] It could have been worse. In Kansas City, two Chiefs walked the picket line with shotguns.[3] New York Jets star Mark Gastineau, who opted to stay on the defensive line and off the picket line, was spit on by his team's center.[4] Striking Oilers smashed windows on the replacement team's bus. When the police showed video of the incident to Jerry Glanville, Houston's head coach recognized the culprits as his striking starting safeties. "Officer, I've never seen those two boys before in my life," he explained.[5] The pair remained free safeties.

Team nicknames took on nicknames: the San Francisco Phony Niners, New Orleans Saint Elsewheres, Chicago Spare Bears. What the players lacked in talent they tried to make up for in enthusiasm, and as in the USFL, Al made the most of an opportunity. With fellow USFL veteran Rick Neuheisel slinging him passes, Al led the Re-Chargers in receiving and placed eighth in the NFL in receiving yards during the replacement games. His receptions for 110 yards against the Tampa Bay Buccaneers helped Neuheisel break Dan Fouts's team record for single-game passing efficiency. Unlike the striking Chargers, the Re-Chargers won. They went undefeated in three road games.

Then the plug got pulled on the Re-Chargers. Al recalls a chance meeting with receivers coach Charlie Joyner the week following that third game. "I was going in the tunnel to the meeting room. I happened to cross Charlie. He goes, 'Where you going?' I said I'm going to our morning meeting. He says, 'Don't go in there.'" Only when he returned to a near-empty locker room did the reality of the situation catch up to him. The strike had ended. Almost all his replacement teammates had been cut. He had been kept. Al had realized his dream of parlaying replacement-game success into a roster spot. Reality just didn't work out the way the dream did.

A vibe of camaraderie quickly shifted to one of enmity. "A few of the players, they would see you in the locker room and just walk by you—not even acknowledging you," he remembers. "That went on for weeks." Dan Fouts appeared to exude the most bitterness. "He wouldn't look me in the eye." Al remembers the bearded and burly gunslinger screaming and swearing at him after overthrowing a route in practice, leaving Wes Chandler to observe, "He just called you every mother effing name in the book."[6] Later Fouts contended, "That's what ruined the team," referring to the nine replacement players who stuck with the Chargers. "We had maintained such strong unity during the strike, but that got pretty tough to do when we had all these little cancers within the locker room."[7] Dehumanized as a "cancer" and a "scab" off the field, Al Williams became a nonentity on the field.

Al Williams, more than a quarter century after he stood on the other side of the picket line, finds himself joined together with the men who once stood against him. Al and more than 4,000 other professional football players have united to sue the National Football League. They seek financial relief for head injuries suffered during their league tenures, however brief.

Al joined a suit at the suggestion of former St. Louis Cardinal Mel Gray, a similarly small but speedy receiver who played alongside Al on the Arizona Outlaws. Gray played in 169 NFL games. Al played in three. He insists that the concussions he suffered in the NFL—rather than the hits he endured in Pop Warner, high school, college, the USFL, or the CFL—have left him with symptoms such as recurring headaches and insomnia. Williams cites medical documentation of his ailments that predates the wave of lawsuits. He insists, "I'm not trying to jump on no bandwagon and get free money."[8]

There's certainly a lot of money to be had. The master suit encompassing the many smaller ones points out, "The NFL generates approximately $9,300,000,000.00 in gross income per year." Surely the layman could grasp the point without those gratuitous two zeros the lawyers threw in at the end: the NFL has more money than Monopoly. In fact, the NFL's GDP outranks that of Zimbabwe, Guyana, and Bhutan.[9] The sixteen host stadiums of NFL Nation average a population of 67,509 on fall weekends. The fans buy everything from hot dogs to jerseys to parking spots. But, as the lawyers point out, the real lucre comes from television: "The NFL earns billions of dollars from its media deals with, inter alia, ESPN ($1.1 billion), DirecTV ($1 billion), NBC ($650 million), Fox ($712.5 million), and CBS ($622.5 million)."[10]

One could make the case that Al Williams—a genuinely nice guy, talented receiver, and sacrificial lamb from the NFL's strike season—deserves a settlement more than, say, Bruce Smith. The Buffalo Bills defensive end spent nineteen years in the league—but he got paid. Smith's last contract with the Washington Redskins awarded him $23 million, including a $4.25 million signing bonus. The Redskins released him before the final year of the five-year contract, but still paid him close to $20 million.[11] Football players reap such enormous salaries in part because of the risks, and brevity (Bruce Smith aside), of their careers. What's a millionaire chaser of quarterbacks doing chasing personal injury attorneys?

Al endured hits—*on and off the field*. He never really got paid. And though striking players may have resented Al for taking a paycheck when they went without one, their paychecks benefitted greatly from the competition Al and other USFL players provided the NFL. That, more than anything gained by the union in the two strikes of the 1980s, boosted salaries. "It may have been the greatest thing that ever happened to NFL players," reflects punter Sean Landetta on the USFL. "If you look at a graph, it took sixty years for that NFL average salary to get to about $75,000. And in three years, it triples."[12] Al never truly enjoyed the dollars the USFL injected into NFL players' wallets. Bruce Smith absolutely did.

Of course, the other side of this argument shouts louder to us. Bruce Smith crashed into men larger than him on every play for nineteen NFL seasons. It's probable that banging into other large men thousands of times a year for decades impaired not just knees, fingers, and joints but the brain, too. It's rarely a pillow fight for a defensive lineman as it sometimes is for a receiver. Bruce Smith's cheers, adrenaline, and paychecks departed. The pain stuck around.

Juxtaposing Bruce Smith with Al Williams may make Al's case seem frivolous. But it's not as though Al, who hung on as a practice squad player into the 1988 season, experienced the violence of the league less than all the other litigants. In fact, Al looks like a grizzled NFL veteran in comparison to hundreds of men who have joined the class-action lawsuit. Roughly 10 percent of the plaintiffs never even played a down in an NFL game. A perusal of the *Washington Times*'s NFL Concussion Lawsuits Database shows that 414 (and counting) plaintiffs appear nowhere on the official roster of any National Football League team.[13] Never has getting cut seemed so much like hitting the lottery in retrospect.

Bruce Smith is the outlier, not Al Williams. Just two players suing the NFL entered more NFL games than Smith. More than 500 litigants touched the field less than Williams. Most of these players didn't touch it at all. These John Doe athletes attaching their names to the suit, while Dick Butkus, Mean Joe Greene, Art Donovan, and Jack Youngblood stay out of the litigation, makes sense perhaps if inflicting damage somehow made a player ineligible for settlement damages. Equal justice under law demands recognition that not all NFL careers, or the pain suffered from them, were created equal. Should the suit prevail, hundreds of plaintiffs whose tenuous connection to the NFL consists of trying out for a team may become the wealthiest never-was-beens in the history of sports.

Al acknowledges, "There are players who are out there faking it and just trying to seek out money. It's not like that for me."[14]

The sheer number of litigants—greater than a third of all living NFL players—ensures a Rod Tidwell–quality to the lawsuit. The *Jerry Maguire* character, a caricature of the spoiled professional athlete played by Cuba Gooding Jr., looms over the proceedings. He whispers, nay, he shouts: "Show me the money!" The plaintiffs, many accustomed to their pleas for easy money not falling on deaf ears, shout the irresistible catchphrase with him. It conjures up a pleasant image, so it's pleasing to say. This is particularly true when you say it enthusiastically, earnestly, and ear-splittingly—the way Tom Cruise did in the movies. *Show ... me ... the ... money!*

Thomas Brown, who in 1942 played nine games for the Pittsburgh Steelers, somehow managed to live into his nineties to sue the NFL over its deleterious effect on his health. *Show him the money!* Danny Miller kicked in five NFL games for two teams in 1982. *Show him the money!* Robert DiRico played three games for the Giants as a replacement player in 1987. *Show him the money!* Richard Van Druten got cut by the Kansas City Chiefs in August of 1989. *Show him the money!* Brett Basanez, a backup to the backup of Jake Delhomme, played during the fourth quarter of a blowout for the Carolina Panthers in 2006.[15] *Show him the money!*

If they were given the chance to do it all over again, assuredly the plaintiffs would gladly give back the money and cup their ears to the roar of the crowd in exchange for healthy heads, right? Pat White, out of the NFL for three seasons, answered that question in the negative in the spring of 2013. The fleet-footed quarterback's lawsuit against the league alleged "repeated and chronic head impacts" that resulted in "[c]ognitive and other difficulties, severe headaches, speech issues, memory loss, depression, isolation, mental anguish, and diminished self-esteem." But when a contract to play for the Washington Redskins appeared, the lawsuit disappeared.[16] *Show me the money!*

"Jerry, doesn't it make you feel good just to say that?" a dancing Rod Tidwell asks his agent. "Say it with me one time, Jerry!"[17] Training camp cuts, replacement players, clipboard holders, kickers, and personal injury attorneys, you know the words. *All together now...*

Cuba Gooding Jr. won an Oscar for commanding Tom Cruise to "Show me the money!" Is it so preposterous that real football players could win a lawsuit making the same demand?

Willie Sutton famously claimed that he robbed banks because that's where the money's kept. If he were around today, he might sue the NFL. It surely has more money than the Corn Exchange Bank and Trust Company. The concussion lawyers, like the concussion doctors, know where the money's kept.

The lawsuits started in the summer of 2011 when Vernon Maxwell, 1983's defensive rookie of the year, filed suit along with scores of defendants against the NFL in a California court. More than 200 lawsuits and 4,000 players followed Maxwell's lead. The next year, a federal judicial panel, seeing the similarity in the many cases, ordered their consolidation in one master lawsuit to avoid tying up multiple courts from hearing essentially the same case. The plaintiffs are many. The defendants are essentially two: the National Football League and Riddell, the leading manufacturer of football helmets.

The Riddell portion of the lawsuit might surpass the NFL portion in its flimsiness. At least the NFL knows that 90 percent of the people suing it actually played in their league. A large chunk of the players suing Riddell didn't wear their helmets. Ken Stabler, who led the Oakland Raiders to their first Super Bowl victory in 1977, may be suing Riddell today. In 1977, the Snake appeared on the cover of *Sports Illustrated* wearing a Wilson helmet.[18]

Players, at least when a diversity of brands competed for their allegiances, shifted from MaxPro to Wilson, from Wilson to Riddell, and so on. Wearing one helmet in one picture didn't preclude a player from changing helmets when the photographer put the cap back on the lens. "If you had an oblong-shaped head, like a Tony Dorsett," then you might seek out unique gear, explains Curtis Worrell, who specializes in recreating vintage football headwear for man caves, movies, and museums. "He wore a Rawlings helmet. Rawlings helmets were longer. They weren't as round."[19] He may have worn MacGregor at Pitt and Rawlings entering the NFL. But as a plaintiff, Tony Dorsett prefers Riddell. There's Denver Broncos linebacker Karl Mecklenburg wearing a BIKE helmet in his 1986 Topps card. And there's his name on a pending lawsuit against Riddell. *Sports Illustrated* celebrated current litigant Eric Dickerson breaking O. J. Simpson's single-season rushing record on its December 17, 1984, cover. There, and seven years later when Dickerson last graced *SI*'s cover, the Hall of Fame running back appeared wearing the same style of BIKE/Schutt headwear. He's a litigant against Riddell, too.[20]

Lawyers may lie. Football cards don't.

The master suit charges, "Prior to 2002, the Riddell Defendants made no attempt to design a helmet to protect against concussive injuries.... Even the Riddell Revolution Helmets (introduced in 2002) were not designed to sufficiently protect against concussions."[21] But what helmet is? Helmets protect skulls. They don't do all that much to protect brains from shaking inside of, and against, skulls. To do that, Riddell would have to develop a helmet to place inside the skull that surrounds the brain—an innovation lost even on God. The lawyers might have been better off employing doctors to write their brief. One such doctor, Robert Cantu, cites "helmets prevent most concussions" as one of eight basic concussion myths in his recent book. The players' attorneys evidently didn't read it—or much else of the literature on concussions. "Will helmets ever prevent concussions in football?" Cantu asks. "For that to occur, the manufacturers would have to do a lot more than tweak the design. They'd have to overcome the laws of physics."[22] Alas, they don't teach physics in law school.

The *Jerry Maguire* quality that colors the suit's motivation against the NFL yields to a *Da Vinci Code* vibe within its text. The master suit depicts a massive conspiracy dating back to the earliest days of the league to withhold accurate medical information to preserve profits. "Since the NFL's inception in the first half of the 20th Century," the complaint alleges, "the NFL has been aware of the growing body of scientific evidence and its compelling conclusions that professional football players who sustain repetitive MTBI [Mild Traumatic Brain Injury] during their careers are at greater risk for chronic neuro-cognitive illness and disabilities both during their football careers and later in life." It contends that the NFL has long "suppressed" and "concealed" such scientific information.[23] In a free society, how?

Doubtless, some claims within the suit have merit. The master complaint, for instance, points to the NFL's creation of a Mild Traumatic Brain Injury Committee in 1994. The chair of the committee was a specialist in rheumatology who served as the New York Jets team physician. A conflict of interest, and a question of competence, plagued the committee from its origins. No neuropathologist sat on that original committee. At least initially, the body appeared more as a servant of the league's business interests than its players' health interests.[24] The suit also alleges that the NFL profits by marketing violence. The brief cites such NFL Films releases as *Crunch Course II*, *Big Blocks and King Size Hits*, *The Best of Thunder and Destruction—NFL's Hardest Hits*, and *NFL Rocks: Extreme Football* to buttress this claim. The lawyers point to a Michael Irvin quote—"Hey, you know I'll trade a concussion for a reception!"—from one of the videos to demonstrate the NFL's recklessness.[25] The problem with this argument isn't that it's false but that it's obvious. Even the league, one thinks, would plead *nolo contendere* to the charge that it sells hard hits.

Does not this charge contradict the earlier charge that the NFL concealed and suppressed the dangers of its game? Surely *Crunch Course II* convinces the viewer of football's risks more persuasively than anything written in the concussion lawsuit.

And Riddell, assuredly blameless for head injuries to litigants who didn't wear their helmets, deserves blame for underwriting a "scientific" study touting protections that their Revolution helmets provide against concussions. Other scientists found the benefits marginal if not dubious. If a Riddell employee—identified as such in the article—serving as one of the coauthors doesn't spark thoughts of ImPACT's studies touting its own product, then the awkward presence of ImPACT's Lovell, Collins, and Maroon as coauthors assuredly does.[26]

But given that a majority of plaintiffs suing the NFL played before the release of this Riddell-sponsored study, just as they played before the formation of the MTBI Committee, how is this actionable?

What do the players want? The same thing Rod Tidwell wanted. The master complaint "seeks a declaration of liability, injunctive relief, medical monitoring, and financial compensation for the long-term chronic injuries, financial losses, expenses, and intangible losses suffered by the Plaintiffs and Plaintiffs' Spouses."[27] *Show them the money!*

Al Williams and other replacement players uniting with the striking players who once hurled eggs at them radiates irony. Time heals all wounds—money more so. A greater irony encompasses the strikers, who largely ignored the interests of retirees during their strike, suing once in their retirement for the benefits that they left on the table so long ago. Players have the retirees' backs—just only when the players themselves become retirees.

"The bottom line is I don't work for them," NFL Players Association (NFLPA) head Gene Upshaw once controversially said of retired players. "They don't hire me and they can't fire me. They can complain about me all day long. They can have their opinion. But the active players have the vote. That's who pays my salary."[28] In other words, the late union head would have considered their interests only once retirees paid union dues.

In 1987, NFL players struck for free agency. Today, those same players sue for free health care. Athletes whose careers started during the 1980s, an era marred by a nasty adversarial relationship between labor and management that culminated in two strike-shortened seasons, comprise a quarter of the plaintiffs.[29] Had they considered long-term interests instead of short-term greed during the 1987 work stoppage, the current lawsuits might not have been necessary. But professional athletes, from Johnny Unitas to Brett Favre, rarely envision themselves as *retired* professional athletes.

In 1987, the players struck for *now* without thinking about *later*. The disastrous strike, which witnessed Joe Montana, Lawrence Taylor, and Steve Largent eventually joining Al Williams across the picket line, failed athletes, present and future. The 1987 strike didn't deliver for players in 1987—and it isn't delivering for those same players in retirement today. Suing the 1987 versions of themselves just isn't a viable option. So they have hauled the NFL to court, even though 10 percent of the litigants never actually saw action in an official NFL game, and have sued Riddell, even though many wore helmets by other manufacturers when they played.

The concussion lawsuit represents collective bargaining by other means. NFL retirees have demanded better health care benefits for years. The NFLPA, focused more on the desires of current players than retirees, never won the benefits for them. What players didn't win in the negotiating room, they might win in a courtroom, using a cause du jour of American sports journalists to do so.

"Why does the most lucrative professional sports league in the world have the worst pension and disability plan?" Joe DeLamielleure asked in 2007. "My answer is: Gene Upshaw. He's the one running this thing." A longtime foe of Upshaw, and ferocious advocate for the interests of former players, the Hall of Fame guard allegedly sparked the other Hall of Fame guard's ill-advised "I don't work for them" comments. In the *USA Today* piece, DeLamielleure cited simple justice, not concussions, as a reason for the NFL to offer more generous benefits to retired players.[30] But now that concussions grate on the national conscience, they work as a rationale, too. The reasons have shifted. The conclusion hasn't. *Show me the money!*

If any player embodied Rod Tidwell in the public's perception, Deion Sanders certainly did. The late author David Halberstam eulogized a supposedly retired "Prime Time" in 2001 as "emblematic in team sports of me-first self-promotion." The two-sport star's habit of tracing a dollar-sign in the dirt with his bat and of celebrating touchdowns with imaginative soft-shoe end-zone dances enraged purists of both games. Halberstam spoke for many when he concluded that "people like Deion do not sacrifice, they always take."[31]

Anyone nodding over the sentiments expressed in Halberstam's "Deion, We Hardly Knew Ye" piece might expect to see the defensive back's name atop any of the myriad lawsuits. But the bitter article's title, not its content, foreshadowed the real-life Rod Tidwell's stance on the concussion lawsuits. Deion Sanders emphatically refuses to take part in the litigation lottery at the expense of losing friends and making enemies.

"The game is a safe game," Sanders declared on a Super Bowl XLVII pre-game show. "The equipment is better. I don't buy all these guys coming back with these concussions. I'm not buying all of that. Half these guys are trying to make money off the deal. That's real talk. That's really how it is. I wish they'd be honest and tell the truth, because it's keeping kids away from our game."[32]

Deion, we hardly know you, indeed.

If only to satisfy a sense of cosmic justice, Al Williams, a receiver too talented to have left all that money on the field way back when, should finally get to pick up his paycheck in the courthouse today. But more down-to-earth considerations of fairness insist that NFL profits remain in the hands of owners and active players. Reasons beyond Deion's exist for wishing that the retirees and their lawyers lose their suit.

A courtroom victory would unjustly reward players who have already been more than justly compensated for the risks of a line of work not nearly as risky as other male-dominated professions (police officer, fisherman, fire fighter, construction worker, soldier, and so on). It would incentivize the litigious culture that absolves individuals of responsibility for personal actions in favor of punishing an organization that didn't compel the personal actions. It would pretend away the plaintiffs' exponentially greater football experience outside the NFL by focusing exclusively on the wealthiest league in which they played. It would legitimize claims lacking evidentiary support, such as the suit's reliance on "latent neurodegenerative disorders and diseases" lurking undetected within the plaintiffs and damage caused by ancient undiagnosed concussions, by awarding a settlement without determining the cause, or even the existence, of injuries that in large part can be neither proved nor disproved.[33] It would inflate ticket prices, depress salaries of active players, and potentially threaten the existence of a source of joy for hundreds of millions of people.

The worst aspect of the lawsuit winning won't be its effect on the league the players are suing but on all the leagues they aren't suing. Deion has a point. The suit harms football more than it harms professional football.

The *New York Times* reported that as an unintended consequence of the NFL lawsuit "colleges, high schools and club teams may be forced to consider severe measures in the face of liability issues, like raising fees to offset higher premiums; capping potential damages; and requiring players to sign away their right to sue coaches and schools. Some schools and leagues may even shut down teams because the expense and legal risk are too high." An insurance broker explains, "A common misconception is that no one's going to sue their youth league or nonprofit, but that's not the case." A professor of sports law tells the *Times*, "Insurers will be tightening up their own coverage and make sports more expensive."[34] Youth football, a get-away ticket to college for project denizens and farmboy yokels alike, will lose its appeal to its natural constituency once the entrance fees exceed a country club's.

In a sense, the lawyers have already performed a dress rehearsal for the NFL litigation. In 1977, Riddell settled for $3 million with a player paralyzed at fifteen in a game six years earlier. The $1 million in lawyer fees extracted from the quadriplegic's settlement undoubtedly turned on light bulbs over the heads of many a personal injury attorney.[35] "Right or wrong," Chris Nowinski points out in *Head Games*, "this began a trend. Payouts from lawsuits against helmet manufacturers reached $22 million in 1981–1982, when the gross income of the entire industry was $20 million."[36] According to *Sports Illustrated*'s John Underwood,

Riddell faced $1.5 million insurance premiums in 1978 after paying just $40,000 three years earlier.[37] The legal costs, and the inflated insurance premiums, forced athletic equipment companies to abandon football headwear. Helmet manufacturers dwindled from fourteen in 1975 to a handful of companies—Riddell, Schutt, Xenith, Rawlings—that mass produce them today.[38] Ken Stabler's name doesn't appear on a lawsuit against Wilson because lawsuits already put Wilson out of the football helmet business. "Riddell is on the chopping block," Helmet Hut's Curtis Worrell observes. "As soon as they go down, Schutt comes right up. Then Schutt will be on the chopping block. This is the way of the world."[39]

The helmet lawsuits made helmet manufacturing cost prohibitive just as the current lawsuits will make football cost prohibitive. The helmet lawsuits drove out competition, which inevitably curtailed innovation and inspired designers to play it safe for their employers rather than for the players. They ensured that the design and technology remained stuck in the '70s through the '90s. Helmet Hut's Worrell maintains, "It's always the same issue: liability insurance. It will probably be the demise of our company, and people don't even wear our helmets," which are sold to collectors.[40]

Opponents hope, and enthusiasts fear, that the retired player suits will have a similar effect on football as a whole. "As a school board member," Dr. Paul Butler explained of his proposed ban on football, "I don't want to put the Dover taxpayers at risk for the lawsuits that you might engender. I don't want to spend the money to defend them and I don't want to spend the money on payouts because I want that money to go to teaching the children how to read and write and how to think."[41] Chris Bowler, the football father coaching his son's Arlington, Massachusetts, Pop Warner team, notes that he could foresee the War on Football eventually forcing his program to consolidate with a neighboring town just to field a squad.[42] Win or lose, the suit increases insurance premiums for youth football, discourages participation, and encourages future suits against leagues with less cash than the NFL. Even if the risks of football don't strike parents as prohibitive, the fee to play will.

Football may not be for everybody, as Coach Bergstrom conceded. But can't former football players too old for the game allow it to remain for Cam, Brendan, and Jack?

Football is a kids' game. It won't be for long if the adults have their way.

Concussions serve as the rationale but not the reason for the retired players' attack upon the game that once made them rich. Rod Tidwell could shout the real reason over his cell phone; or Deion Sanders could spell it out in the dirt with a Louisville Slugger.

$

CHAPTER FOUR

2013 IS THE NEW 1905

"I realize that you are an exceedingly busy man," Doc Pollard meekly wrote Walter Camp. Asking "pardon" for intruding on Camp's "valuable time," the head coach at the University of Alabama sought an authoritative voice—*the authoritative voice*—on whether several complicated formation shifts he employed in games passed muster. "I would greatly appreciate your ruling."[1] New Haven, Connecticut, once served as the Rome of the football religion, and Walter Camp served as its first pope. Even the head coach of the University of Alabama kissed his ring.

Before Walter Camp invented football, he played it. He loved the game so much that after he received his undergraduate degree from Yale in 1880 he spent the next several years studying at his alma mater's medical school, thereby extending his collegiate career to six seasons. Unsurprisingly, the football player didn't become a doctor: "I can't bear the sight of blood."[2] Instead of pursuing medicine, Camp worked for the New Haven Clock Company. He devoted his time away from time to football, which tellingly adopted a clock rather than innings to pace the acts of the play.

Camp officially coached Yale teams to three unofficial national championships. In an advisory capacity, he oversaw several additional championship squads. But his legacy to the game came more as rule maker and evangelist. In the early 1880s "when some of the American colleges were endeavoring against all odds to establish the sport of foot-ball, I undertook the then extremely unpleasant task of begging for space in daily papers, weekly periodicals, and magazines in which to exploit the advantages of the sport."[3] Mainly as a gridiron propagandist, Camp wrote several hundred articles and more than two dozen books over the course of his nearly sixty-seven-year life. His establishment of a paper team of "All Americans" at the end of every season remains a tradition whose popularity hasn't waned. Camp's rule making innovations include such taken-for-granted aspects of the game as downs from scrimmage, teams of eleven men, the snap from center, the two-point safety, and the requirement that offenses gain a predetermined number of yards to earn a new set of downs.[4]

In football, change and violence remain the only constants. The game evolves. A round ball elongates, a kicking game becomes a running game becomes a passing game, and posts extend atop the soccer goal to form an "H" goalpost. The man most responsible for transforming the ancient, barely recognizable game into the current one is Walter Chauncey Camp.

In the nearly half century between 1878 and his death in 1925, Walter Camp, in various roles, annually attended meetings of the various incarnations of football's rules committee.[5] Initially a student body, the committee morphed into a plaything of former players. Mirroring his station as a postgraduate player vis-à-vis undergraduate competitors on the field, Camp in the committee room kept getting older as the other rules committee members stayed the same age. This undoubtedly enhanced his influence. Camp ruled as only a man among boys could. By 1885, for instance, underclassmen, save for Yale's representative, exclusively peopled the committee.[6] Later, under pressure to add a western representative to his eastern clique, Camp chose Amos Alonzo Stagg, a former player who continued scouting for Yale long after he started coaching the University of Chicago.[7] Thus did the most influential figure in the game's most influential period retain influence. The secretary of football's rules committee ruled football.

Walter Camp took the English game of rugby and made the American game of football. His reshaping of an existing sport outraged purists. Then he became the outraged purist.

In the beginning, they tossed a coin. What followed wasn't so familiar.

When Rutgers hosted Princeton on November 6, 1869, for the first football game in history, twenty-five men faced twenty-five men. That iconic oblong pigskin appeared, to the time traveler from the future at least, compressed into soccer-ball roundness. Players could catch but not throw or run with the spherical bladder, which delayed the contest by periodically exhaling. Scoring required kicking the orb *beneath* a crossbar between two posts—hence, *foot*ball—which Rutgers did six times to Princeton's four. An amalgamation of soccer, rugby, and street fighting, football soon prohibited tripping and holding but permitted pretty much everything else.[8]

"From the very beginning of its history Foot-Ball met with such strenuous opposition even to the extent of the passing of laws making it an offense to engage in this sport," Camp recalled in 1903, noting that "in the natural order of things it should have passed rapidly out of existence."[9] When no intercollegiate games took place in 1871, it seemed that it would. But it didn't. The following year, Columbia and Rutgers further transformed the fledgling sport by agreeing to kick the ball above rather than below the crossbar.[10]

The American game developed as much from without as from within. In 1873, Yale played the English boarding school Eton under foreign rules dictating eleven players to a side.[11] That same year elite schools met to impose uniform rules on the anarchic game. Harvard, insisting that its Boston Game that permitted running with the ball differed too greatly to be reconciled with competing kicking versions of football, balked at attending. Shunned by natural competitors, Harvard welcomed Canadian opponent McGill to Cambridge, where in 1874 the Crimson learned to embrace the Canuck prolate spheroid over the round Yankee ball.[12] When neighborhood playmates eventually agreed to indulge their spoiled peer, Harvard got its reward for having taken its ball and gone home. Not only did the other schools agree to adopt Harvard's running game, but Harvard learned, significantly, that it could get its way in the future if it decided to throw a fit. Even in the 1870s, you could tell a Harvard man, but you couldn't tell him much.

With Yale deferring on several rules to its older academic sibling, the two schools agreed to play for the first time. In 1875, prep school student Walter Camp watched a game between Harvard and Yale that used a soccer ball. The next year, he played for Yale in a game that adopted Harvard's rugby one.[13] Harvard's running game, which emphasized blocking, forbidden in rugby, and tackling, forbidden in soccer, gave football its American stamp, inviting frightening hits and turning a kicking sport into a collision sport. Football gradually resembled a game that didn't resemble its name.

The violent amusement's arrival in the immediate aftermath of the Civil War can hardly be understood as coincidental. Less than five years earlier, young men, the same age as the players in that initial competition, fought on battlefields not all that different from the campus football field in New Brunswick, New Jersey. By accident of birth, the student athletes had missed out on the glory and the gory. Football initially served as mock warfare. Student-athletes whose older brothers tested their manhood on the battlefield now tested it on the football field. Pretend war strangely inspired more abolitionists than the genuine article.

The diversion earned its bellicose reputation. "Football was a brawl without the rules of the boxing ring: anyone with fisticuffs experience had a great advantage," recorded rules guru David M. Nelson.[14] If the impromptu fistfights didn't clue the spectator into the game's wild nature, then certainly the hippie heads of the combatants did. In the days before helmets, players protected themselves with long hair.[15] Linemen were rock stars before rock stars were rock stars. And only in 1899 did football legislators decree ejection for players "striking with the closed fist."[16] The game they played was rarely lethal. It was always combat.

The relationship between football and war may have existed merely at the subconscious level in 1869. But in time spectators understood the strategic, violent competition as a civilized substitute for war. "Football IS war on a mimic scale and it will continue just as long as the nation is virile enough to fight," Camp, promoting the Daily Dozen exercises for the military, noted during the First World War.[17] Stadiums took on the architecture of imperial conquest and their names—Memorial Stadium, the Vet, Legion Field, Soldier Field—paid tribute to those who waged football by other means. Society venerated star athletes in a manner akin to the honors bestowed upon war heroes. Tactics and strategy, devised by older men distant from the rigors of combat, more often proved the difference between winning and losing in football than in any other sport. Competitors marching into battle, backed by uniformed bands playing martial music and protected by modern-day chain mail, underscore the metaphorical connection to warfare. So does the football lexicon's inter-changeability with the military lexicon.

As the late comedian George Carlin reminded, "In football the object is for the quarterback, also known as the field general, to be on target with his aerial assault, riddling the defense by hitting his receivers with deadly accuracy in spite of the blitz, even if he has to use the shotgun. With short bullet passes and long bombs, he marches his troops into enemy territory, balancing this aerial assault with a sustained ground attack that punches holes in the forward wall of the enemy's defensive line." On the other hand, "In baseball the object is to go home! And to be safe! I hope I'll be safe at home!"[18]

But at the turn of the last century, baseball players weren't arriving home safely.

On a sunny Saturday in 1905, Henry Diehl stepped to the plate on a Wooster, Ohio, diamond to face Bert Thorne. The pitcher let a curveball get away that struck the twenty-year-old batsman above his right ear. As Diehl trotted to first base, he kept his sense of humor, announcing: "I've got it on the noodle." But he collapsed and then died within an hour.[19]

More than a century later, nobody much talks about Henry Diehl or of a crisis in American baseball. Terrifying violence doesn't fit the narrative of a game often described as bucolic but never as barbaric. Instead, Henry Diehl's death-by-curveball coincided with the great crisis in American *football*.

In 1905 and 1906, twenty-nine football players lost their lives directly and indirectly from play at all levels of competition.[20] The most remarkable but least remarked upon fact regarding football's great crisis is that baseball's great non-crisis claimed more lives. History may not have noticed. But Robert Coughlin, a New York–based physician, did. His study counted 943 sports deaths in the United States from 1905 to 1915. Baseball was blamed for nearly a third of those fatalities, more than any other sport.[21] During the 1905 and 1906 seasons, the *Chicago Tribune* counted twenty-nine football deaths. Coughlin tabulated baseball's body count for those years at thirty.[22]

Baseball's great non-crisis eclipsed football's great crisis by a single death. Thankfully, baseball's extinction never loomed.

In *Death at the Ballpark: A Comprehensive Study of Game-Related Fatalities, 1862–2007*, researchers Robert M. Gorman and David Weeks painstakingly detail hundreds of baseball-related deaths. Though the numbers include tangentially related fatalities such as those from lightning strikes and bleacher collapses, the book convinces that swinging bats, speeding pitches, and charging outfielders can be every bit as deadly as colliding helmets.

- Dennis "Big Dan" Brouthers raced from third to home in the fifth inning of a semi-pro game in 1877. The 200-pound, six-foot-two pitcher crashed into the opposing catcher, John Quigley, who died one month later. A despondent Brouthers contemplated leaving baseball. But he overcame his grief, batting .342 over nineteen seasons in the major leagues. The Hall of Fame accepted Brouthers posthumously into its ranks in 1945.[23]

- On September 26, 1909, Eugene Swinbank got hit in the chest after moving behind the count 0-2 with the bases loaded. "I'll force one run in, anyway," the seventeen-year-old Chicagoan testified upon trotting toward first. He never made it—to base or the hospital.[24]

- Pitcher George Wesley endured a beaning in his first-inning at-bat against a rival Utah team in 1915. He responded not by plunking the opposing pitcher but by hitting a homerun off of him in the sixth inning. He crossed home plate and promptly collapsed. Wesley, whose last conscious act involved the completion of the ultimate hitting achievement, died the next morning.[25]

- Grapevine High School pitcher Chris Gavora threw batting practice behind a screen to a teammate within a batting cage on February 22, 2007. In another nearby cage, a player "hit a line drive that went through an opening in the net, across an open area, and through the other batting cage's opening" to hit Gavora in the back of the head. The Dallas-area high school junior died two days later.[26]

Freak accidents, of the type that ended Chris Gavora's life, happen during any number of otherwise benign activities. Still, few experiences pose the danger that a cowhide orb spinning toward your unprotected head at 95 mph does. To limit such risks, baseball reformed, at least in a manner in keeping with the traditionalist nature of the sport. Governing authorities mandated protective equipment and banned dangerous practices. Nobody tried to ban baseball.

Death at the Ballpark tells the story of America's most dangerous game evolving into a relatively safe one. So complete has this transformation become that stating the fact that baseball once killed more of its players than football surely would elicit widespread disbelief if not scorn. Fans don't think of baseball as a deadly game. But it sometimes is and often was. Theodore Roosevelt, the president of the United States when Henry Diehl collapsed on the diamond, had as a federal bureaucrat applauded *Scribner's Monthly*'s "reprobation of brutal base ball" in a letter to Walter Camp.[27] Baseball brutal? Really?

George Carlin may have believed that baseball isn't a contact sport. Ray Fosse doesn't.

Baseball never endured an existential crisis. Football, in *Groundhog Day* fashion, repeatedly experiences the same existential crisis—*2013 is the new 1905*. Before that, 1909 was the new 1905—and 1905 the new 1894. Reform never satiates an abolitionist.

More than one hundred years ago, players suffered grave on-field injuries, medical doctors prescribed euthanasia for the sport, and politicians made a federal case out of a ball game. The national uproar that today greets Pop Warner concussions and NFL bounties isn't as loud as the national uproar that met the rough game in the first decade of the last century. But glimpsing at 1905, one can't help but notice uncanny resemblances to the current controversy.

Though doomed to periodically face extermination, the crises bless the sport with the tools to avert extinction. Unlike, say, its antecedent soccer, whose fixed rules make today's game familiar to the ghosts of George Best and Ricardo Zamora, association football's unrecognizable offspring now plays unrecognizable to those who birthed it. Football is a revolutionary game of violence and change. The former quality necessitates the latter. Ares and Proteus share equal claims as its deity. More than a century after 1905, football has grown habituated to breaking its habits.

The sport they played then certainly *resembles* football now. Despite the same name, it wasn't the same game. It took five yards to get a first down. There was no end zone. Referees penalized coaches for, well, coaching. On a change of possession, players simply changed position: the offense became the defense and the defense the offense. The rules required six men, not seven, on the line of scrimmage. There was no neutral zone. Most players didn't wear helmets, even leather ones. Instead of merely snapping the ball backward, centers could kick it forward. Stranger still, the quarterback to whom a center snapped the ball could not pass it forward.[28] Without the threat of the pass to keep them honest, defenders bunched close to the line of scrimmage. Many teams lined up, for instance, in a 7-3-1 defense. One back could get a head start through forward motion, a vestige of the mass momentum plays restricted in 1894. Running backs, without much hope of overcoming the beef amassed on the line of scrimmage, relied not solely on their legs but in great part on their linemen pushing and pulling them forward—so much so that running backs once employed seamstresses to sew handles on their uniforms.[29] Such a cramped game injured players less than spectators, who could barely follow the ball in the brawl.

"Never before has a football season ended amid such a well-nigh universal chorus of denunciation of the game, or with such a record of fatalities," reported the *Nation* following the 1905 season. "At least our college presidents have found their voices; some of them at least have got beyond the fear of losing students by attacking what has become an intolerable evil, and are ready to follow [Harvard] President [Charles] Eliot's lead in demanding change." The piece described football as a "grave menace" that merited immediate abolition.[30]

Harvard's president got a jump on the 1905 season by addressing "The Evils of Football" during the spring semester. "Some danger attends almost all of the manly sports, and taking their risks makes part of the interest in them," he conceded, "but the risks of football are exaggerated and unreasonable." The college president downplayed the game's roughness by noting that "the risk in riding horseback, driving an automobile, or boating and yachting" exceeded the risks in football. For Eliot, if not his cheerleaders at the *Nation*, "the main objection lies against its moral quality." He decried the game's trickery, coaching from the sidelines, and bunched-up mass play that concealed violent shenanigans. The inability of referees to police so many players, in effect, rewarded rather than punished a circumvention of the rules.[31]

Charles Eliot and the *Nation*, like the game they despised, came to America's attention in the immediate aftermath of the Civil War. Eliot had become Harvard's president in 1869 at age thirty-five and had transformed higher education by deemphasizing the classics in favor of utilitarian training for the professions. The *Nation*, founded in 1865, was then and is now a leading voice of progressivism. Though the game's appeal, then as now, trespassed across political boundaries, a progressive ideology vaguely united many of football's opponents at the turn of the last century.

The War on Football very much fit into the crusading spirit of the times. Do-gooders earnestly sought to right every wrong through top-down reform. The paternalism dictated who could breed through a wave of eugenics legislation. It dictated which liquids could be imbibed through an alcohol ban. This we-know-best mentality extended to overseeing the games people played. Certainly few university professors, social gospel ministers, or settlement house volunteers watched, let alone played, football. They nevertheless voiced strong opinions about it.

Thorstein Veblen, scourge of walking sticks, duels, classical languages, and other anachronisms, similarly judged football a "one-sided return to barbarism." Veblen's *Theory of the Leisure Class* seconded the notion that "the relationship of football to physical culture is much the same as that of the bull-fight to agriculture."[32]

"Should an alleged sport that necessitates taking such chances receive the sanction and encouragement of sane and sensible people?" asked Congressman Charles Landis, whose brother became the first commissioner of baseball. "Possibly so. I desire to register my opinion, however, that dog fighting, cock fighting, and bull fighting are Sabbath school games in comparison with modern football."[33]

"Football to-day is a social obsession—a boy-killing, education-prostituting, gladiatorial sport," contended social gospel theologian Shailer Mathews. "It teaches virility and courage, but so does war. I do not know what should take its place, but the new game should not require the services of a physician, the maintenance of a hospital, and the celebration of funerals."[34]

Within this toxic atmosphere, even the partisans of football recognized that change must come. Among them was a young politician named Theodore Roosevelt. He confessed to Walter Camp in a lengthy 1895 letter, "Of all the games I personally like foot ball the best, and I would rather see my boys play it than see them play any other."[35] Ten years later, Roosevelt was president of the United States and used his office to reform the game that he loved.

"I want to talk over certain football matters with you," Theodore Roosevelt wrote Walter Camp on October 2, 1905, "and I very earnestly hope that you will be able to come."[36] Twenty-nine years earlier, Harvard freshman Theodore Roosevelt, along with a few hundred other spectators, traveled to New Haven and watched Yale freshman Walter Camp and his teammates win by scoring one field goal to Harvard's two touchdowns. The game, as the strange scoring suggests, had changed a lot between 1876 and 1905.[37] Being there at football's beginning, Camp and Roosevelt, graduates from the class of 1880, shared an interest in not seeing its end.

Roosevelt, as his characterization of the meeting to son Kermit as an attempt to eliminate "mucker play" suggests, believed the sport's problems could be solved by enforcing existing rules rather than creating new ones.[38] He never threatened to abolish the sport, as a stubborn myth holds.[39] The president pledged to stand by football but noted that the sport could do itself a favor by more faithfully adhering to the principles of sportsmanship. The president, at the White House luncheon of October 9, 1905, recited examples of unfair play by Princeton, Yale, and Harvard, each of the schools represented at the two-hour meeting.[40] Afterwards, the principals released a joint statement pledging their universities to "carry out in letter and in spirit the rules of the game."[41] Football, like the Russo-Japanese War, had become a federal concern.

Getting Harvard and Yale to break bread at the White House wasn't in the league of cajoling the Russians and Japanese to sit down for peace in Kittery, Maine, as Roosevelt had famously done a month earlier to win the Nobel Peace Prize. But, as the milquetoast statement released in the meeting's aftermath suggests, getting the Ivy rivals to agree on anything substantive required a power higher than the president of the United States. When Harvard Coach Bill Reid sat down with Walter Camp alongside the president in Washington, beating Yale, not reforming football, dominated his thoughts.

Reid had defeated Yale by scoring two touchdowns as a player in 1898. He had defeated Yale in 1901 in his first coaching stint. But without Bill Reid as player or coach, the Crimson had won just two of the twenty-five other football contests against the Bulldogs. As Reid explained to his players before the 1905 season, their task was to uplift the university from "the most disastrous Athletic year that Harvard has ever known: beaten [by Yale] in baseball, football, tennis, track and crew, and in fact everything that really counts."[42] Bill Reid had Yale on the brain.

Reid's obsession inspired several trips to New Haven to scout the opposition's equipment ("For shoulder pads, Yale is away ahead of us.").[43] He investigated a Bulldog player he suspected of being a ringer.[44] He scheduled opponents for the purpose of providing Harvard with the most advantageous path to that final, crucial contest.[45] Before the season started, and as it progressed, Reid attempted to maneuver Paul Dashiell, a referee friendly to Walter Camp, out of officiating the rivalry game.[46] Even when Harvard played Dartmouth, it was about beating Yale.

Such an outcome certainly would have pleased Roosevelt. "Did you ever know anything more disgraceful than Harvard's record in football this year?" Roosevelt asked his son in 1903. "I think it has been one of the most humiliating things I have ever heard of. Imagine being beaten on her own ground by both Amherst and Dartmouth."[47] The Harvard Man in the Oval Office now had an added interest in his alma mater's athletics. His son played on the Cambridge school's freshman team. The president took pride in his namesake's participation. When Theodore Roosevelt Jr. suffered a minor cut at practice, journalists made it a major story in the newspapers.[48] The son's rough go of it on the field fueled speculation regarding the father's reform efforts off the field. The presidential scion dismissed media reports that Yale's freshmen eleven had targeted him for injury as "a lie," "rotten talk," and "all bosh." The broken-nosed boy reported to his father, "I am very glad that I made the team anyway. I feel so large in my black sweater with the numerals on."[49]

His father felt rather large in the White House. This paradoxically amounted to paying big attention to small concerns. A man empowered to direct generals in war zones focused instead on generals directing pseudo-battlefields, a domain over which the president possessed little legitimate authority. The minutiae of a boys' game increasingly occupied the thoughts of the most powerful man in America.

The coaches overseeing the game viewed Roosevelt's attention as validation rather than intrusion. Camp, to whom football ranked in importance somewhere below his wife but above clocks, congratulated the president for focusing on football reform but opined that "the opponents of the game will make it just as difficult as possible for us to improve upon the spirit of the sport." If football reformers "fritter away their energies in manifold suggestions" such as "forward passing," Camp complained to Roosevelt, then "they will never accomplish their purpose."[50]

The man most responsible for the introduction of the forward pass was a nineteen-year-old halfback who neither threw nor caught a ball during his brief playing career. Harold Moore, a native of the northern New York border town of Ogdensburg, studied engineering at Union College. He worked summers for the electric company. A brother in the Phi Delta Theta fraternity, Moore's sunny disposition inspired the ironic nickname "Blue." The sophomore's athleticism—in addition to varsity football he ran track and played basketball and hockey—made him a big man on campus. "His ability as a football player won him many friends almost as soon as he entered college, and he was one of the most popular men" at Union.[51] More than the cheers of his fellow students, Moore craved the presence of his father at the final game of the season. The running back was just a year older than Theodore Roosevelt Jr., and, like many teenagers, wished for his parents to share in his enthusiasms. William Moore's only son wrote to petition his father to attend the game. He accepted and traveled several hundred miles to the Bronx to watch.[52]

So when Blue Moore fell and never got up on a dreary fall day, the cheery sophomore couldn't help but become the Junior Seau of his day, a smiling symbol of the dangers of the game he loved. Football would never be the same after November 25, 1905.

The play that changed football forever came during the first half of a scoreless contest. What happened remains something of a mystery. A spectator gauged that "Moore tackled his opponent too high."[53] NYU's coach maintained that "a Union man who attempted to help Moore stop the play struck Moore on the chin with his knee, which resulted in Moore's death."[54] The manager of the Union team contended that during the tackle "both the New York University man and the Union man fell on Moore. We knew as soon as the play was stopped that Moore was badly hurt, for his head hit the ground with a great deal of force."[55] In the *New York Times* telling of the story the next day, the Union star died trying to score a touchdown: "Moore got the ball at the 30-yard line and started toward the goal. He was tackled and thrown by a New York University man. The next moment there was a pile of men on the field, with Moore at the bottom of it."[56] A History Channel article depicts a teammate inadvertently kicking Moore in the head.[57] Another modern account claims that the pile crushed Moore to death.[58]

Though several accounts read as contradictory, it is possible that numerous collisions—with a cleat, a knee, the ground, the runner, a teammate, the pile—occurred on the same down. Without the benefit of instant replay, one can't conclusively say much more than Blue Moore suffered a brain injury. No such mystery surrounded the injury itself. So evident was Moore's unconsciousness that several doctors, as well as the police, apparently stormed the field immediately. "Detective Sergeant Darcy, who had been doing special duty with twelve policemen, broke through the lines and cleared the players away," the Old Gray Lady

colorfully reported. "Moore was lying flat on his face on the field uncon-
scious." The presence of an automobile—a contraption unavailable just
a few years earlier—to rush Moore to the hospital ultimately made no
difference.[59] The popular player died that evening of a brain hemorrhage
with his father bedside.

A few facts remain fairly consistent across the *Rashomon* vantage
points, fog of time, and second-hand reports. Harold Moore suffered a
concussion earlier that season. He had been told by his doctor not to
play football. He played anyway. Beyond that, the story gets convoluted.
"After the accident a Union College professor told me that Moore had
been injured in a football game three weeks ago and that he had a clot
of blood on his brain," a parent-spectator explained.[60] "Moore's head
was injured in the game between Wesleyan and Union a month ago,"
the *New York Tribune* reported. "It was thought he had completely
recovered."[61] Other accounts suggest that the malady prompting the
earlier doctor-ordered exile from the field may have involved something
other than the previous head injury. "It was learned that Moore had been
ill, that he had been warned against football some time ago by his own
physician in Schenectady, who said that he was not in condition to play.
His death was directly due, however, to concussion of the brain."[62] One
needn't have read obscure medical journals to understand the dangers
of concussions in the fall of 1905; they appeared on the front pages of
America's most widely read newspapers.

If Blue Moore had been the only player to fall that Saturday, football
would still have experienced a public relations nightmare. But after
reporting Moore's death, newspapers detailed several other casualties,
increasing the urgency of reformers and abolitionists alike. Carl Osborne,
a high school senior, died in a Rockville, Indiana, game after a tackler
drove Osborne's rib into his heart. Robert Brown, a fifteen-year-old
player paralyzed that day in a game in Sedalia, Missouri, passed away
three days later.[63] A Columbia running back suffered a serious spine
injury.[64]

The headlines in the week leading up to that dreary Saturday reported that Harvard's captain had experienced a head injury in a game against Dartmouth.[65] The sandlot fatalities of anonymous teenagers stirred public heartstrings only so much. The captain of one of the nation's powerhouse football programs being sidelined with a major concussion and the president's son suffering from the game's violence fixated everybody's attention on the ferocious nature of the sport. Who could fix football? Was football even fixable?

Harvard coach Bill Reid discovered that his star player Daniel Hurley was "a little out of his head." Understanding the seriousness of a "concussion on the brain," both medically and from a public relations standpoint, Harvard's coach removed the team leader from the field and downplayed why. Harvard brought in a specialist, who recommended hospitalization.[66] "John, I'm going to play in the game if I have to jump through that window," a hospitalized Dan Hurley told his brother. "To play against Yale this year has been the ambition of my life and there will be a fight if they don't let me out."[67] Harvard men sang him fight songs and sent him telegrams.[68] But Harvard didn't let him play.

Coach Reid demanded his players report every injury, no matter how minor. Team doctors not only took meticulous care of their athlete-patients, they studied them, leaving detailed records for posterity. Two doctors assigned to the team counted 1,057 practice and game days missed due to injuries. They treated eight dislocated shoulders, thirteen sprained ankles, one broken leg, and nineteen concussions. That last injury vexed the pair. Anticipating the concerns of their profession more than a century later, they expressed frustration about concussed athletes like Hurley returning to play, and wondered what permanent damage the temporary condition unleashed. "Concussion was treated by the players in general as a trivial injury, and rather regarded as a joke," the doctors concluded. "The real seriousness of the injury is not certain. Our own experience with the after-effects of the cases is not sufficient for us to draw any definite conclusions, but from conversation with various neurologists, we have obtained very various opinions in regard to the possibility of serious after-effects."[69]

A team doctor, as reported by Reid in his diary, had earlier lectured the varsity that "in case any man in any game got hurt by a hit on the head so that he did not realize what he was doing, his team mate should at once insist that time be called and that a doctor come onto the field to see what is the trouble, also that every man on the squad must make up his mind in case he gets hurt, to have a friend with him from the time the injury occurred until noon of the next day, to prevent any serious results from beginning without anybody being around."[70] By the time of Hurley's concussion, the doctors adopted a more stringent policy of confining concussed players to the infirmary overnight.[71] Harvard's treatment of, and reaction to, their concussed captain could be used as a model for teams today. Our ignorance of the past prompts us to assume the past's ignorance.

Without their on-field leader, Harvard's team ventured across the Charles on Saturday, November 25, 1905, to take on their archrivals. Demand skyrocketed $2 tickets to $30.[72] Paul Dashiell, the Walter Camp lackey whom Reid had tried so hard to prevent from refereeing, officiated. When a Harvard player called for a fair catch at the opposition's forty-yard line, a rushing Yalie slugged him in the face. The referees recognized neither the blow nor the signal, a crucial oversight given the rule allowing for a fair-catch free kick.* Henry L. Higginson, who had donated the land for the newly constructed Harvard Stadium, demanded that Reid remove his team from the field in protest. The twenty-seven-year-old coach ignored the entreaty—as he tried to ignore Camp's post-game handshake.[73] Harvard, as had been their usual lot in *the* game, went on to lose: Yale 6, Harvard 0.

Two days before the game, Harvard's president told a correspondent that "intercollegiate football ought to be forbidden to Harvard students"

---

*A free kick allows the receiving team to opt to try an unobstructed field goal on the down immediately following a fair catch. The NCAA has since eliminated the obscure rule. An NFL team hasn't converted a free kick since 1976. Given the positioning of the uprights on the goal line, the greater bounce of the more rounded football used, and the four rather than three points awarded for field goals, the Dashiell crew's non-calls likely harmed Harvard significantly.

but that he remained unsure whether the school's governing boards yet held that opinion.[74] Very soon after the controversial season-ending game he became quite sure of the agreement between his views and their views.

Poor sportsmanship and brutality on such a big stage underscored the problems plaguing football. About a week following the big game, Harvard's All-American tackle, Karl Brill, announced his retirement and denounced the sport as "brutal" and "gladiatorial." An injured Brill noted that "the human body was never meant to withstand the enormous strain which football demands."[75]

Save for Yale, no subject abraded Coach Bill Reid more during the 1905 season than Karl Brill. Reid agonized in his diary over "Brill's absolute worthlessness," "dreamy nature," "queer ideas," and "impossible temperament."[76] Brill's weeklong summertime disappearance on the high seas, which led Reid to speculate on his drowning, reinforced the coach's dim assessment of his player as a flake.[77] But Brill better understood the correct priorities of a student-athlete than his coach did. The athletically gifted loafer confessed to a teammate, "I would much rather get an 'A' in Calculus than to score a touch down against Yale." The comment left his coach "thoroughly disgusted."[78] When a class caused the oft-tardy lineman to arrive late for practice, the coach told him to skip it next time.[79] Brill's suffering grades, as much as his suffering body, hastened his exit from the sport. In his diary, Reid pondered cutting Brill.[80] In the newspapers, Brill cut Reid.

The game had survived the assaults of academics, preachers, and scribes. Could it long endure attacks from its stars?

The week after the Harvard-Yale game, President Roosevelt attended the annual Army-Navy game, bringing "a peculiar importance to the contest." If the game momentarily distracted the president from the indignities suffered by his alma mater the previous week, he needed only to glance down upon Navy's head coach, the same Paul Dashiell who had so controversially refereed the ferocious Harvard-Yale game.

The coach's confident midshipmen had publicly wagered $6,000 on themselves. But Army and nightfall conspired to hold them to a tie in a game called because of darkness.[81]

Princeton hosted the event, and away from the gridiron Princeton President Woodrow Wilson entertained President Roosevelt. Though eventual political enemies, they shared a deep love for football and a desire to save the game from itself. "Unless brutality and danger to the lives of players is reduced materially," the *New York Times* reported after the game, Roosevelt "realizes that the sport is practically doomed."[82]

The Monday following the game, the president met with Harvard Coach Bill Reid at the White House. Surely the president's beaten and bloodied son, as well as the pending extinction of the game he loved at the school he loved, weighed on his mind. But the coach refused to divulge what the president had said—at least for several decades.[83] He later recalled, "The President was in great humor, and everyone felt perfectly at ease. He would lean and look down the table at me, and make facetious remarks from time to time, like, 'You getting enough to eat down there, Reid? My wife doesn't know what these football appetites are like, you know.'"[84] The two Harvard alums discussed, among other topics, a Harvard player slugging a Penn player subsequent to the earlier White House fair play agreement and the savagery and unfairness of the previous week's Harvard-Yale game.[85] Roosevelt, who had earlier declined Reid's request to assign an alumnus in the armed forces to a Boston Harbor fort so that he could help coach the Crimson, remained true to his school here.[86] Paul Dashiell—Navy coach, referee, and member of Walter Camp's Intercollegiate Rules Committee—felt the commander in chief's wrath. Up for appointment as a professor of chemistry at the Naval Academy, Dashiell waited and waited and waited.[87]

Dashiell's patron felt the pressure, too. Walter Camp played by his own set of rules. By coaching a game whose penalties and prohibitions he largely devised, the secretary of football's rules committee cultivated champions—*and resentment*. Small colleges and big Western universities wondered why a few men unelected by them deigned to make rules for their contests.[88] Rivals questioned whether the rules committee didn't regard its charge as keeping the game safe for the Yale Bulldogs.[89] After Harvard unveiled the flying wedge to its advantage in a loss to Yale in 1892, and Penn used it the following year to become the first squad to score on Yale in four seasons, Camp spearheaded the ban on the inverted "v" juggernaut.[90] It endangered both players on the field and Yale in the standings. So football's most celebrated and controversial formation became also one of its briefest. But Yale's grinding style of mass play, which bored spectators and bruised athletes, survived. In the same way that the rest of the Ivy League** resented Camp's domination of them, smaller schools resented Ivy League domination of the sport. The tragic events of the fall of 1905 provided the opportunity to loosen Camp's grip on the game he crafted. Beaten by Yale on the field, Reid's determination to beat Camp intensified. A member of the Intercollegiate Rules Committee, Reid nevertheless privately regarded it as "merely a tool of Camp's" that "ought to be abolished at once."[91] Many at Harvard, including its president, board of overseers, and faculty, felt that way about football. In the wake of the brutal season, the school's boards and faculty came out for prohibiting the game on the Cambridge campus.[92]

Metaphorically down 29–13 with 42 seconds left in the fourth quarter, Reid required a miracle. Caught between a calcified, Yale-dominated rules committee impervious to substantial change and a Harvard establishment demanding substantial change as a precondition to reentering the game, Reid essentially had to walk the finest of lines to defeat Harvard *and* Yale on the same field. The amazing story of football's do-or-die comeback witnessed Ivy League espionage, sudden jaw-dropping shifts in allegiance, skullduggery at the highest levels of the U.S. government, shocking *sub rosa* agreements, and a double-cross switcheroo worthy of Machiavelli. Reid relied on the tactics of a coach, but more important, on the *brashness* of a young coach, to rescue the game.

** No such Ivy League existed in any official manner for nearly a half century.

Tipped off through intrigue that the Harvard Corporation had secretly voted to strike down football, Reid and his cohorts released a public letter under the coach's name that recycled the school president's criticisms of the game to urge reform instead of abolition.[93] Channeling his inner-Eliot, Reid's early-November missive lambasted the "distinct advantage to be gained by the brutality and evasion of the rules" and called for an overhaul.[94] Reid hoped his epistle would prompt the board to reconsider. It prompted many friends of the game to reconsider whether Reid remained on their side.[95] The coach, who affixed his name to sentiments not wholly his own, clearly loved the game more than his reputation. The football friendly Harvard group set about devising its own set of reforms to save the game from itself. "We took great pains in the preparation of that letter, discussing the probable effect of each sentence and word before letting it go," Reid recalled two decades later. "We secured a copy of President Eliot's criticism, and embodied all of his suggestions in the letter, with a manner of expression as close to his own as we dared use."[96] The letter undermined Eliot and one-upped Camp.

A vehicle for reform appeared the next month in the form of the Intercollegiate Athletic Association, an outfit launched by NYU Chancellor Henry MacCracken to rid campuses of the autumnal menace. Stung by his hometown newspaper conveying a grisly image of burly NYU players piling on Harold Moore, MacCracken went into public relations overdrive to exonerate NYU and indict football.[97] MacCracken publically petitioned the coroner examining Moore's body to determine that a collision, rather than a pig pile, caused the player's death. The coroner found what MacCracken, and probably what the truth, had demanded.[98] The chancellor denounced the game's "homicidal feature" in a speech before students and judged football players "below the band of gladiators in the coliseum" in their "exaltation of bulk and brawn over brains."[99] He wrote Harvard University president Charles Eliot to organize a conference considering the game's abolishment. Eliot curtly, and somewhat strangely, balked.

"Deaths and injuries are not the strongest arguments against football," Harvard's president told his peer. "That cheating and brutality are profitable is the main evil." Striking at the game while the gridiron was hot appeared to the septuagenarian-going-on-centenarian as a form of the very cheating he railed against in sports. While Eliot's punt disappointed MacCracken—who thought a man of Eliot's stature could influence trustees—it created an opportunity for Reid to score.[100] Once again, the twentysomething Cantabrigian would outwit the man who had assumed Harvard's presidency almost a decade before his birth.

The chancellor of NYU plunged ahead without Harvard, calling a conference on football that welcomed any institution to participate that had played his school since 1895. The gathering considered whether football should be abandoned or reformed, and, if the former, what game should replace it?[101]

Delegates from thirteen schools attended the first meeting on December 8, 1905. While the conferees addressed the issue of football, unwittingly, they did much more. The organization they created, the Intercollegiate Athletic Association (ICAA), would eventually rename itself the National Collegiate Athletic Association (NCAA) and govern nearly all intercollegiate athletics in the United States. In several meetings over the next few months, they made history and remade football.

The question of reform implied a desire to wrest football legislation from Camp's sclerotic rules committee. But for some schools the problem stemmed not from Camp but from the game that he largely governed. One of the initial meeting's invitees, Columbia University, which had revived football in 1899 after an eleven-year respite only to suffer an embarrassing scandal for employing non-student tramp players, had already decided upon abolition in the wake of the casualties.[102] A university committee, acting over Thanksgiving weekend at the behest of President Nicholas Butler, opined that "the present game of football should be abolished" and "the game [should] be prohibited at Columbia University."[103]

MIT, Duke, and Northwestern jettisoned their programs. Soon Stanford and Berkeley ditched football for rugby. The president of the latter school, which replaced football with its ancestor, doubted that rugby's American offspring could survive. He predicted before the school's first football-free season, "In my opinion, the whole country will within five years be playing the Rugby game."[104] Stanford president David Starr Jordan, who had hired Walter Camp to coach his fledgling school's fledgling football team in the 1890s, wrote Yale's football honcho in 1905 that "reform is more urgent here than in some other sections of the country."[105] Shortly thereafter, he, like Cal's president, became an evangelist for rugby.[106] At MacCracken's conference, five (Union, NYU, Columbia, Stevens, Rochester) of the thirteen schools attending voted to abolish football.[107] Surely if the oldest and most prestigious school in the nation also dropped the game others would play follow the leader.

Football's survival was in doubt. Though neither the president pushing reform nor the dueling factions presumed the power to abolish football nationwide, the potential abandonment of the burgeoning game by a few key schools risked a cascading effect that might marginalize or end the game. Camp's old guard procrastinated. Deference to Reid's group of Harvard reformers, still working out their own plan, in part explains the delay. Reluctance, at least for the old committee's most powerful member, explains it, too. As the old committee fiddled, MacCracken's group acted. The thirteen schools agreed to the West Point–advanced idea for a new rules committee and cast a wider net for a conference on football reform by extending invitations to upwards of 200 schools.[108] There's safety in numbers.

On the eve of January 1906 meetings by the very different rules committees in the very same city, Reid dramatically resigned his membership on Camp's rules committee and startled the new committee by announcing his intention to join it. The following night, Reid showed up at the competing ICAA gathering and waited in the corridor while stunned members considered his admittance—*and their fortune*.[109] The young coach at the old college had shifted the balance of power. The unlikely character that aided Reid's exodus from Camp's committee was coach/referee/rule maker/chemist Paul Dashiell. With a Naval Academy promotion held in limbo by the president, Dashiell urged the old guard to merge with the new.[110] Eventually, the secretary of the navy signed off on

Dashiell's promotion. He never again, though, refereed a Harvard-Yale game.[111] Just weeks before the Reid-Dashiell coup, Roosevelt had written, in a general sense, to Camp of the "very great importance to get the umpire freed from the danger of unpleasant consequences."[112]

Curiously, representatives of two schools controlled directly by the federal government—West Point and the Naval Academy—did more to further Harvard's, and its most famous alumnus's, reform ends. The president's big stick ensured that he could speak softly, or not at all, and manipulate underlings toward his ends.

The stunning addition of Reid added legitimacy and star power to the ICAA's gathering of mostly smaller schools in January 1906. While the ICAA members failed to get Harvard's president, they got its coach. No longer could Camp's clique legislate for colleges without their representation. The Intercollegiate Rules Committee yielded to the inevitable. The pressure forged the two rules committees into one, with compromise candidate James Babbitt of Cornell assuming the leadership role that Camp had so long occupied. "Or so the old committee thought," records historian John Sayle Watterson. "Reid and Babbitt had worked out a different scenario. Once the two committees joined, James Babbitt startled the old committee by resigning as secretary and designating Bill Reid to take his place. In less time than it took to play one half of a football game, Harvard had unveiled the flying wedge of football politics."[113]

With Harvard promising to go lest change came, Reid issued an ultimatum to the joint rules committee: accept Harvard's reform plan or lose football at America's most important school.[114] The rule makers understood the importance of keeping Harvard on the field and acquiesced. Tricked and out-strategized, Camp had finally tasted defeat.

The 1906 season that followed featured first downs at ten yard intervals, a neutral zone, the end of pre-snap forward motion, an additional referee, and other Reid-driven reforms.[115] It also featured a Crimson team, which won the begrudging blessing of the board Brahmins after

Reid secured the reforms. Like his ally in the White House, Harvard's coach played the conservative reformer, instituting radical change in the spirit of preserving the established order. And Reid, like his fellow Harvard alumnus in Washington, employed means fair and foul to do so.

Harvard, which in the 1870s dragged Yale screaming but barely kicking into the running era of football, now hurled its rival into the passing era. The Yale man who invented football helplessly watched its reinvention. Worse still, his diminished place on the new committee forced him to serve as the revised rulebook's scribe, dutifully writing down the obituary for the game he had created.[116]

The radical changes evoke philosopher John Searle's distinction between "regulative" and "constitutive" rules.[117] Whereas the addition of an official, the subtraction of ten minutes from the game clock, and the requirement to move the ball ten yards to win new downs merely *regulated* an existing game, the introduction of the forward pass *constituted* a new game entirely. The designated hitter and the three-point shot appear minor modifications next to the aerial attack. No rugby-derived game had allowed forward passing. Kicking? Laterals? Runs? Sure. Passing? That's for basketball. What Bill Reid appreciated as preservation, Walter Camp saw as destruction. It's easy for posterity to dismiss Camp as an atavist clutching yesterday. But to many football lovers in 1905, the Bulldog guarding his turf appeared as their paladin protecting their passion from extinction. The reformer of the 1880s and 1890s became the conservative of the 1900s. Somewhere the partisans of the kicking game snickered at their conqueror lamenting the loss of the ground game. If football could remain *foot*ball after running overwhelmed kicking, then surely calling football "football" after the air game overtook the ground game proved no greater offense against semantics.

Forward passes remained a rarity; the revised rules treated incompletions as turnovers. Relying on their running games, much as they had the previous season, Harvard and Yale entered their annual contest unbeaten and untied, amplifying the significance of college football's most significant grudge match. Bill Reid traveled to New Haven in search of vindication. Instead, he found his undoing in the play his rules committee foe so vehemently opposed. "It was not until the Harvard-Yale game that a great forward-pass play appeared," reported football historian Parke Davis, "but with this play Yale won the contest by sending the ball thirty yards to Harvard's three-yard mark, from which the touchdown was quickly made."[118] Yale 6, Harvard 0.

Bill Reid defeated Walter Camp at his own game in the committee. Yale defeated Harvard at Reid's own game on the field. Some losses take a long time to get over. Others take a lifetime.

Bill Reid posted a 30-3-1 record in 1901 and 1905–1906 stints as Harvard's head coach, bettering the winning percentages of Bear Bryant, Joe Paterno, Woody Hayes, and even Knute Rockne. Yet, he resigned his post after the 1906 season believing himself a failure. His perception encroached on reality. Bill Reid never coached college football again. Though the Harvard coach's salary once rivaled the school president's, Reid subsequently scraped together a meager living selling bonds, work that he assumed left his wife "humiliated." His marriage, passionate in those heady Harvard days, cooled until the mother of his four children took her own life.[119]

The man who deftly rescued college football from both its stubborn purists and vengeful abolitionists couldn't quite rescue himself from a moment in time. If there is anything sadder than a jock mired in his glory days, it's a jock stuck in his defeats. In the two seasons of Reid's second coaching run, the Bulldogs held the Crimson scoreless. The teams he coached won all but two other contests. Bill Reid returned to lead his alma mater's team neither to defeat Amherst nor to save college football. He returned to beat Yale. It's not called "the only game that matters" for nothing.

CHAPTER FIVE

SAFER THAN
SKATEBOARDING

Harold "Blue" Moore's death prompted Union College to scrap football only to resume play after a season's sabbatical. The punishing violence of the game took no such respite. Three Octobers after Moore's death, his alma mater squared off with Wesleyan in a fight reminiscent of a football game. Counting zero points on the scoreboard and seventeen knockouts on the grass, the *New York Times*, which had so terribly botched the Moore story, colorfully reported "a football game which for its exhibition of roughness has never been exceeded in the history of college competition." The newspaper reported on its front page that hospitals treated five of the seventeen players temporarily relieved of awareness.[1] The reforms catalyzed by Moore's death benefited spectators more than safety, even if they benefited neither that Saturday in Schenectady. A safer sport, tragically, awaited two, three, many Blue Moores.

Nearly four years after reformers transformed the game, Archer Christian, a running back at the University of Virginia, played his best game. By the time he broke through the line of scrimmage in the second half, the freshman had already kicked a field goal and run for a touchdown against an overmatched Georgetown squad. Known for daredevil leaps over the opposition, Archer played a rough game recklessly. Knowing her son, or knowing football, "Mrs. Christian had not witnessed the game, but had come over simply to be present in case of accident, having had a premonition that her son would be injured."[2] After breaking through the line, the eighteen-year-old suffered a concussion in the open field. Archer died of a cerebral hemorrhage the next day at Georgetown University Hospital. The mother that couldn't bear to watch him play watched him pass.[3]

Similar scenes played out elsewhere that season. West Point tackle Eugene Byrne, the victim of a sustained, focused Harvard attack, succumbed to a spinal cord injury. When the cadet's father broke the news to his mother at a rail station, the *New York Times* reported that "the meeting of the bereft parents was so pitiful that even curiosity seekers turned away."[4] Midshipman Earl Wilson, one of the best athletes at the Naval Academy, had suffered injuries similar to Byrne's while attempting an awkward tackle on a Villanova runner a week earlier. Paralyzed in his four limbs, Wilson for six months bravely fought a losing battle for his life.[5]

Before Wilson's passing, the *Chicago Tribune* counted twenty-six football martyrs for the 1909 season. The body count ultimately increased by nine over 1905, and, crucially, the number of fallen college athletes—participating in contests drawing the largest crowds and receiving the widest coverage—increased from three to eleven.[6] In the absence of a National Football League, teams like Army and Navy might as well have been the Green Bay Packers and the Chicago Bears. Fans knew Earl Wilson as the Naval Academy's quarterback, and his paralysis and subsequent death cast a dark shadow over the football field.

The game becoming *more dangerous* after the 1905 reforms proved an inconvenience to reformers just as it now proves an inconvenience to historians. The progressives had saved lives and a sport, right? Football historian John S. Watterson mocks the narrative: "Teddy Roosevelt, himself a sportsman writ large, descended briefly from the Olympian affairs of state to make lightning crackle with a wave of his hand. In doing so, he sent the colleges scurrying to reinvent the rules of a sullied game. Or so the myth would lead us to believe."[7]

Reformers whose passion exceeded their expertise peopled the ranks of the football prohibitionists, as they did the era's other prohibitionist crusade. Football's founding father understood the ignorance of the abolitionists and the reformers better than most. He noted that opening up the game would likely lead to more, not fewer, serious injuries. "It has been brought out many times already that injuries are more frequent in the open plays than in the so-called close formations," Walter Camp explained in 1905. "That cannot but be apparent even to the ordinary spectator, for, as he looks out over the field and sees a man running unprotected by his fellows and another coming charging down upon him, as, for instance, in the running back of a punt or a kick-off or in the wide sweep around the end when the runner is circling, he cannot help but realize that the impact under those conditions is far more severe than that in the pushing wedge of players."[8] More than a century after Camp wrote this, football reformers have caught up to his logic, if not his conclusions. "As for kickoffs, any viewer knows that a disproportionate amount of serious head and spinal injuries occur on these plays when large, aggressive and armored athletes charge toward each other from great distances," sportswriter Joe Lapointe notes. "For this, it might be best to suggest a radical change: Eliminate kickoffs."[9] The NFL didn't quite eliminate kickoffs after the 2010 season. But by moving the tee from the thirty- to the thirty-five-yard line, the league increased the likelihood of a touchback. This resulted in a 43 percent decline in concussions on the anarchic and exciting play over just one season.[10]

Though football reformers eventually figured out that the open field allows for open season on bodies, they continued to conflate protection of the offense with protection of athletes. The deadliest activity on the football field isn't taking a big hit but delivering one. The few players who suffer paralysis or death tend to be defenders.[11] Yet, rule makers generally ignore reality and indulge a fantasy that Bambi-like offensive players require guardian angels against the likes of Jack Lambert, Chuck Cecil, Bill Romanowski, and other goblins that roam the dark side of the line of scrimmage. This mentality increases scoring. It doesn't always increase safety.

The pressure on football comes largely from people who neither compete nor observe. What alleviates conscience doesn't necessarily alleviate injury. Reformers feel better. Players? Not so much.

Archer Christian and Earl Wilson significantly fell in the open field. Open play made for a more interesting game. It didn't make for a safer one.

"No one has started an agitation yet for the abolishing of the automobile," famed sports columnist Robert Edgren noted at the fatal close of the fateful 1905 season. "Yet where there has been one fatality or serious injury in football and boxing there have been a dozen in automobiles. And the superior deadliness of the motor car stands out even more when the small number of those who can indulge in the costly sport is compared to the millions who play football or amuse themselves with boxing gloves."[12]

A renaissance man who held the world's record in the hammer throw as he sketched political cartoons for media tycoon William Randolph Hearst, Edgren never fully grasped the meaning of what he wrote until twenty-seven years later, when he nearly died in a terrible car accident. The crash led to a long decline that mercifully ended in 1939.

Manufacturers install side airbags, blind-spot detection, and even video cameras to keep motorists safe today. But more than a million people around the world will still die in traffic accidents this year.[13] Nobody, save for squirrels, advocates the abolition of the automobile. People with all sorts of conflicting views agree that motorized vehicles, on the whole, improve our quality of life. This measured assessment might usefully be applied to football, which not only claims fewer lives than cars do, but is less dangerous than other athletic activities. For instance:

- Bicycling kills about seven hundred Americans every year.[14]
- The U.S. averages twenty-five mountaineering deaths per year.[15]
- Eleven people (no numbers on the critters) died hunting during the 2008-2009 season *in Virginia alone*.[16]
- 3,500 American recreational swimmers drown annually.[17]
- Since 1940, more than 150 jockeys have been killed—averaging more than two a year—in horse races in the United States.[18]
- Skateboarders suffered forty-two deaths in 2011.[19]
- Amusement parks and carnivals kill about four Americans every year.[20]
- Skiing/snowboarding on American mountains results in about forty-two deaths per season.[21]

The difference of course is that defensive ends hit quarterbacks with intent. The cars, trees, and waves that claim the lives of cyclists, skiers, and surfers, don't intend any harm at all—but even without intent claim more lives, which presumably is the important thing. And yet there is not a mass movement to ban cycling, skiing, or surfing, or to put out of business those nefarious merchants-of-wheeled-death Schwinn, Huffy, and Diamondback. We know that swimming, surfing, cycling, and skiing, for all their risks, offer enormous rewards of pleasure and even improved health for millions of people. The same is true of football. Oddly enough, while its risks have decreased, the uproar over its risks has amplified.

This year's Winter X Games killed more athletes than the National Football League has in ninety-three seasons.[22] So did San Francisco's "Escape from Alcatraz" triathlon.[23] Even competitors at the Westminster Dog Show aren't completely immune to the hazards of ruff competition. Cruz, a three-year-old Samoyed, died of internal hemorrhaging consistent with poisoning four days after the competition ended. His owner and handler suspect foul play.[24]

We're obsessed with football fatalities not because they happen very often, but because football commands our attention in a way the Winter X Games, and even the Westminster Dog Show, does not. A snowmobiling death at the X Games isn't going to galvanize politicians, journalists, and doctors the way a paralyzing hit in football might.

The *New Yorker*'s Ben McGrath thinks NFL fans secretly fear that "one of these days, millions of us are going to watch a man die on the turf."[25] At least one fan, according to ESPN, harbors this anguish: NFL commissioner Roger Goodell.[26] More interesting than the imagined future is the experienced past: Why *hasn't* a single player died, including the seasons when players weren't required to wear helmets, from a hit in a National Football League now in its tenth decade?[27]

It's not that McGrath's morbid fantasy, or Goodell's nightmare, is far-fetched. Perhaps four or five times a game viewers marvel that NFL players pop up after getting popped. When Baltimore Raven Bernard Pollard crashed into New England Patriot Steven Ridley in the AFC Championship Game in January 2013, to recite one example, the frightening collision left many worrying aloud if Mr. Ridley had met his maker after meeting Mr. Pollard. The game supplies spectators the occasional sick feeling amidst the thrills. At every other level of the sport, where participation greatly exceeds that of the pros, players have perished. Given the violent nature of the sport, and the speed of the massive bodies playing it, it surprises that every NFL player to take a vicious hit has lived to tell the tale.[28]

Major League Baseball can't make this claim. In 1909, Doc Powers, a catcher for the Philadelphia Athletics, died two weeks and three surgeries after crashing into a wall at Shibe Park. Yankees headhunter Carl Mays beaned Cleveland Indians shortstop Ray Chapman to death before thousands of fans at the Polo Grounds in 1920.

The National Hockey League isn't immune from death, either. Minnesota North Star Bill Masterson, who has a sportsmanship trophy named after him, died after being checked helmetless into the ice during a 1968 game. Montreal Canadien Howie Morenz, one of the greatest hockey players to ever lace up skates, died as a result of complications from a broken leg suffered in a 1937 game against the Chicago Blackhawks.

The tragedies led to improvements rather than abolishment. Hockey eventually forced players to don helmets, minimized fighting, and penalized particularly vicious hits. Baseball banned the spitball, required visible white balls, mandated batting helmets, and added warning tracks and padded fences. MLB's two deaths in 138 years, and the NHL's two in 95 years, isn't a particularly grisly track record. But it's four violent deaths more than the National Football League.

Football, though gradually and away from public notice, has reformed, too. Equipment changes, such as the NCAA rules committee mandating helmets in 1939, mouthpieces in 1973, and padding for goalposts in 1988, made for a safer game.[29] So did outlawing dangerous maneuvers on the field, such as the phasing out of forward-motion mass-momentum plays beginning in 1894, and prohibitions against the chop block in 1980.[30] Football's adaptability makes it anything but a staid and conservative sport. "The kicking sport of soccer has not changed its basic rules in two hundred years, but United States football in a little over one hundred years has been a sport in transition," pointed out David Nelson, longtime secretary-editor of the NCAA's rules committee. "The original rules of 1876 numbered sixty-one. Today [1991], there are 738."[31] The reforms Bill Reid foisted on Walter Camp weren't the first game changers. Football evolves.

It's time to face the truth about football—no matter how comforting that truth is. The field witnesses a safer game than it did thirty, fifty, or a hundred years ago. The taken-for-granted safety innovation of the hard-shelled helmet, for instance, would likely have saved the life of Archer Christian. Consider that Walter Camp advised in "How to Play Football" that "doing away with the heavy head protectors will be a great step in advance and will probably save many injuries."[32] Clearly, football isn't as hazardous as it once was. It's also not as hazardous as any number of activities that parents don't regard as particularly hazardous. The sport offers greater protection to the lives of its enthusiasts than dozens of other activities that parents allow their children to participate in without concern. Statistics paint a very different portrait of the game than its critics do.

Football averaged seventeen play-induced deaths per year from 1931 to 1965. Brain trauma, spinal cord injuries, and heart-stopping hits caused most of the fatalities. From 1966 to 1970, the numbers spiked dramatically to an average of more than twenty-seven fatalities per year stemming directly from contact. Nineteen sixty-eight, a year of assassinations, riots, and peak casualties in Vietnam, also witnessed frightening violence on America's football fields. Thirty-six players died as a result of on-field contact during games and practices.[33]

The on-field carnage led directly to off-field changes. In 1971, player safety was dramatically improved when the NCAA made "spearing"— dangerous, head-leading hits—a fifteen-yard penalty; in flagrant cases, a player could be expelled.[34] Equipment innovations helped, too. John T. Riddell's webbed-suspension design that cradled heads inside of hard-plastic shells, conscripted during World War II for military use lasting well into the twenty-first century, fell out of favor with football by the mid-1970s. Whereas head protection for the game that mimics war raced into the Space Age, the head protection for actual warriors remained mired in the Stone Age. The transition in helmets from harnessed interiors to padded ones saved lives in the 1970s—on the football field if not the battlefield. Nelson Kraemer, Riddell's chief engineer, credits the National Operating Committee on Standards for Athletic Equipment (NOCSAE) established in the wake of that brutal 1968 season, with improving helmets by setting industry standards. "A lot of the helmets that were out there would not comply and a lot of new design efforts were put in place to comply not only with the standard but beyond the minimum requirements of the standard," Kraemer notes. "So that did a couple of things. It started sorting out the good helmets from the bad helmets that were in existence and gave a lot of people some design direction on how to make helmets better."[35]

By 1990, when millions of American boys sacked, upended, and decleated opponents, no one died. Unlike the concussion controversy, the moratorium on mortality elicited a great big yawn. Since athletic and educational organizations began tracking football injuries in 1931, they had not reported a season in which every player made it out alive. And since 1990, there hasn't been a year in which the grim reaper hasn't roamed the gridiron.[36] So, 1990 remains something of an outlier. But even if it's an anomaly, 1990—not 1968—represents the direction the game heads.

The last decade has experienced as few as one player perish from contact in 2006 and as many as seven die from it in 2008. Whereas football averaged more than twenty-five deaths per season in the late 1960s, the game now averages less than four collision deaths every year. There hasn't been a season with double-figure deaths in more than a quarter century. The change between the 1968 peak and today is glaring, not glacial. In 1968, ten times more football players died from collisions than have died from collisions during the average season among the last ten.[37]

The game may still be too dangerous for some. It's not as dangerous as it once was.

Neuropsychologist Christopher Randolph puts the data in perspective. "In reviewing 10 seasons of American football at all levels of play (ending in 2006)," he explains, "there were a total of 50 cases of permanent disability and 38 deaths from cerebral injuries. The great majority of the deaths were from acute subdural hematoma. Based upon an annual participation rate* of 1.8 million, this corresponds to 88 instances of permanent disability or death for 18,000,000 player-seasons, or one instance for every 205,000 player-seasons. For a squad of 100 players, this would translate to one such injury every 2,050 seasons."[38] Put

---

* The most recent "Annual Survey of Football Injury Research," relying on a more thorough count of youth participants, puts the number of American players in organized football at 4.2 million.

another way, a child's chances of suffering grievous harm on a football field aren't very high.

More kids died getting struck by lightning on football fields last season than died getting struck by other players.[39] During a year in which the *New York Times* screamed such headlines as "If Football Is So Dangerous to Players, Should We Be Watching It?," "Should Kids Play Football?," and "Dying to Play," not a single Pop Warner, high school, college, or professional football player died from an on-field hit.[40] In fact, contact caused just two total deaths—both in adult leagues—at all levels of football in 2012.[41] Given the 4.2 million participants in the sport this makes dying from a football hit not even a one-player-in-a-million occurrence.[42] Given the thousands of hits those millions of players endure during a typical season, contact causing death in football might be more accurately termed less than a one-hit-in-a-billion occurrence.

Football isn't less safe. Americans are more squeamish.

The media interest in head injuries has increased as they have declined, at least in their most quantifiable and lethal form. Tabulating concussions relies on guesswork dependent on the reporting of the concussed, who might be fifteen-year-old boys or professional athletes on a roster's margins. The subjective nature of the injury, and the confused or conflicted nature of the injured, suggests that many concussions go undiagnosed. Some competitors, weary of the obstacles of reentering play if diagnosed with a concussion, simply won't report them. Last season, for instance, backup New York Jets quarterback Greg McElroy tried to hide concussion symptoms from his coaches after winning the starter's job. Earlier that season, quarterback Alex Smith reported his concussion to the San Francisco 49ers. Smith, enjoying a great season, nevertheless lost his spot to backup Colin Kaepernick, who demonstrated why starters hide their medical conditions by leading his team to a Super Bowl.[43] The intense media interest in concussions has, as one coach told me, led some young players to assume that almost every hit leads to a concussion.[44] It's also led to tabulations of NFL concussions—the Patriots led the league in inflicting them; the Raiders in receiving them—akin to statistics on touchdowns or sacks. The 2012 NFL regular season witnessed 156 reported head injuries, slightly more than half a concussion per game. Tellingly, Greg McElroy, whose concussion symptoms made headlines but not the injury report, appears nowhere in the "official" concussion count.[45] A firm retained by the players' union counted 266 the previous season and 270 in 2010, so concussions, if not concussion coverage, trends downward in the league.[46]

While concussions don't lend themselves to precise counts—doctor estimates vary by a factor of ten[47]—there aren't any doubts about death or paralysis. They either happen or they don't—and we know that deaths and spinal injuries from contact on the football field have declined dramatically in recent decades.[48]

Strangely, the Fourth Estate has simultaneously averted its gaze from a far deadlier pigskin problem as it has exaggerated a declining pigskin problem. It's not the pressure on heads but on hearts that results in the greatest loss of life. Football's indirect deaths—fatalities that have occurred while playing but not necessarily because of play—have increased in recent years. Causes include sickle-cell anemia, heat stroke, congenital heart defects, and even H_2O verdose. The most common characteristic is obesity, which is increasingly becoming an American characteristic. Americans eat too much and exercise too little. We are the roundest people on a round planet.

Obesity is heartbreaking.

During the 2012 season, Hartsville, South Carolina, senior Ronald Rouse, a six-foot-three 320-pound player who liked singing "Purple Rain" for friends and attempting flips that he could never complete, dropped to the ground twice after calling timeout during the second quarter of his squad's homecoming game. The lovable giant died in the emergency room. An autopsy found an enlarged heart.[49]

When William "the Refrigerator" Perry became a pop-culture phenomenon during his rookie season it had more to do with size than skills. Americans marveled that a professional athlete could be so large. In 1985, three-hundred pounds appeared as a novelty, even in the NFL. The Bears behemoth played at almost the exact size of Ronald Rouse.

Today, sandlot pee-wee leagues have to turn away twelve-year-olds nearly as heavy as Rouse and the Fridge.[50] Letting them play proves dangerous not just to the opposition but to the plus-sized players themselves.

Traditionally, the gridiron offered oversized kids a place to shine. Sports like soccer and basketball almost seemed, to the class fat kid at least, a conspiracy devised by the lean to exclude the large. But football showcased their advantages of strength and size downplayed in other contests. When our fathers played football, oversized meant husky, burly, brawny, and bruising. In twenty-first-century America, oversized means morbidly obese. Three hundred pounds weighing down on a heart and the heat of August make for a lethal combination. Deaths on the field mostly pertain to bellies, not brains.

- In August 2008, a sixteen-year-old player, who had spent two days in the hospital for heat exhaustion several weeks earlier, dropped to the ground during practice only to die a few days later. The six-foot-five player, whose body temperature registered 108 degrees at the hospital, weighed 360 pounds.[51]
- On August 18, 2009, thirteen-year-old Anthony Troupe Jr. collapsed while running a lap before practice. The suburban St. Louis youngster weighed 360 pounds. Despite his youth, Anthony died from high-blood pressure—as his father had.[52]
- In October 2010, a sixteen-year-old collapsed during the warm-ups for a no-contact helmet-and-shoulder-pads practice. The deceased player stood five-foot-eight and weighed 300 pounds.[53]

Whereas just two players died from contact during the 2012 season, football witnessed Ronald Rouse and twelve other players' indirect deaths, the kind often facilitated by obesity.[54] Don't look at football. Look in the mirror. Our waistlines have expanded.

At roughly the same time that football collision deaths started to decline, American tummies began to grow—and grow. Obesity affected one in twenty teenagers four decades ago. Today, it afflicts almost one in five.[55] The Big Gulp, the Chalupa Supreme, and king-size Kit Kats kill more young football players than linebacker helmet-to-helmet hits. But the latter, smaller danger rather than the former, greater danger preoccupies parents, coaches, and critics. Misinformation misguides them. Death lurks more ominously in the cupboard than on the grass.

Football, a magnet for oversized athletes, plays a constructive role in combating obesity. The fact that head injury deaths have declined dramatically, or that they pale in number to obesity-related fatalities, doesn't register for those who have it out for football. To them, two deaths last season in what amounts to an amusement is an unacceptable price. And maybe it is. But if we ban football for two fatalities, how many more fat-kid fatalities will we have? How many other amusements will we ban? Skateboards? Carnival rides? Bicycles?

The season after Archer Christian, Eugene Byrne, and Earl Wilson fell on the field, a twenty-two-year-old Norwegian-American walked on the field at Notre Dame. Knute Rockne made his name, and his school's, by upsetting West Point four years and a day after cadet Eugene Byrne's death. The player did so not through the brutish means used by Harvard to beat West Point, but by a mastery of the air game that Harvard's former coach Bill Reid helped introduce. *Coach* Knute Rockne's strategy relied on shifts, misdirection, the forward pass, and other elements that made a strongman's game also a thinking man's game. Like Archer Christian's death, Knute Rockne's life forces us to rethink the past. And rethinking the past necessarily compels us to rethink the present.

"There will never be but one Rockne, here at Notre Dame or anywhere else," Ronald Reagan's George Gipp proclaims in 1940's *Knute Rockne, All American*. "He gives us something they can't teach in schools, something clean and strong inside. Not just courage, but a right way of living that none of us will ever forget."[56]

Rockne's star player Gipp's "way of living" included pool-hall hustling, bootlegging, and playing professional sports when he wasn't playing for Notre Dame.[57] It wasn't right but it was a way of living. He didn't learn this from his famous coach. But he could have.

Contrary to Reagan's cinematic assertion, two Knute Rocknes did indeed exist. Repeatedly upheld by the hagiographic biopic as a paragon of sportsmanship, Rockne boxed professionally and played semi-pro football under aliases while a Notre Dame student-athlete.[58] "We haven't got any use for gamblers around here," Pat O'Brien's Rockne lectures a bookie in *Knute Rockne, All American*. "You've done your best to ruin baseball and horse racing. This is one game that's clean and it's gonna stay clean."[59] But the other Knute Rockne, the one who existed off the silver screen, gambled on the Fighting Irish—and much else—just as his star player did. George Gipp biographer Jack Cavanaugh writes that, like his subject, "Rockne, while a player and coach, would place bets on Notre Dame for gambling friends from downtown South Bend and himself, even though Rockne, so far as is known, did not come close to Gipp when it came to gambling and breaking university rules."[60] The coach even habitually employed a far-from-impartial referee for his "clean" contests in South Bend.[61]

"Any player who flunks in his class is no good to his coach or the school he attends," Pat O'Brien's Rockne sermonizes, as ancient coaches Pop Warner, Amos Alonzo Stagg, and Howard Jones look on approvingly in cameo roles. "And any coach who goes around trying to fix it for his athletes to become eligible scholastically when mentally they're not is just, well, a plain everyday fool."[62] But the greatest player in the history of Notre Dame didn't really go to school at Notre Dame. George Gipp averaged 6.3 yards per carry for the Fighting Irish. The tramp athlete's grade point average came in quite a bit lower, as in nonexistent. *The Gipper* notes that the Gipper "had gone through two academic years without receiving any grades and had failed to take final examinations in any of his classes." Gipp's final two-and-a-half years conformed to the template of truancy, expulsion, and readmission.[63] Nights in the pool hall preclude days in the lecture hall.

All of the college football programs on probation today don't combine to violate the protocols of sportsmanship as much as Knute Rockne's program did. The Fighting Irish bet on games, fielded professionals to play as amateurs, waived eligibility requirements for older tramp athletes, and employed hometown officiating. It would be easier to name the few rules they followed than to name the many they broke. This sets Rockne's Notre Dame apart from college programs today. This doesn't set Rockne's Notre Dame apart from other football powerhouses of long ago.

Sports ethics then weren't as strict, or as codified, as they are today. In an 1893 game against Minnesota, Wisconsin's team manager dispensed booze and ten-dollar bills to players in the locker room after collecting a fortune at the gate and a loss on the field.[64] In 1894, the University of Michigan's eleven featured seven lacking even an affiliation with the educational institution.[65] The 1905 Andover-Princeton cheating affair witnessed a varsity-sweater-wearing prep-school jock scribble "205 pounds" atop a blank entrance exam to win admission to the Ivy League school.[66] Leonard Wood, Rough Rider who conquered San Juan and Kettle Hills with Theodore Roosevelt, helped conquer Georgia for Georgia Tech as a thirtysomething unenrolled guard.[67] Corrupt was the football world Rockne inherited.

Hollywood's saintly portrayal of Rockne is about as believable as Rockne's famous portrayal of Gipp's last request that the Fighting Irish win one for him. It's more likely that he implored Rockne to win a bet on Notre Dame for the Gipper, one teammate later quipped.[68] The cinema, a creature of imagination, tends toward a "golden days" idealization of days gone past. It shows life as viewers want it to have been rather than how it actually was.

Our minds similarly play tricks on us. When we nostalgically recall a game of football without the violence, hits, and injuries that plague today's game, we rely on imagination and not reality. Those who invoke the good old days aren't old enough to remember them. Kids play a safer game of football than has ever been played. One gleans the exact opposite idea from the media hype. But the numbers don't lie. Newspapers found eighteen deaths, including Blue Moore's, in the controversy-plagued 1905 season. In 1909, the season which lost Archer Christian, Earl Wilson, and Eugene Byrne, twenty-seven indirect and direct deaths were blamed on the sport.[69] As recently as the late 1960s, football averaged more than twenty-five deaths per season just from hits. During the last decade, football has averaged 3.7 deaths a year from contact. Just two players died from collisions in 2012.[70]

Notice a trend line?

Notice the media not noticing the trend line?

Fewer deaths on the field tell part of the story. Longer lives off the field tell another part of it. That's the untold story told in the next chapter—all those bodies sprinting, jumping, and wrestling for sixty minutes does a body good. Unfortunately, the football-equals-longevity story enjoys the longevity of a mosquito. Like the declining number of football fatalities, the notion that playing football contributes to one's health complicates the football-is-bad-for-you meme.

Football will never be as safe as foosball. But as Frank Gifford and Chuck Bednarik will soon show, football pumps hearts, fills lungs, and strengthens muscles in a way foosball can't. Foosball does a party good. Football does a body good.

CHAPTER SIX

FOOTBALL DOES A BODY GOOD

"Maybe I should station a policeman out there with you," New York Giants Coach Jim Lee Howell suggested to kicker Pat Summerall. The specialist had just dodged three Philadelphia Eagles strangely rushing him "presumably with crippling intent" on a kickoff. Summerall balked at the idea of an on-field protector.[1] But at Yankee Stadium on November 20, 1960, even policemen needed protectors.

Frank Gifford certainly could have used one. The Hall of Famer played in two of the National Football League's most consequential games. They both happened to have been played in a park made famous by an outfielder resembling a linebacker. The first one, 1958's championship game against the Baltimore Colts, made the league's future. The second, less famous contest against the Philadelphia Eagles *foretold* the NFL's future.

On December 28, 1958, forty-five million people tuned in to the NFL championship game between the Giants and the Colts. The record-setting audience didn't include a single viewer in the nation's largest media-market. NFL Commissioner Bert Bell, who, a season earlier, had catered to black-and-white set viewers by mandating white uniforms for visitors and colored uniforms for the hosts, justified blacking out games with seats still available. "If we ever start valuing the TV audience more than the paying public," Bell explained, "we'll be in trouble."[2] If the NFL wouldn't favor the TV audience, NBC would. After Raymond Berry caught an eleven-yard pass from Johnny Unitas on the fateful overtime drive, electromagnetic noise filled television screens. Stomping fans had unwittingly jarred loose a cable that stayed that way for more than two minutes. To buy time, an NBC employee played drunk and meandered onto the field to cause a delay. Not for the last time did the millions at home take precedence over the thousands at the stadium. The original TV timeout enabled the network to fix the problem without missing the entirety of a single down.[3] Three plays later, the Colts defeated the Giants in the "Greatest Game Ever Played" on an Alan Ameche dive. In the aftermath, Colts players spotted NFL Commissioner Bell—whose father, as a mutinous member of Walter Camp's rules committee clique, had seen football's future in the forward pass—crying in the recesses of their locker room.[4] Bell, who died less than a year later, had glimpsed football's future just as his dad had a half century earlier.

Consequently, two years later in the second pivotal game, selling out the House That Ruth Built posed no great task. The *New York Times* noticed fans congregating near the box office at 6:30 a.m., more than seven hours before the 2 p.m. kickoff. The Giants, cognizant of the line that more than circled Yankee Stadium, estimated that they could have sold 90,000 tickets if they had the seats. "Several hundred ingenious nonticketholders found a happy solution," the *Times* explained. "They crowded five rooftops of buildings that towered above the walls ringing right and right-center field. Seventy-two fans were counted on one roof."[5] Louis Wallach, a Queens assemblyman worried about the Big Apple losing big-time football, pointed to the overflow to call a proposed ballpark in Flushing, which became Shea Stadium, "inadequate, ill-conceived, and entirely unworthy of New York City." The assemblyman wanted 90,000 seats at least.[6] The game was getting bigger. The next day's announcement of a new NFL franchise, the Minnesota Vikings, and the addition of two games to the 1961 regular season schedule, affirmed this. No longer did professional football play second fiddle to its collegiate cousin or offseason timewaster until baseball's spring training. Professional football—now with two leagues competing for fans—commanded America's attention like never before.

The stadium teeming with fans hinted at the league's bright future. The stadium teeming with fans hinted at another, darker future as well. Even by football standards, the game in the Bronx on the Sunday before Thanksgiving was exceptionally violent, and perhaps, as the Summerall anecdote suggests, gratuitously so.

The Giants opened a ten-point lead in the first half. In the second, the Eagles scored seventeen straight points, including ten in four-and-a-half minutes. The Giants out-rushed and out-passed their opponents. But the Eagles out-muscled Big Blue and forced more turnovers, including a crushing Chuck Bednarik hit on Giants fullback Mel Triplett that resulted in a fumble returned for a touchdown by Jimmy Carr. These trends converged on Frank Gifford in the fourth quarter as he attempted to step out of bounds after a reception to stop the clock. Instead, the Eagles stopped his clock—and the Giants' playoff hopes.

Hit by six-foot-five safety Don Borroughs low and roofed by 235-pound linebacker Chuck Bednarik high, Gifford lost the ball and lost consciousness. The iconic photograph of the aftermath shows a gleeful Bednarik dancing midair in celebration over Gifford's lifeless body. As the beast bounced above the beauty, Bronx bystanders booed. The linebacker maintained that causing the fumble, not the unconsciousness, made him "emotional." The play meant we "knew we had just won."[7] And win they did—that day, the following week in a déjà vu rematch, and against Vince Lombardi's Packers in that season's championship game. Perhaps Bednarik envisioned that future as he danced in Yankee Stadium.

Diverging personalities separated the players joined in history. Gifford acted in Hollywood in the offseason. Bednarik sold concrete. The former's good looks made him a sought-after pitchman by the likes of Lucky Strikes, Palmolive, and Vitalis. The latter's face resembled a topographical map of Bethlehem, Pennsylvania. Following their careers, Bednarik's outspokenness exiled him from the Eagles for most of the 1970s; Gifford's eloquence made him a staple of ABC sports broadcasts for three decades.[8] But the violent collision wasn't a case of opposites attracting. Concrete Charlie and Hollywood Frank adhered in ways beyond that brutal stick. Bednarik, the last of the 60-minute men, played both linebacker and center the day he acted as the sandman to Gifford, who earned Pro Bowl nods as a running back, defensive back, and wide receiver. The hulking Bednarik occasionally kicked and punted. Gifford threw more touchdown passes (fourteen) than any non-quarterback in league history. Bednarik and Gifford, two men who differed in every way imaginable off the field, arrived cast from the same mold on it. In an era of minute specialization, the pair remained anachronistic reminders of a dying breed: the complete football player.

Frank Gifford, the team doctor soon discovered, wasn't the patient in most dire need of medical care that afternoon. "It was a busy day for Dr. Francis Conway, the Giants physician," the *Times* reported. "Jack Stroud, a guard, suffered a mild concussion when kicked in the head. Roosevelt Brown, a tackle, hurt an elbow." Defensive tackle Jim Katcavage, third on the Giants all-time sacks list behind Michael Strahan and Lawrence Taylor, broke his collarbone.[9]

If November 20, 1960, demonstrated football's brutal potential, it also provided perspective. Frank Gifford, who would spend several decades in the *Monday Night Football* booth and marry Regis Philbin's television cohost, didn't endure the worst injury that day. James Cooper, a veteran New York City policeman from Coney Island, suffered a heart attack on the sidelines. As Gifford arrived in the locker room on a stretcher, Cooper died there.[10] The coincidence confused many into believing that the motionless running back had lost his life.[11] But the famous athlete survived. The unheralded cop did not. Some occupations put more stress on the heart than three-hundred pounds of brawn. Chuck Bednarik, an aerial gunner on thirty missions over Europe during

World War II, certainly knows this.[12] Football is a game and a profession. Unlike truck driver, fireman, or electrician, NFL player isn't a deadly profession. Still, as Frank Gifford's, Steve Young's, or Troy Aikman's concussions show, it's dangerous.

"Gifford will remain at St. Elizabeth's for three weeks," the *Times* informed. "In addition to an acute deep brain concussion, he also suffered a contusion of the occipital region of the skull and neck."[13] Bednarik denied allegations of a dirty hit—then and forever after—and sent the hospitalized Gifford a fruit basket and his regrets.[14] When a medical consultant seconded the doctor's opinion that Gifford couldn't play for several weeks, the halfback Hall of Famer derided him as a "crepe hanger."[15] But Gifford not only stayed out of the NFL for the remainder of the 1960 season. He didn't play in 1961, either.

The notion that concussions have only recently become a concern, or that they had been previously dismissed by a primitive medical profession, doesn't withstand a reading of the Gifford-Bednarik hit. Through a two-and-a-half-week hospitalization, the medical refusal to allow a return to the field in 1960, and the 18-month semi-retirement, Gifford and his doctors showed a comprehension of the dangers of concussions that goes far beyond treating it with smelling salts or laughing off a brain injury with a "stinger" diagnosis. The past wasn't nearly as backward as our understanding of it is.

November 20, 1960, foreshadowed both football's current popularity and its current controversy. The spectators on Bronx rooftops, if they looked far enough, could see the sellouts and the brutality. And if they thought hard enough, they realized that the former derived in large part from the latter.

Would you exchange twenty years of your life for tens of millions of dollars, the adoration of screaming throngs, and sports-legend immortality? In the wake of linebacker Junior Seau's suicide, critics, and a few fans of football, asked such uncomfortable questions. Football, like acid rain or Y2K or shark-infested beaches or SARS, has become hazardous to your health. Don't trust me? Trust the media. They don't lie. They're about facts, not hype, right?

"The average life expectancy of a retired football player is 58 years, according to the NFL Players Association," ABC News informed us in 2012. "That stands in contrast to the average American man's life expectancy of 75 years, according to government data based in 2006."[16]

"The fact of the matter is this," the *Huffington Post*'s Will Bunch asserts. "The average American lives to be 75. The average pro football player lives to be 55. And statistics suggest that the longer a player stays in the game, the more likely he is to die at a young age."[17]

Dr. Michael Arnold Glueck erred twice when he wrote, "It is not a widely disseminated, downloaded or discussed fact that the average life expectancy for all pro football players, including all positions and backgrounds, is 55 years. Several insurance carriers say it is 51 years."[18]

"The NFL is killing its players, literally leading them to an early grave—and now the NFL is trying to kill them even faster. That's a fact, people." So says CBS Sports' Gregg Doyel in a column about the possibility of expanding the regular season. He continues, "Players want to play, yes. But they want to enjoy their lives after football. Hard to enjoy all that money, all that fame, when you're dead at 55."[19]

"For all players who play five or more years," George Will explained in America's most widely read column, "life expectancy is less than 60; for linemen it is much less."[20] The *Seattle Post Intelligencer*'s Dan Raley described professional football as "a violent sport characterized by startling[ly] low life-expectancy rates, depending on playing position, of 53 to 59."[21] LZ Granderson wrote on ESPN.com, "The average life expectancy of an American male is about 75. The average life expectancy of a retired NFL player is 53-59. And yet, we keep watching, like first-century spectators at the Coliseum."[22]

Why does America so enthusiastically give the thumbs up to such a sanguinary game? Performers dying for our entertainment reads like something out of ancient Rome or the futuristic *Hunger Games*. But it doesn't seem very twenty-first-century America.

It turns out that it's not. The notion that NFL player life expectancy falls short of sixty is as widespread as it is false. Talking heads say it loud. They say it often. But they say it without any basis. The commentators referenced nameless studies, never citing any. That's because no study said any such thing. But the idea of such a study—demonstrating that football lops years off one's life—proved so appealing to writers that they continued to amorphously reference the phantom study and its nonexistent findings. The myth of football's fiftysomething lifespan, like an athlete obsessed with diet and training, proves hard to bury.

Did George Will, ABC News, and LZ Granderson simply make up the numbers so comforting to their jaundiced view of football? The genealogy of a lie rarely reveals so uncomplicated a creation story. In 1988, Ron Mix, a Hall of Fame tackle, spoke to a Scripps Howard reporter about "compiling" a study on player deaths and disabilities. The former San Diego Charger had reinvented himself as a workman's compensation attorney specializing in injured athletes, so his interest in documenting early mortality in football players may have stemmed as much from his legal work as it did from his previous athletic endeavors. The Hall of Famer pegged life expectancy at fifty-five for NFL players.[23]

Like Mix, Len Teeuws never published a study. Teeuws, an NFL lineman turned insurance agent, similarly told the news service that he found a life expectancy of sixty-one for 1,800 athletes who had played five or more years during the NFL's first forty seasons. "I think, after seeing how young some of the guys are dying now, in the next five to ten years, some of the numbers will be astounding," the former Cardinal and Ram explained. "With steroids and artificial turf, life expectancy will go down."[24]

People grinding dull axes appear sharp to other people with the same dull axes to grind. Teeuws's and Mix's research, dubbed "small and unscientific" within Scripps Howard's sympathetic 1988 article, nevertheless caught on more than two decades after first appearing in the print press. Though never published, and admittedly preliminary, the research of two activists standing to gain financially and professionally should the premature-death charge prove accurate nevertheless won evangelists instead of skeptics. When hunches suit a crusade, intuition passes for science.

The pair catalyzed media mischief. They also ensured a scientific hearing.

The speculation inspired a government study to determine whether suspicions regarding early player mortality and increased cardiovascular disease would hold up after inquiry. In response to the activism of Teeuws, Mix, and others, the NFL Players Association (NFLPA) sought to check the National Football League by turning to the only outfit bigger than it: the U.S. government. The NFLPA petitioned the National Institute for Occupational Safety and Health (NIOSH) to determine the workplace safety of their profession. The government examined more than 3,000 players who spent five or more seasons in the league between 1959 and 1988. What they found turned conventional wisdom on its head.

It turns out that all that running and jumping, pushing and pulling, tackling and wrestling, and throwing and leaping does a body good. So does the training table by not offering jelly donuts, Doritos, or Ho Hos. Athletes, even (especially?) ones who put their bodies at risk, take great care of their bodies. NIOSH found in 1994, and again in a 2012 follow-up, that NFL players live longer than American males outside of football and suffer from various life-threatening ailments at lower rates. Football is good for you.

Everett Lehman, an author of the study, wasn't surprised by the conclusions that surprised so many. "You have a very select, highly fit, almost like a Superman cohort," the doctor points out. "To be able to play football you have to be above physical average to get in to begin with. So in terms of cardiovascular disease—training, fitness, their medical care—it would be expected when you're comparing them to the general population that they would have much better cardiovascular disease mortality."[25]

Bill Barnwell from Grantland.com thought as much. He likened the NIOSH paper to "a comparison of apples and oranges," so he conducted his own apples-to-apples study that examined football players alongside other professional athletes, i.e., Major League Baseball retirees. Barnwell found a significant difference in the mortality rates of baseball (16 percent) and football (13 percent) players who had plied their trade for five or more seasons between 1959 and 1988.[26] NFL veterans, despite their heft, outlive not only their peers in society but their peers in baseball, too.

NIOSH expected to find 625 deaths among the football retirees based on the actuarial tables for comparable American men. Instead, it found 334 deaths. Longer lives held true not just for quarterbacks and kickers, but for linemen, too. The rate of cancer—leaving aside Gifford's endorsement of cigarettes in magazines and Bednarik's endorsement of them at halftime[27]—for players was 42 percent less than what it was for the general population. Fatal cardiovascular disease afflicted players 32 percent less than it did non-players. Respiratory disease, unsurprisingly, struck down players at just one-fifth the general rate.[28] When you run up and down a field for sixty minutes, it apparently has health benefits for the heart and lungs. Who knew?

Science didn't cooperate. So even scientists ditched the science. "Growing evidence demonstrates that both the lifespan and quality of life of NFL players is significantly reduced," claimed a report by Harvard University's Dr. Lee M. Nadler released after the NFLPA's 2013 pledge of $100 million to his school. "Whereas white males live to 78 years and African-American males live to approximately 70 years, it appears that professional football players in both the United States and Canada have life expectancies in the mid to late 50's. This is not true for other professional athletes."[29] The *Boston Globe* then regurgitated this false claim in the lead of a front-page story on the nine-figure NFLPA promise to Harvard.[30] If the NFLPA gave you $100 million, you might peddle their fictions, too.

The duh quality that colored the scientific "discovery" that athletes possess healthier hearts and lungs also applied to diseases of the sensory and nervous system. Just as running and jumping influences health, so, too, does crashing and colliding—and generally not for the better. The study found twelve deaths among the 3,439 NFL veterans from nervous system and sensory diseases, constituting a 24 percent higher rate than expected.[31] In other words, though a prolonged football career may keep the big killers—cancer and heart disease—at bay, it invites several smaller killers. Periodic high-speed head-on collisions over a career that spans from Pop Warner through at least five seasons in the NFL result in a higher-than-normal rate of disease to the brain and nervous system.

A second study focusing exclusively on neurodegenerative diseases appeared soon after the first. The same scientists researched the same cohort but reached more dramatic conclusions by applying different methodology. Instead of focusing on the underlying cause of death as the first study did, the second study also included contributing causes of death. It also pared down the nervous system and sensory ailments category to focus exclusively on neurodegenerative diseases. Within this redefined template, the authors reported a more pronounced rate of neurodegenerative fatalities than their first study indicated. The nervous system maladies concentrated on skills position players. Linemen, whose receipt of repetitive subconcussive blows has sparked theories of greater CTE risks, experienced neurodegenerative disease fatalities at rates not discernibly different from non-football players. Neurodegenerative causes of death for the entire cohort outpaced the general population's rate by 3-1, with Alzheimer's and Lou Gehrig's disease showing an even more pronounced ratio. Parkinson's displayed "elevated" levels in the players but did not achieve "statistical significance" in its departure from the norm.[32]

The percentages alarmed. The numbers underwhelmed. Two Alzheimer's deaths, six from Lou Gehrig's Disease, and two from Parkinson's among 334 total deaths within a pool of 3,439 players—or seventeen total deaths if one includes contributing causes and not just underlying ones—might signify a trend.[33] But because the number of deaths remains so thankfully small, it may, in the case of Parkinson's especially, represent an anomaly. Had there been one Parkinson's death instead of two, for instance, the player rate would have come in lower than the population's.

And while millions of boys play football every year, just a few thousand men receive paychecks to do so. The heightened number of neurodegenerative ailments afflicting former NFL skills position players doesn't translate to elevated problems for players in other positions or at other levels of the game. A 2012 Mayo Clinic study of midcentury high school football players, for instance, found rates of ALS, Parkinson's, and dementia in line with rates from non-athlete members of the glee club, choir, and band. The findings, which disproved the authors' hypothesis, suggest that the neurodegenerative risks that a prolonged football career reaching the pinnacle of competition entail do not apply to high school players.[34]

Regardless, Alzheimer's, ALS, and Parkinson's afflict retired professional football players at elevated rates. Playing football leads to healthier hearts and lungs. Healthier heads? Grown men crashing into one another at full speed don't do their brains any favors.

Just as it's important for football's critics to listen when science speaks on the health benefits of the game, it's important for partisans of the game to listen when science tells us of the game's health drawbacks. The science on the game, like the game itself, isn't neat and doesn't exclusively favor one side. It's there to inform, or, if you've just scored a $100 million grant, to ignore.

The discoveries regarding football's beneficial relationship toward cancer, heart disease, and vascular health ignited controversy. The study's explosive findings separating football from suicide so confounded as to invite disbelief. Everyone knows that football players are more likely kill themselves, right? They *know* this because they've heard it over and over and over again—and then some more. One sports publication reports that "the pattern of NFL players that have ended in suicide is alarming."[35] GamesOver.org, a foundation helping players adjust to retirement, informs: "The suicide rate among former NFL players is nearly six times the national average."[36] The suicide statistic found its way into the *Washington Post,* the *Boston Globe, U.S. News & World Report,* the *San Diego Union-Tribune,* Tony Dungy's memoirs, and a book on Tom Brady.[37]

Certainly a number of high-profile players have ended their own lives in recent years. The most depressing of the suicides may have been that of Junior Seau. For twenty NFL seasons, mostly with the San Diego Chargers, Seau played linebacker, the position that experienced the most concussions in one study.[38] For twelve seasons, the NFL named Seau a Pro Bowl selection. He played in two Super Bowls. Unlike, say, Ray Lewis or Chuck Bednarik, Seau didn't personify the position. Quite the opposite, he came across as a gentle giant who would rather help you than hit you. This may not have suited a linebacker's image. But fans identified more readily with a player who laughed rather than growled.

Fans remember the smiling surfing Samoan hanging ten on Southern California beaches in the off season. Perhaps the play that best exemplified Junior Seau came when an inebriated Patriots fan sacked him on the snowy sidelines during a New England 47-7 drubbing of Arizona shortly before Christmas in 2008. Rather than throttle the trespasser, the blind-sided linebacker laughed his head off from the ground. Whereas fans pelted the intruder with snowballs, #55 characteristically refused to press charges. Seau quipped, "He got an unassisted tackle whoever he is."[39]

That happy-go-lucky attitude left friends and fans stunned at his suicide. Former Chargers teammate Mark Walczak spoke for many: "It would be easier for me to believe that you were from Mars than it would be for me to believe that Junior killed himself."[40]

But with Junior Seau, as with football suicides, all was not what it seemed.

The *San Diego Union Tribune* reported that Seau "drank heavily, at least five or six days a week, according to some of his friends. He gambled excessively, in Las Vegas and San Diego-area casinos, on the golf course and in local San Diego card games. He had an insatiable appetite for women, especially those in their 20s, stringing together a series of casual-sex relationships with young girlfriends (his pals jokingly referred [to] them as 'Junior's harem'), and he never was able to remain completely faithful to any one woman." Seau relied on Ambien, and other aids, to fall asleep for just three or four hours a night. An autopsy found no alcohol but traces of four prescribed drugs in his bloodstream. Despite earning nearly $60 million dollars during his career, Seau experienced financial problems. Several of the eateries he invested in hemorrhaged money. San Diego's Seau's the Restaurant, for instance, closed within two weeks of his death.[41]

Football fans may not have known any of this. They did know that Seau spent twenty years of his life crashing into other professional athletes at top speed. So, naturally, spectators linked the spectacle they saw with the sorrow that they didn't. Professional athletes lead lives off the field that fans never see. The idea that someone so extraordinary could find himself ensnared in problems so ordinary seemed a slur against his greatness. Better to cast Seau as a martyr to the game he loved than to accept that a man so universally beloved didn't follow the crowd in this regard. Junior Seau may have been the only one in the stadium who didn't love Junior Seau.

Questions arise: did the hard times cause the suicide, did the hard hits cause the suicide, or did the hard hits cause the hard times that caused the suicide? Scientists have discovered, for instance, that depression follows traumatic brain injuries more so than any other psychological disturbance.[42] It's plausible that a damaged brain may have led to the damaging choices that ultimately led to that final, irreversible choice. But it's impossible to prove or disprove. One can't isolate, for instance, Junior Seau's brain damage caused by drinking to excess almost nightly, or driving his car off a cliff, on the one hand, from the damage caused by three decades of football, on the other.[43] Furthermore, connecting the dots from CTE to suicide requires a naked leap of logic not based on any established science. We know Junior Seau killed himself. We don't, and really can't, know why.

Next to concussions, no medical concern so animates the conversation on football more than CTE. Called punch-drunk syndrome when first discovered in prizefighters in 1928, CTE has only in the last decade been linked to players who have never stepped inside a boxing ring.[44] It manifests under a microscope as dark protein deposits called tau. Markers in a living person include poor decision making, depression, dementia, and memory loss. Though doctors have made advances in the quest to identify the degenerative brain condition in the living, they presently can only diagnose it in the dead.[45] A 2011 study pointed out that "the incidence and prevalence of CTE is currently unclear.... To date, there have been no randomized neuropathological studies of CTE in deceased athletes, and as such, there is a selection bias in the cases that have come to autopsy."[46] In other words, the suspicion of disease often serves as the impetus for donating a brain. Hamstrung by the limitations imposed by postmortem diagnosis and the limited and relatively monolithic sample, the scientists immersed in studying CTE strike a more cautious tone than football's naysayers, admitting that the field remains in its "infancy" and has developed more slowly than the public's interest in it has.[47]

Why do laymen pretend to have all the answers? Scientists don't yet fully know what to ask.

Why does a certain genetic marker found in about a quarter of the general population appear in about three-fifths of CTE cases?[48] What percentage of the brains of non-athletes contains tau deposits? Does CTE merely mimic Alzheimer's, Parkinson's, and ALS, or does it also cause them? If subconcussive blows unleash CTE, as a Purdue scientist insists, and CTE encourages suicide and neurodegeneration, why does the position—lineman—that bears the brunt of such repetitive trauma not show elevated rates of suicide and neurodegenerative disease?[49] Why do many athletes who've endured a severe amount of brain trauma never develop CTE?

The shared experience of repetitive head trauma links CTE cases. Beyond this, CTE, like Junior Seau's suicide, provokes more questions than answers.

The suicides of other fearsome players meshed neatly with the death-by-football narrative. But when inquisitive journalists got to know the people rather than the mere players, they discovered nagging troubles of the sort that often drive people to depression. In other words, the marital, financial, and health problems that drag down normal men also hamstring millionaires once cheered by normal men.

- The *St. Petersburg Times* described Andre Waters as "a person who projected an upbeat demeanor but concealed bouts of depression; a person who was engaged in a prolonged and emotionally draining court fight involving custody of his daughter; a person who harbored some deep-seated feelings of frustration about his career."[50] The hard-hitting Philadelphia Eagles safety killed himself in 2006.

- Indiana's Mr. Football 1979 became football's Mr. Suicide 2011. Four-time Pro Bowler Dave Duerson inflicted punishment on the field. He endured it off the field. In 2004, a court forced Duerson Foods into receivership. In 2007, a bank foreclosed on his home. A few months before his suicide, with creditors and an ex-wife demanding money, Duerson, an integral component of the Chicago Bears' only Super Bowl victory, filed for bankruptcy, listing liabilities of nearly $15 million.[51] The self-inflicted gunshot to the chest coupled with the last request to donate his brain to science shifted attention to NFL brain injuries.[52]

- Ray Easterling, a defensive back as fearless but not as skilled as Waters or Duerson, committed suicide in April 2012 after filing a class-action suit against the NFL. The former Atlanta Falcon experienced financial distress, early-onset Alzheimer's, and chronic knee, hip, elbow, and shoulder pain.[53]

- Mike Current played thirteen professional seasons as an offensive lineman, mainly for the Denver Broncos. A bold sub-headline upon his death described his suicide as "due to the inability to deal with the traumatic brain injury caused by concussions."[54] But the fine print explained that when Mike Current stuck the wrong end of a shotgun to his head, he faced more than thirty years in prison for allegedly molesting three children.[55]

How long until the media declares CTE, rather than O. J., "the real killer" of Ron and Nicole?

The question is not, unfortunately, a rhetorical one. After released Detroit Lion Titus Young allegedly completed a one-man crime wave that resulted in three arrests for drunken driving, burglary, assaulting a

police officer, and other transgressions, the wide receiver's father pointed
to a concussion as the source of his son's troubles during that wild week
in May 2013. "He's always been temperamental," the concerned dad
conceded. "But he's changed. It's different now."[56] A concussion defense
may prove the difference between freedom and seven years in jail for the
disturbed athlete. The day after Boston Marathon Bomber Tamerlan
Tsarnaev died in a spectacular firefight, researchers working a mile or so
from the carnage he unleashed urged CTE testing on the amateur boxer's
brain. "If they don't do it," Robert Cantu warned, "something could be
missed."[57] A local doctor took to the pages of the *Boston Globe* to second
the one-track minds confusing a malady of the soul for one of the brain.
"The driving narrative, the one garnering the most national attention, is
about radicalization and the influence of an alien culture set on terror-
izing us," Michael Craig Miller wrote. Out of sight from that focus, the
psychiatrist laments, is "the biology of violent behavior."[58] The defense
for a Massachusetts high school football player, accused of hanging his
girlfriend by a bungee cord and slitting her throat, argued that CTE, not
their client, should be held responsible for the teenage girl's death.[59] Ideas
have consequences.

One tragedy overlooked amid the saturation coverage of player suicides was that of Enzo Hernandez. Enzo may have played futbol growing
up but he certainly never stumbled across a football in Valle de Guanape,
Venezuela. Standing five foot eight and weighing just 155 pounds, Enzo
homered twice in more than 2,300 lifetime at-bats. In 1971, Hernandez
lost the Triple Crown—he finished last among all qualified batsmen in
homers (zero), batting average (.222), and RBI (twelve). In fact, that
season he set the all-time mark for the fewest RBI for any player who had
the requisite number of plate appearances to qualify for the batting title.
If the woeful plate statistics tell us something about his bat, they tell those
listening something more about his glove. The San Diego Padres put him
on the field to play the field. And if by good fortune Enzo got on base,

his speed might propel him from first to second. During his eight seasons in the majors, he stole 129 bases. A three-tool player, Enzo lacked the two tools—power and hitting—that casual fans appreciate. But rabid fans in Jack Murphy Stadium nevertheless made a cult hero of the short-stop upon hearing the public address announcer introduce, "Number eleven, *Enzoooooooo* Hernandez!" On January 13, 2013, thirty-five years after he last heard such an introduction, Enzo Hernandez, suffering from severe depression, killed himself.[60]

Though he hunted groundballs on the diamond on the very field where Junior Seau hunted running backs, Enzo Hernandez didn't even merit an obituary in the same *San Diego Union Tribune* that fixated on Seau's death for months. A search of the paper's site reveals two articles—focusing on other baseball matters—that mention Enzo's passing in passing.[61] Granted, journeyman ballplayer Enzo Hernandez never cap-tured the attention of San Diego the way future Hall of Famer Junior Seau would. But a lesser contributing factor to the disproportionate (obsessive versus aloof) coverage surely pertains to the way each story fit the script. Seau's did. Hernandez's didn't. Baseball suicides usually earn an obituary at least. Then the press moves on. Football suicides become reference points in the overarching narrative months after the fact. The coverage conveys the unmistakable impression that football drives men to suicide.

Nobody wondered whether baseball killed Enzo Hernandez because the question was just too stupid to ask. No one sees a relationship between suicide squeezes and suicides. Otherwise sane people connect sacks to suicides. The relationship between a violent game and violent ends may make sense to people on an anecdotal level. It doesn't survive a statistical analysis.

During the last quarter century, Enzo Hernandez and eleven other former Major League Baseball players have killed themselves. During that time, thirteen former NFL players took their own lives. For every Junior Seau, there is a Mike Flanagan; for every Jovan Belcher, a Donnie Moore. Given that football fields more franchises than baseball, that athletes cycle through the NFL more rapidly, and that NFL rosters boast more players than even the expanded September MLB rosters, the suicide rate among major league players actually ranks higher than the suicide rate of NFL players.[62]

Like the great football crisis of 1905–1906, when more died on the diamond than the gridiron, today's football suicide "epidemic" says more about sensationalistic reporting than it does about the dangers of the game. Hype overwhelms fact. There is a football suicide crisis because the media repeatedly says that there is. There isn't a baseball suicide crisis because the media never says that there is. Maybe once a narrative about the dangers of sunflower seeds or chewing tobacco develops, the media will proclaim a baseball suicide epidemic. But right now there's a Fourth Estate fixation on concussions, so there's a football suicide epidemic—even though baseball players kill themselves at a higher rate.

And it's not as though baseball players end their lives in any exaggerated number the way Jack Kevorkian's acquaintances once did. A small fraction of their ranks, just like a small fraction of doctors, accountants, and waitresses, decides that life is just not worth living. A fraction of athletes who wear shoulder pads and helmets reaches that conclusion, too. Since they invaded our television screens on any number of Sundays, they invade our television screens upon their deaths. If you weren't on TV when you lived, chances are you won't be on TV when you die. So for TV talking heads, waitressing and accounting don't induce suicide, but football does.

If football players killed themselves at a higher rate than the general public, sensible people might blame the game. But retired NFL players commit suicide at a *lower* rate than the general public.[63] Knowing this truth might lead sensible people to examine the failing aspects of a fallen player's life—divorce, bankruptcy, depression, ailments, addiction—that help explain the suicides of so many people who never played a down of football. But since the assumption, even among sensible people, remains that football contributes to suicide, impulses direct us to blame the blows of a game rather than those from life when an NFL player hits the off switch.

When the NFL Players Association asked NIOSH to look at more than three thousand retired league veterans, the researchers found nine suicides rather than the twenty-two they might have expected to find. NFL players commit suicide at *less than half the rate* of other American men. For every ten suicides that occurred within a similar demographic, pension-vested NFL players experienced just four.[64]

The familiar statistic that players kill themselves at six times the national average didn't dematerialize because a federal government study demanded by the players union rebutted it. Months after NIOSH scientists proved that the suicide rate for men outside of the NFL exceeds the rate for NFL veterans by two-and-a-half times, Frank Bruni repeated the NFL sixfold-suicide canard in a *New York Times* column charging fellow football fans with being "morally compromised."[65] A lie is easier to repeat than to refute.

Dr. Lehman, a coauthor of the study that showed NFL players outliving other American men, wasn't bewildered by the discovery that players accustomed to the high-intensity, high-profile world of professional football emerge better equipped to deal with everyday stresses. He isn't bewildered by the fact that people don't believe that either. "People can believe what they want," Lehman allowed. "I've read a lot about how people assess risk. They're going to focus in on the people who are out of the norm, the people who have died young. That's going to draw more attention than people who are continuing to live. You don't hear about the people who are continuing to live. You don't hear about some football player who is now eighty years old."[66]

"You know what I wish?" Chuck Bednarik reflected after his career. "That God made us so we could play until we were 65. That would've been just long enough."[67] God didn't make us that way. But participating in athletics helps athletes live to sixty-five and beyond.

Good news isn't to everyone. "I think it's bogus," said Hall of Famer Joe DeLamielleure of the NIOSH study. "Just think of the guys who have died before they got into their 60s or 70s. Don't tell me we live longer. I don't believe it."[68]

But the lives of octogenarian Frank Gifford, who survived the most brutal hit in league history to act in films and star in the sports broadcasting booth, and the 1925-born Chuck Bednarik, a ferocious two-way "60-minute man" who missed just three games in fourteen seasons, suggest that the government study's findings aren't as outlandish as its critics charge.

CHAPTER SEVEN

THERE *IS* CRYING IN FOOTBALL

In Shrewsbury, Massachusetts, invisible even to longtime residents, lies a sylvan fortress of football. There, a high wall of trees surrounds a square plane of mud and grass. Accessible by a circuitous dirt road at one end and a stony footpath at the other, the secluded practice field of the St. John's Pioneers remains blind to the sights and deaf to the sounds of the outside world. A blocking sled and a decrepit goal post suggest its purpose. The burnt orange, red, and yellow foliage further hint that football season has arrived in New England.

At about quarter to three, the young congregants of the Church of Football arrive for daily services. The faithful chant. They receive instruction from the high priests. They partake in the rituals. But mostly, they sacrifice.

"It's a great day for football," a coach barks. It's a bad day for everything else. Drizzling, raw, and gloomy, the weather fits the activity. Football is a game of grit and glory. Players occasionally enjoy the latter on game day. Practices, which are more numerous than games, emphasize the grit. The possibility of glory on game day so inspires that young men endure the certainty of the grit of practice.

Nobody likes a football practice. Everybody likes a football game.

"Looking good today, Sully, looking good today," assistant coach Pat White yells. "Haven't washed those pants in four years." Andrew Sullivan looks every bit the football player. Dirty wardrobe aside, the defensive end stands at six foot three and weighs 220 pounds. From his Johnny Unitas-style high-top cleats to his red wiffle haircut, he appears all football and no flab. A sport increasingly classified as hazardous to one's health producing so many pictures of health surely ranks as one of the great paradoxes of the War on Football. Watching St. John's practice helps explain how football produces so many young men like Sully. It's shocking that large segments of the population find it shocking that doing what Sully does in the fall for twenty falls—as many of the NFL players in the NIOSH study did—lengthens lives, strengthens lungs, and reduces heart attacks. The mental health benefits obvious to practice observers aren't so obvious to game detractors. Keeping up with a strenuous exercise regimen doesn't just release endorphins temporarily; it enhances self-worth permanently. Play instills purpose. Players set goals and achieve them. The NFLPA-sponsored NIOSH study's findings that NFL veterans commit suicide far less often than men outside of the NFL doesn't seem so strange to anyone who's ever become part of, or hung around, a football team. Teammates lift each other up and guard each other's backs.

Practice also underscores why the sport that took thirty-six lives in 1968 took just two during Andrew's senior season—and none at the high school level. Coaches are smarter. Equipment is better. Players are cognizant of the costs of gratuitous hits. The game isn't particularly lethal anymore. That doesn't mean it's not rough.

"Don't avoid the collision," a coach barks. "Make the collision." Fifty-seven times during practice, Sully collides violently with fellow teammates. Seven times Sully launches himself against blocking sleds and padded tackling dummies. Hits include open-field tackling drills in which Andrew crashes into and wraps up ball carriers and scrimmages in which Andrew plays against teammates in game simulations. On some scrimmage plays, Andrew registers two or three significant hits. On others, the contact amounts to standing wrestling matches with offensive linemen.[1] When researchers tracked seventy-eight high school players over 128 practices and thirty-eight games, their helmet sensors registered 54,247 total hits resulting in thirteen concussions. In other words, a concussion appeared in one out of every 4,173 head jolts. Although high school players like Andrew—or, more accurately, slighter ones unlike Andrew—exhibit lower tolerance levels for impacts, their concussion rates, perhaps because they generate less force, don't deviate much from the rates of their collegiate and professional counterparts.[2]

Andrew, despite playing since the eighth grade, has never experienced a football concussion. His strong neck may have something to do with this. More so, the way Coach John Andreoli manages the lead up to game day—dressing his squad for contact in full pads just twice during the week—reduces the risk for such injuries. For practices the team embraces a thud-tackling approach in which a defender hits and wraps but doesn't bring the offensive player down. Facemasks collide frequently. Because Andrew plays in the trenches with his head up, the scary crown-to-crown hits that now elicit flying yellow laundry rather than cheers don't appear at practice. Nevertheless, the banging, jolting, crunching, clashing, and smashing make the unseen preparation contain more, if less intense, contact than the game watched by students, parents, girlfriends, and alumni.

In the distance, a group of smaller teenagers trots through the practice field to the path behind it. It's the St. John's cross country team. While the runners don't possess Sully's beach muscles, their after-school activity undoubtedly produces healthy bodies. And they stay fit without head-to-head collisions at top speed. Shin splints, not concussions, haunt cross country teams. The distance runners running in the distance spark a thought: What would young men lose, and what would they gain, if they dropped their cleats for sneakers, the field for the forest, football for the finish line?

The superficial differences between football and cross country spark thoughts of obvious costs (fewer teammates) and benefits (fewer injuries) that ditching the violent competition for the serene activity might foster.

But a full realization of the substantive differences between the two sports would wait until game day. For now, the juxtaposition of the graceful striders with the armored combatants prompts a strange sense of the alikeness of both activities. The sports share a basic gene: running.

Despite football's violent reputation, the primary activity players engage in during practice is running. The players run when they stretch: straight-leg kicks, karaoke, high knees, and back peddling for thirty yards warm-up Sully for the real workout. After warm-ups, the practice shifts to a series of efficient, position-oriented, tightly-scheduled stations that emphasize blocking and tackling. A three-station tackling drill features short, explosive running. So, too, do the blocking sleds, agility drills, and crash pads that Sully encounters when he divides off with other linemen. When Sully lines up for plays against air, as he did for seven downs during the practice's special-teams component, he runs thirty to forty yards at full speed to cover the punt. The forty-seven plays in which Sully lines up against a scrub-squad feature aerobic activity combined with the anaerobic blocking, driving, and hitting that characterize the workmanlike existence of life on the line. Practice's climactic moment features a team session emphasizing defense or offense depending on the day. At the end of practice, players endure "the beast"—fifty-yard liners run back and forth six times with rest buffering three explosive repetitions.

Because, as one coach loudly reminds, "Nobody walks on the practice field," activity as incidental as running to the water fountain accumulates into significant exercise. Andrew actually jogged more than a half mile between drills.[3] For many Americans, that movement, which Andrew considers transportation to the workout rather than the workout itself, would exhaust. But the physicality of football makes it all relative. Our exercise is their rest.

Practice is hard work. But the more closely I watch Sully practice, the more cognizant I become that I am missing the real work. Sully tells me that when he entered high school he stood five-foot-ten inches and weighed 170 pounds. His frame has added five inches and fifty pounds. Training had much to do with the physical transformation.

The football team lifts weights two days a week during the season. During the offseason, Andrew, like many football players, joins the track and field team partly as a way to continue running and lifting. He does a variety of exercises but emphasizes a few core ones. "Bench press, dead lifts, squats, power cleans," he points out. "That's all you need, really." For three months during the offseason, Andrew follows the cult-like exercise regimen of CrossFit, a fitness phenomenon that utilizes primitive equipment to stress athletic lifts and explosive movements. When his coaches tested him as a sophomore, Andrew bench pressed 135 pounds nineteen times. Now as a senior he benches 185 pounds for twenty-one reps, which calculates to a 300-pound-plus max. Despite his size, he runs the forty-yard dash in 4.8 seconds.[4] Most of the preparation for game day doesn't occur during practice. It comes during the offseason.

To be a starting, let alone elite, high school football player requires an outlier's dedication to wellness in the United States of Obesity. When he's not going to the beach or partaking in all-you-can-eat pancakes at Denny's, Sully spends his time training. Even his hobbies (reading *Muscle & Fitness* and weightlifting) and his job (working at a local batting cage) revolve around sports.[5] One senses that Andrew burns more calories at work than the rest of us do at play. Andrew is a grown up Cam, the overactive Pop Warner pee-wee we met in chapter one, or perhaps a male version of fellow CrossFit enthusiast Danielle, the Boston Militia player who works at two gyms and plays collegiate soccer. Sitting in front of a computer doesn't have the same appeal to everyone. Some people need activity, physical activity that challenges their limits and imposes the will of the mind over the cries of the body. Football attracts such people. Football creates such people.

Hang around a high school football practice at the risk of seeing upended stereotypes. There's beef but no obesity. The amoeba-like teenagers resembling doughy grandmothers that one encounters near the local mall's Hot Topic don't play football. The rebels against Generation Text show themselves neither soft nor spoiled but ready to perform dirty work. Going to practice every day is a prerequisite to making the team.

Starting on the team involves training every day when nobody's taking attendance, when no coach looks over the shoulder, when the person forcing you to work is yourself.

This becomes apparent in the lead up to the St. John's game against Leominster, Andrew's home-city high school that he spurned to attend a private institution in a leafy hamlet. Both schools, pulling from a similar talent pool of about 1,000 boys, appear evenly matched on the field if not in the classroom. St. John's charges nearly $12,000 in tuition and selects or rejects students on the basis of grades, an entrance test, recommendations, and an essay. Recent graduates of the football team have gone on to play sports for Yale, Bowdoin, Stanford, Fordham, Cal, Oberlin, and MIT.[6] Leominster High, in contrast, opens its doors to all comers. A 2012 ranking of Massachusetts high schools pegged it at 232 out of 350.[7] A few months before the game, Leominster police arrested one of its high school's English teachers for allegedly selling cocaine. The city's mayor reassured parents, "There is no indication that she was selling to minors at this point or to anybody who was a student or staff there as far as we know."[8] Sully's family paid for him to get an education at St. John's despite Leominster High offering them one for free.

Sully's opponents aren't just his friends. They are offseason workout partners and former teammates. "We throw a lot," explains John Giacoppe, who, like Andrew, lives in Leominster but plays for St. John's. "One day during the summer, we'll just call each other up and say, 'Wanna throw down at the Pop Warner field?'"[9] Summer friends morph into fall opponents.

In eighth grade, Andrew and John's Leominster Pop Warner team made it to the local Super Bowl. Andrew's dad coached the team. John's dad battled cancer. "Football was very special to my father and me," John recalls. "Pop Warner—I used to be terrible, terrible. He just pushed me. I came back one year after not being able to catch anything—I came back and had close to a thousand yards in Pop Warner in receiving."[10]

Andrew recalls that in the Pop Warner Super Bowl, "John had the best game I have ever seen him play."[11] John remembers it that way, too. "It was a really emotional time. My dad actually died that night before the Super Bowl. I went and I played. They were all so supportive. I think I played one of the best games I'll ever play in my life. I was just cracking people and catching everything." Rather than a weight on his shoulders, his father's death served as an inspiration. John recalls more of his team's performance at the funeral home than on the field. "They were so supportive through everything. During the wake, they were there the whole time. They didn't leave. They didn't just say 'sorry.' They stayed with me the whole time."[12] He struggles to name the team they played in the championship game. But he remembers that.

As if the Leominster-St. John's game didn't have enough added drama, the powerhouses had played in the previous season's Central Massachusetts Division 1 Super Bowl. The public school kids, as they had done every time they played St. John's during Andrew and John's high school careers, beat the private school kids in the season-ending game. In fact, the Super Bowl victory tied Leominster with Brockton for the most titles in Massachusetts history. Nevertheless, the Leominster game remains one the Pioneer players look forward to. "I love it," Giacoppe explains. "I played Pop Warner with them for like six years. So I grew up with them. They're my best friends. I see them on the weekends. Playing them is crazy. I can't explain it. It's so emotional."[13] This game turned out to be just that: emotional.

Those introduced to high school football through *Friday Night Lights* might find a St. John's game more spartan than spectacle. The squad doesn't enjoy a voter-approved, tax-funded 19,032-capacity stadium, charter jets taxiing the athletes to road games, or a part-time football coach making more than full-time teachers. "Pepettes" don't worshipfully bake sweets for the players, beauty-queen cheerleaders don't root them to victory, and a band doesn't serenade their success.[14]

St. John's does enjoy the enthusiastic support of several costumed teenage boys—one dressed as a banana, another as a red-devil within a fried egg—who also attend the single-sex school. What St. John's lacks in off-field accoutrements they make up for in on-field product. It's exciting, fast-paced football.

The Pioneers live up to their name by running a Chip Kelly/Oregon Ducks–style blur offense that remains trailblazing for colleges, let alone high schools. On the sidelines, back-up players hoist four two-sided placards with easily identifiable icons—the Kentucky Fried Chicken logo, the Clemson Tigers insignia, Coach John Andreoli's face—that direct the action on the field or distract the defense's attention away from the field. Who knows what placard means what? The quarterback, lining up four yards behind the line, enjoys a long-distance relationship with his center. If you want to glimpse the team's fullback, you'd be better off spending your money on a milk carton than a ticket. Huddles? They are so twentieth century.

It may not seem very old school. But, in keeping with history's everything-old-is-new-again dynamic, the St. John's no-huddle hurry-up harkens back to the origins of football. Once downs from scrimmage replaced the down-and-dirty scrummage, quarterbacks began employing signals, rather than today's huddle, to direct movement. Encrypted words or numbers, much like today's audibles, eventually overtook signals as the preferred method.[15] In 1896, when Amos Alonzo Stagg's University of Chicago team played the University of Michigan indoors, the coach overcame the crowd noise by utilizing a huddle. Outdoors, Stagg's innovation hampered rather than hastened his track-meet team's progress, so the huddle remained dormant for another fifteen seasons.[16] Ancient football without huddles hints at a game that valued stamina as much as strength. St. John's very much plays cardiovascular football.

The frenetic pace, and the system's complexity, would seem advanced for a 1980s professional team (if not an 1890s amateur one). But it suits the 1990s-born Giacoppe just fine. Whereas defensive end Sully plays a position still more or less how Walter Camp described it—"assisting at the edge as much as possible"[17]—offensive end Giacoppe plays a position unrecognizable to football's anti-pass founding father. The receiver splits beyond-the-numbers wide, catches passes, and appears more bone than beef. St. John's is pass-happy and the lean and lanky John Giacoppe is happy with that.

St. John's strikes early after Giacoppe catches a 35-yard bomb from quarterback Drew Smiley. The catch helps set up a Shadrach Abrokwah touchdown run, the tailback's first of three on the day.

Sully makes an impression on his hometown opponents by sacking the quarterback to force a fourth and eleven, which Leominster converts into a 31-yard touchdown pass to receiver Neal O'Connor—the same guy who almost single-handedly defeated them in last year's Super Bowl. In the second quarter, Sully stops two consecutive runs that end a Leominster drive. Despite a quadriceps injury, Sully raises his game. The previous week, Shrewsbury High School tailback Zach Dionis rushed for 301 yards and four touchdowns against the Pioneers in an upset that left their undersized defensive line dejected and defeated. The 4-4 defense seeks redemption.

Sully pressures the quarterback, makes numerous tackles, and sets the edge as the weak side end in the St. John's four-man front. As his father tells me, "This is Andrew's Super Bowl."[18] He plays like it, and even from the press box, it's evident that his opponents don't like it—or don't like that he spurned their team for St. John's. Andrew and the offensive linemen taking him on play *through* the whistle. The referees eject one Leominster player after he takes a swing at a St. John's player. The skirmishes on the line grow increasingly chippy and, though inaudible from the grandstand, the players jaw. As Andrew observes, playing Leominster is "emotional."[19]

It's a football game. It's a fight. The participants in that first 1869 Rutgers-Princeton football game wouldn't recognize the passing, the uprights, or even the oblong ball as deriving from the competition they staged. They would recognize the fighting and the physicality. Football has always been combat.

Leominster plays catch-up for most of the game. But after a clock-eating drive that also devours the Pioneers' lead, Leominster finds itself sitting on a 29-28 edge with the better part of the fourth quarter past. It is times like these—when time ticks away—that remind the Pioneers why they run the blur. With the efficiency of a professional offense, quarterback Drew Smiley marches the St. John's eleven down the field.

St. John's gains composure. They recognize they have a six-foot-three receiver and Leominster doesn't even have a six-foot defensive back. With 114 ticks left on the clock, the shotgun quarterback slings the ball to John Giacoppe in the back corner of the end zone. The athletic receiver leaps above the defender and snatches the ball from its falling trajectory. He comes down awkwardly on one foot before tumbling out of bounds. The referee signals touchdown. The home bleachers explode. St. John's 34, Leominster 29. Giacoppe has stuck a dagger into his Leominster friends' hearts and avenged the St. John's loss in last year's Super Bowl.

But his buddies on the opposing squad have different ideas. With less than two minutes on the clock, Leominster's offense starts from their twenty-five and immediately moves thirty-five yards downfield on a Garrett DelleChiaie pass to Neil O'Connor, whose gain is half throw and half run. A quarterback draw brings the ball from inside the forty to inside the twenty. Three runs grind the ball down inside the ten yard line. With seven ticks left, the Blue Devils find themselves second and goal from the six. They call timeout, and Leominster's coach turns the playbook over to his players.

This isn't a throwback to Pop Warner but to schoolyard football. The home team's bête noir O'Connor, who burned St. John's with a halfback pass to his brother in last year's Super Bowl, volunteers that he can get open on a hitch route. The Pioneers and Blue Devils line up aware of the possibility that this play could be the roller-coaster-of-a-game's last. An isolated O'Connor stands split to the left lined up against an equally isolated St. John's defensive back. The center snaps the ball, and Sully struggles in vain to pressure quarterback Garrett DelleChiaie. O'Connor sprints to the goal line, stops abruptly, spins inward, catches a bullet on his outside shoulder, and falls into the end zone. The play is too quick, and too perfectly executed, for the Pioneers to stop. The third lead change in the final five minutes would be the last. Appropriately, kids playing sandlot football together since grade school conclude their competition with a play drawn in the sand. It ends as it began.

"It started before the season started—throwing routes," the game's hero Garrett DelleChiaie tells me. "It was definitely an emotional game. It's personal. John Giacoppe—he's my brother."[20]

The opposing quarterback, who saw his senior season nearly ruined when Giacoppe grabbed a touchdown from the air with less than two minutes on the clock, calls his adversary his "brother." Indeed, one of the receivers the undersized DelleChiaie threw routes to during the off-season was the split end who lit up Leominster's defense for nearly one hundred receiving yards that October day.

The visitor side's feast day cruelly coincides with the home team's funeral. The high priest offers consoling words. The congregants speak in hushed tones if at all. Loved ones offer condolences. Approaching the same end zone where just minutes earlier he had caught what screaming fans assumed would be the game-winning touchdown, Giacoppe slowly walks with a face like a dam: hard but holding back. He nears the spot where he had enjoyed brief glory. His face collapses into tears as his body falls to a knee on the grass. A single teammate approaches, takes a knee, and puts his hand on Giacoppe's shoulder. It's Sully, the physical specimen I have been tracking to get a sense of the physicality of the game. "I didn't say anything," Sully explains to me of his end zone moment with Giacoppe. "I just got down on one knee with him."[21]

I didn't say anything, either. It seemed a bit heartless to permit curiosity, let alone my digital recorder, to intrude on the very private moment in a very public place. So the tear ducts let flow a mystery: Why was the watery-eyed athlete down on a knee, head down, back toward the spectators, breaking down?

Perhaps it had something to do with all those routes Garrett threw to John during the offseason, a deceptive word that in football parlance refers to the time when players drop gallons of sweat without the weekly reward of a public performance. Is there really an "off" season? Investing all that time and energy away from the eyes of spectators only to come a few points short once the crowd has gathered might make anyone cry.

Then again, the fact that football offers so few contests—the NFL regular season features fewer than one-tenth the games of Major League Baseball and one fifth the games of the NBA—heightens the emotions. The physicality of the game, which necessitates week-long breaks between games, also fosters an intensity of play. John may have realized that "tomorrow's another day" doesn't apply to football, whose games prove too grueling to play every day. A game means more when it's played less.

Perhaps the adrenaline dump after the fight unleashed the tears. Players battle alongside one another not in a metaphorical sense as in other sports but in a literal sense. The bonding that occurs when others have your back, and you have theirs, supersedes the bond created by checking in for another player at the horn or grabbing the baton in a relay. It creates that unspoken understanding between two teammates commiserating over a loss. John looked defeated because he had been defeated. Sully felt it, too.

Could it be the brotherhood established by the sport? The red uniforms tell us they're the St. John's Pioneers. Without the benefit of a roster, you can't tell them, like brothers, apart. From the facemasks masking faces to the pile providing the cloak of anonymity, evidence of the collective nature of the sport appears every time a player disappears from view. It's a game of self-abnegation in which the sum trumps any of its individual parts. Some players never touch the ball, let alone score. The quarterback helps determine John's success, and the offensive line helps determine the quarterback's success, and so on. One weak link renders the chain broken and ineffective. If Andrew's defense can't stop Leominster's offense, the scoreboard negates John's on-field acrobatics. One man's success can't help but be interpreted as the group's success because his success never occurs in a vacuum. John played a great game. John doesn't find that a consolation. The team wins together. The team fails together, too.

Maybe the sense of something coming to an end overcame John. Football plays as a post-industrial passage rite. Boys enter bleached fields of crabgrass under the unforgiving August sun. They emerge as men once the stark, leafless trees, first snowfalls, and abbreviated daylight signal the end of the lifecycle. Under the long shadow of the goalpost, John could clearly see his high school football days growing shorter. A boy forced into manhood before his teammates surely understood that the joys of childhood don't last forever.

Maybe all of it weighed John down to his knee after the defeat. John only knows what grounded him. And maybe only a teammate like Andrew could truly empathize.

That postgame drama wouldn't have happened had John and Andrew put on cross country sneakers instead of football cleats. The unforgettable end-zone image demonstrates why the century-old War on Football remains an ill-fated crusade. Football initiates its players into its cult. Intellectual briefs against a game inscribed on the soul ultimately fall on deaf ears. Arguments from the head don't persuade the heart. The congregants of the Church of Football don't lose the faith once they leave the game. Memories serve to intensify devotion.

The gridiron that day imparts the lesson that football isn't primarily a physical sport. It's an emotional one. The brutal component assuredly gives rise to the emotional component. The glaring violence may blind spectators to the emotion of the game. It binds players to it. In exploring the physical side of football, one finds a tender spot unknown to those who only know the game as fans. Like practice, where I discover that the work in front of my eyes builds on the work done away from eyes during the offseason, game day similarly surprises. Football involves strategy devised by brilliant tacticians. It requires the power, quickness, and endurance of young bodies. But it's mostly about a spirit, passion, *thumos*.

A discussion with Sully and John's head coach John Andreoli on the eve of the epic contest foreshadowed the profound postgame image—and DelleChiaie's virtuous take on the fraternity of opponents. "Stepping outside of your comfort zone is something that is done on a daily basis in football," Andreoli, a former professional linebacker, explained. "You're challenged physically. You're challenged mentally. It's a game of self-discipline. It's a game of sacrifice. It's a game in which the greater good is really more important than the individual accomplishments. That is something that stays with people. They understand through their entire lives having played the game. That's why there is a great camaraderie and brotherhood among the people who have played the game—whether you have played with someone or against."[22] Andrew and John played with Garrett before they played against him.

Football isn't a game of the body. It's a game of the soul.

There may be no crying in baseball. There is plenty of it in football.

CHAPTER EIGHT

THE ABOLITION OF BOYS

"The true man wants two things," Nietzsche concluded, "danger and play."[1] Football, like women, gives him both.

With snow falling and darkness encroaching, St. John's and Leominster reconvened for danger and play in 2012's Central Massachusetts Super Bowl. The rematch of their emotional contest from earlier that season unfolds as a repeat. John Giacoppe catches a thirty-five-yard bomb to set up the first St. John's touchdown. Sully intercepts a pass for a fifty-three-yard touchdown. Leominster erases the St. John's lead in the second half when quarterback Garrett DelleChiaie again takes over the game with one arm and two legs. The final score leaves Giacoppe visibly devastated. "That's my brother," Leominster's quarterback says of Giacoppe postgame. "We grew up with him."[2]

Despite the best efforts of Mother Nature, and the intensity of competition, nobody left in an ambulance. Everybody had fun. The Leominster players exhibited class in victory and the St. John's players accepted defeat as men. All over America last season, football was more about fun than fractures. For the first time since 1994, gridiron hits killed not a single high school athlete.[3] The paradox at the heart of the War on Football involves the demonstrable but rarely demonstrated safety improvements that have strangely coincided with growing outrage over the sport's dangers.

Why the sudden hysteria over the sport?

Football hasn't grown especially hard. Society, as the St. John's Pioneers' supersized Super Bowl runner-up trophy suggests, has grown soft. The ranks of the primary football constituency, children, have been decimated; their rough and muddy ways strike overprotective adults as increasingly foreign. A paradigm shift in the ideal man has marginalized, or perhaps redefined, masculinity. Pop culture, when in a kind mood, depicts the manly man as a Neanderthal; when in a cruel mood, as a gorilla. These societal changes, which have next to nothing to do with football, nevertheless influence the way we process the game as a culture.

Existential threats remain a permanent part of football's existence. The current challenge contains elements unique to our times. Walter Camp, Bill Reid, and Theodore Roosevelt operated in a culture that venerated manly virtue, embraced a more libertarian form of child rearing, and exalted rugged individualism. Today's indoor, antiseptic, over-monitored childhood stands anathema to the outdoor upbringings of yesteryear. So, too, do Metrosexual Man and a trophies-for-everybody mindset. This wasn't the soil from which sprang the player voted at midcentury the game's greatest.[4]

On an unseasonably hot October day in 1924, University of Illinois coach Bob Zuppke issued the unusual order to his team to remove their stockings. So unsettling did their bare legs appear to their opponents that University of Michigan athletic director Fielding Yost delayed the game to allow the team's captain to inspect the calves of the Illini players. No socks? No problem. The University of Michigan fielded not only the best team in the country but perhaps the best team in the history of the school. They had shared the previous season's Big Ten title, and a mythical national championship, with Illinois. So, fans anticipated the matchup in Urbana more than any other on the schedule that season. Yost had already proclaimed that containing running back Red Grange, the Illini's best player, posed no problem for the nation's best defense. The University of Illinois coach sagely reminded Grange, with annoying frequency, of these unwise utterances.[5]

Number 77 returned the opening kickoff ninety-five yards for a touchdown. A few plays later, Grange took a direct snap sixty-seven yards. By the time he reached the end zone, no player in chase came within twenty yards of him. A few downs later Grange reversed field on a handoff designed to go around the right end. He again used a combination of speed and smarts to leave an over-pursuing Michigan defense behind in his dust cloud. Before the first quarter expired, the explosive Grange had straight-armed, spun, and cut his way to four touchdowns. He returned for an encore in the second half that included passing for a touchdown and yet another rush for six points.

Michigan suffered more touchdowns from one player that day than they had from every team they played that and the previous season.[6] When a cheerleader at a high school game in nearby Chicago announced through his bullhorn that Grange had scored on a kick return, the crowd erupted. As he repeated touchdown announcements every few minutes, the enthusiastic cheers turned to frustrated cackles of disbelief.[7] Who could single-handedly post twenty-four points on the Wolverine defense in a single quarter? WGN's radio announcer, during the station's first-ever broadcast of a football game, struggled for words to describe the spectacle before him.[8] If seeing is believing, not seeing enticed listeners to fantasize an otherworldly athlete, a Galloping Ghost who raced through defenders as though they weren't there.

The defining moment in Harold "Red" Grange's life occurred not on any of the six touchdowns he hung on the University of Michigan that day. It happened when he was four. Harold's mother died. The family escaped west. Harold escaped through sports.

Red Grange thrived in the male enclave of professional football because, even when a boy, Red Grange knew only a man's world. In the wake of his mother's death, the two Grange sisters departed for maternal relatives, leaving a Y-chromosome club comprised of Red, brother Garland, and father Lyle, Wheaton, Illinois's chief of police in a department of one. The steady paycheck came in exchange for unsteady hours that left the boys alone as their protector protected others. The brothers fended for themselves in a second-floor apartment. Garland shopped for food. Red cooked it. They alternated cleaning the dishes.[9] Circumstances compelled a teenage Red to work on a farm one year. He labored for four hours before bicycling to school for a day's lessons followed by an afternoon's farm chores.[10] When he didn't work, he played. The indoor existence held no charms for such a boy.

"I never went out on dates with girls, because I didn't have any money or a decent suit of clothes to wear," Grange recalled.[11] The whole truth may have been too embarrassing to admit. Within that hypermasculine upbringing, terror came not in the form of older boys picking fistfights but from pretty girls seeking affection. After a high school basketball game, for instance, three girls waited at the locker room door. Rather than face the trio of female admirers, a red-faced Grange escaped out a window.[12] The athlete eluded fawning girls as successfully, if not as deftly, as he did frothing tacklers.

The boy unsurprisingly found comfort within the masculine settings that he had become accustomed to within his broken family. Grange reflected that "the more important part of living came after school when I was able to play football, basketball and baseball with my pals."[13] Name the sport, he played it. When bruising battles with older boys left his body battered, Red confessed to his father that he might be better off trading in the pigskin for marbles. His father encouraged him to continue, noting that the roughhousing would turn him into a man. A fatherly promise of twenty-five cents for a first-place finish unleashed a mania for entering footraces and a collection of quarters. Both brothers earned reputations as sandlot superstars before earning NFL paychecks. In the absence of other children, young Red attempted tackles on the family dog and explored the outdoors.[14] Like so many boys, Red possessed something inside him that made sitting still impossible. Fortunately for the hyperactive Red, he inhabited a world more understanding and tolerant than ours of the widespread medical condition known as boyhood.

Then an actual affliction threatened all that youthful vigor. An irregular heartbeat resulted in doctor's orders to refrain from sports. The boy risked losing the activity that had replaced his mother and had forged a bond with the remaining parent. The prescription seemed a fate equally bad as the possible outcome of ignoring the prognosis, so Red secretly returned to play. A reluctant father ultimately gave his imprimatur to Red playing and paying the medical advice no mind. As biographer Lars Anderson points out, "He understood that the rewards of his boy playing were far greater than the risks."[15] Some boys need sunshine on their faces, mud on their clothes, and the exhilaration of violent collision like the rest of us need oxygen. Red Grange was one such boy.

That world exists the way Red Grange does, as a quaint memory of a yesterday that appears surreal to today. During Grange's Wheaton boyhood, children constituted almost two in five Americans. In the America in which Sully and John came of age, the under-18 set number just one in four Americans—and dropping.[16] More American households shelter a dog than a child.[17] Parents spoil kids with video games, smartphones, and obnoxiously priced sneakers. Rarely do they give them what they want most: a sibling.

Like so many creatures, American children have joined the list of endangered species seldom seen roaming in the wild. Children play by appointment under the watchful eyes of adults. Sports exist as over-supervised de facto daycare, not spontaneous competitions orchestrated informally by the children themselves. Walking to school now represents neglect, not a step toward independence. A simple bike ride compels a parent to dress up a child as though he were Evel Knievel jumping the Grand Canyon. Paid work, an initiation into the adult world of savings and responsibility, somehow strikes society as anachronistic, exploitative, and taboo. Children seemingly need protection from everyone but their protectors. We have met the boogeyman, and he is us.

Football necessarily presents a culture clash. The game is not of this century or even the last. Although football legislators incessantly revamp the sport, the basic nature of the game remains mired in the nineteenth century. That distance rather than the danger inspires the War on Football. It's dirty, aggressive, physical, and quite reluctant to indulge individuality—all the things that we're not. It's surely more hazardous than basketball, baseball, soccer, and other great sports. But it's dramatically safer than football as played by our dads, granddads, and dads' granddads. The profound decline in deaths and paralysis stems from the greater protections offered by way of equipment, rules, and coaching. The improvements in player safety make the War on Football a non sequitur, akin to responding to Pearl Harbor by declaring war on Canada—*in 1985*. The casus belli of the War on Football isn't the harshness of the sport but the softness of society.

Theodore Roosevelt's enlistment in the War on Football as a partisan of the game sprang from a more comprehensive notion that institutions standing as bulwarks against general enfeeblement needed bulwarks, too. "In Roosevelt's estimation, the foes of football were wrongheaded idealists who simply refused to accept the risks that are attached to virtually any human endeavor," John J. Miller writes in *The Big Scrum: How Teddy Roosevelt Saved Football.* "They threatened to feminize an entire generation. At stake was nothing less than the future of the United States."[18] Now that the future has arrived one needn't be clairvoyant to glean what the Rough Rider from the past might think of the smooth ride demanded by our present.

America has drifted. This necessarily alters our perspective. It doesn't alter the facts. Five young boys lost their lives to sandlot football hits in 1967. None did last season. Twenty-three high school boys died from hits in 1970. None did last season. Eighteen players at all levels of competition suffered fatal collision injuries in 1976. Just two did last season.[19] These inconvenient truths don't mesh with the narrative of the War on Football. So, they don't make their way into the conversation. More players died from hits inflicted on the day that Harold Moore lost his life in 1905 than died from hits in every game played in the United States during 2012.[20] The game has changed. The pace of the game's change hasn't been as quick, though, as the pace of the culture's change. We have grown intolerant of the rough pastimes of boys.

Anti-football propaganda has already taken its toll on the sport and on sports in general. Resilient myths that football leads to suicide, heart disease, or a truncated lifespan necessarily suppress the numbers at try-outs. But it's hard not to see the concussion controversy as the main culprit for the rapid decline in youth football. A Portland, Oregon-area league that fielded 270 teams in 2009 fielded just 233 by the 2012 season.[21] A league in fast-growing Fairfax County, Virginia, reported losing 10 percent of its player population from 2010 to 2012.[22] The local anecdotal accounts mesh with national statistics. Youth football leagues, the kind in which Scott Lazo coaches and Cam plays, witnessed a 6 percent drop in participation last season. Around 2.8 million kids, down from 3 million the previous year, played in organized tackle football leagues in 2012.[23] The lawsuit by the former players hasn't dented the NFL's popularity. It has unleashed tremendous harm on kids' leagues.

The same appears to be true, though by a smaller degree, in America's high schools. Instead of serving as ambassadors of the game, the litigious retirees have instead become propagandists against it. Teens desperately needing an outlet and activity increasingly stay on the sidelines. The 2011–2012 academic year was the first in almost twenty in which fewer boys participated in high school sports than had the previous year. Waning interest in football served as the greatest contributing factor in the overall decline. About twelve thousand fewer high school students played football during the 2011–2012 school year than did the previous year. With 1.1 million participants, football still tops all other high school sports in attracting students. In fact, it nearly doubles its closest competitor (outdoor track).[24] But the War on Football has clearly succeeded in scaring some parents away from the game. Who wants their kid to end up like Junior Seau?

A more interesting question: What kind of men do parents hope their boys become?

We don't allow boys to be boys. Why are we so surprised when males denied a boyhood fail at manhood? It's easy to find a dude, a bro, a lad, or a guy. A man? Physically matured males prolonging adolescence through inordinate attention to video games, periodic marijuana-induced escapes from reality, delayed marriage, and less-than-enthusiastic quests for gainful employment advertise the bitter fruits of a culture that no longer sees childhood as preparation for adult responsibilities. Men will remain boys so long as parents forbid boys to be boys.

One finds an alarming number of young men just a few years senior to Sully and John devoid of spark and ambition. A big part of the problem involves the refusal to recognize the problem.

The most recent college commencement ceremonies granted roughly three diplomas to women for every two they awarded men. "A Google search of 'College Women's Centers' finds almost 6,000 links on the Web," Professor Mark Perry points out. "A Google search of 'College Men's Centers' finds almost no links on the Internet (fewer than 10), and asks the question: Did you mean: 'College *Women's* Centers'?"[25] The life expectancy for American women exceeds that of their male counterparts by five years.[26] The U.S. Department of Health and Human Services boasts a womenshealth.gov website. A menshealth.gov site doesn't exist. Instead, one of the six tabs on womenshealth.com redirects the browser to nineteen subtopics, one of which brings the user to "men's health."[27] Throughout the economic downturn that started in 2008, men consistently posted worse unemployment rates than women. The job gender gap, engendered by the collapse of construction and manufacturing, peaked at 2.7 points in August 2009.[28] Amidst this reality, the current presidential administration held a "White House Forum on Women in the Economy" touting "a wide range of policies, programs, and legislative initiatives ... supporting women and girls at all stages of their lives and careers."[29] The fellas?

Everybody benefits from greater opportunities for women to grow healthier, wealthier, and wiser. But the wide-open, wonderful world in which a cheerleader can become a cornerback isn't so welcoming for energetic, aggressive little fellows craving action and adrenaline. Not all males come as rough-and-tumble as Red Grange, and that's okay. Life is more interesting when people aspire to be themselves and not an archetype. But if we celebrate youngsters who defy gender norms, can't we tolerate the ones who conform to them? Boyhood isn't a medical illness cured by Ritalin or a social illness repealed through interdictions on traditional red-blooded folkways. It's an age to come of age, to develop from a child into a man.

They quite literally don't make men like they used to. Masculinity doesn't just appear defeated in such superficial trends as chest waxing, perfumed body sprays, skinny jeans, and beta-male sit-com characters. The levels of testosterone in American males have been falling rapidly for several decades.[30] The male cosmetics industry, virtually nonexistent a few years ago, approaches $3 billion in sales of bronzer, concealer, and other products mainly by calling makeup anything but "makeup."[31] A lingerie company even markets bras, thongs, and teddies specifically for males.[32] Foppish is the new manly. "At the same time that men have been ridiculed in the public square," *Save the Males* author Kathleen Parker notes, "the importance of fatherhood has been diminished, along with other traditionally male roles of father, protector, and provider, which are increasingly viewed as regressive manifestations of an outmoded patriarchy. The exemplar of the modern male is the hairless, metrosexualized man and decorator boys who turn heterosexual slobs into perfumed ponies."[33]

C. S. Lewis certainly had a bead on the direction of males when he wrote his short book *The Abolition of Man*. "In a sort of ghastly simplicity we remove the organ and demand the function," Lewis famously observed. "We make men without chests and expect of them virtue and enterprise. We laugh at honour and are shocked to find traitors in our midst. We castrate and bid the geldings be fruitful." In other words, too often modern man appears all head and no heart or all stomach and no chest. Between big-brained, hollow-hearted "cerebral man" and big-bellied, undisciplined "visceral man" stands the man of spirit, courage, passion, and virtue, a creature more bred than born.[34]

Classrooms don't do a particularly good job of fostering what the Greeks called *thumos*. Athletic fields do. Sully fighting through a quadriceps injury, players jawing back-and-forth, Garrett's second-half heroics, Giacoppe's emotional crash, and the postgame magnanimity between the teams all derive from the thumotic part of the soul. Just as schools don't uniformly foster great intelligence in pupils, sports fail to instill the lessons of the field in every athlete (See Jovan Belcher or Rae Carruth). But in habituating young people to endure pain, and withstand the temptations of pleasure, sports do a better job than other social constructions in developing men with chests. Boys need sports to become men.

As far as passage rites go, football operates within a comparatively tame dimension. It certainly poses fewer hazards than the Maasai lion hunt or the Mardudjara circumcision/dinner ceremony. To take one recent example, twenty-three South African boys seeking initiation into manhood died at government-registered sites over a nine-day period during May 2013. The boys, caked in chalky lime, endured the elements, herbal elixirs, and circumcision, which caused most of the deaths.[35] Rites of passage appear everywhere but do not everywhere appear equal. Anthropologist Joseph Campbell observed, "Boys everywhere have a need for rituals marking their passage to manhood. If society does not provide them they will inevitably invent their own."[36] That our native coming-of-age ritual strikes so many natives as barbaric, beyond the pale, and foreign attests to the alienation of so many toward not only their culture, but to their biology as well. If they talked about soccer the way they do about football, their friends would condemn them as culturally insensitive. But our game is fair game.

We can abolish football. We can't abolish the laws of nature. Males produce twenty times the amount of testosterone as females. The post-pubescent infusion of hormones makes those teenage years especially volatile for young males. Their angst and aggression may be channeled in any number of ways, both maladaptive and adaptive.

"Among the activities through which men seek release from everyday life, games offer in many ways the purest form of escape," Christopher Lasch observed. "Like sex, drugs, and drink, they obliterate awareness of everyday reality, not by dimming that awareness but by raising it to a new intensity of concentration. Moreover, games have no side-effects, produce no hangovers or emotional complications. Games satisfy the need for free fantasy and the search for gratuitous difficulty simultaneously; they combine childlike exuberance with deliberately created complications."[37] When one appraises the various escapes from the mundane in modern life, football appears more constructive than narcotics, sexual conquest, fistfights, computer gaming, and other male-dominated pastimes.

It's no accident that so many team sports originated in the nineteenth century. Urbanized living in the wake of the industrial age relieved males of the responsibility to hunt dinner. To fill the void of the exhilaration of the hunt, men created games that replicated the strenuous act of chasing game. Modern physical recreation acts mostly as a re-creation of ancient living. Hunting and athletics share the name "sport" for good reason. In the immediate aftermath of his presidency, Theodore Roosevelt, a sportsman of both sorts, pursued his passion to Africa where he and son Kermit killed 512 animals while on safari.[38] "While the white men hunt elephants for recreation," Harvey Mansfield points out, "the natives hunt for food and do not kill for fun. Manliness is their way of life, not a relief from it."[39] Sports provide males a respite from a world that devalues strength, stamina, endurance, and other advantages manly men possess over techies and other beneficiaries of modernity. Just as the industrial age forced men to invent sports, the post-industrial digital age forces men to rethink their existence.

The same phenomena that help explain the hostility to football also demonstrate why we need the sport now more than ever. The anachronistic nature of football that makes it so off-putting to our overprotected culture also makes the game, and its players, incredibly popular. In an era when males struggle to be men, fall Sundays offer a reminder that being a man has something to do with masculinity. Hearing an exaggerated version of Ray Lewis metaphorically shout, "We must protect this house," gives the listener the idea that, yes, Ray Lewis could indeed perform this most basic duty of an adult male. But one rarely gets that impression from pasty passersby, necks cranked downward from looking at screens all day. Men have changed so much that it's helpful to have a few reminders of what they are (were?). We don't admire the ordinary. Football has never appeared as extraordinary as it does right now. That it clashes rather than meshes with the culture makes it popular. It also makes it a target. Has it ever not been?

"Who the devil is making you all this trouble?" Frederic Remington asked his old teammate Walter Camp during the sport's 1894 crisis. "Football, in my opinion, is best at its worst—to be Irish. I do not believe in all this namby-pamby talk, and hope the game will not be emasculated and robbed of its heroic qualities, which is its charm and its distinctive quality. People who don't like football as now played might like whist—advise them to try that."[40]

Camp's most famous teammate remains one of America's most beloved artists. The boisterous and burly man's brief career as a blocker surprises no one. It's his artistic endeavors—you know, the stuff he's known for—that seem out of place. One of the few males at Yale's art school, Remington continued to defy stereotypes of the "starving" or "effete" artist. Anything but was the overfed, hard-drinking raconteur. In Plato's tripartite theory of the soul articulated in C. S. Lewis's *Abolition of Man*, Remington didn't fit one archetype but combined all three: he boasted a big brain, a big belly, and a big chest.

The man's man became that way by being a boy's boy first. His biographers note, "Remington was a hyperactive, physically oriented boy, the leader through his imagination and inventiveness as well as his strength. He was given to outrageous behavior at times."[41] The big little boy's antics included painting a neighbor's cat green, habitually pinching schoolgirls' bottoms, and breaking friends' bones in impromptu wrestling matches.[42] Military school couldn't tame his spirit. Football channeled it.

Remington played alongside Camp on Yale's 1879 team, the last of its fifteen-man squads. He exhibited an artistic flair even on the field. Before Yale's contest with Princeton, the blocker brought his uniform to a slaughterhouse "to make it more businesslike" by dipping it in blood.[43] Fittingly, his artistic and athletic passions combined in his first published work, a self-portrait, which appeared in a Yale student newspaper, of a lineman nursing gridiron wounds in a dormitory room. A few years removed from his days as a pioneering football player, Remington left home to capture the Old West before settlers civilized it into extinction. Remington's depictions—cavalrymen by firelight, Indians watering their horses, bison stomping the plain into further flatness—appear so distinct in style, and so singular in subject, that once you've seen one piece you can readily identify any other by the artist.

By helping to create the Teddy Roosevelt legend in sketches for an 1888 book showing the Eastern aristocrat as a Western cowboy, Remington also made his own legend. The Yale-man-turned-rancher initially found the Harvard-man-turned-rancher perhaps too much like himself for his liking.[44] But the double act grew as close in affection as they already had in appearance, outlook, and biography. In the last year of Roosevelt's administration and Remington's life, the president confided in the painter that he remained "one of the men whose friendship I value."[45] Roosevelt regarded Remington as a national treasure for having "portrayed a most characteristic and yet vanishing type of American life."[46]

His zeal for preserving the wild and the untamed extended from the American West to American football. Like the disappearing landscape that captivated his hand, the game that captivated his body seemed like a vestige of a bygone era especially vulnerable to the march of modern progress. More than a century after Frederic Remington's 1909 death, football enthusiasts issue the same plea the former lineman made to his quarterback-turned-rules-guru: "You're not going to civilize the only real thing we have left, are you?"[47]

CHAPTER NINE

FOOTBALL BRINGS US TOGETHER

"**I** was smitten," glows Keith Gilbert about meeting his wife. "My first impression of Stacy was that this is the coolest, most beautiful woman I have ever seen."[1] The feeling wasn't mutual. "Keith and I met at the Harvard-Yale game twenty-seven years ago," Stacy told me at the 129th rivalry meeting in 2012. Traveling to New Haven with girlfriends from New York, Stacy stumbled upon a flask-drinking man in a varsity sweater and coonskin coat. It wasn't very Don Johnson, very Emilio Estevez, very 1985. "At halftime, we were walking around. He was in his full regalia, and I said, 'What an asshole!'"[2]

Twenty-seven years later, when I stumble upon the married couple in a tent designated as the meeting place for Keith's Yale's class of '84, the two appear very much in love. "It's nostalgic," Keith says of coming back to The Game. "It's like, 'Oh my gosh! Here I was twenty-seven years ago! And there's my nearly twenty-year-old daughter.' It's just fun. It makes me remember—good memories."[3] Stacy revels in the tradition, the schools' and her own. "This is a big deal for us."[4]

Football made a family.

It's not just Stacy and Keith. And it's certainly not just Harvard-Yale. Tailgate at Lehigh-Lafayette, Alabama-Auburn, Michigan-Ohio State, USC-UCLA, Grambling-Southern, Army-Navy, or Cal-Stanford. You won't find a story. A story will find you.

Fifty million fans will pour into college football stadiums on Saturdays this fall. They won't all find the girl of their dreams there. And if they do, there's no certainty that the head cheerleader will call them instead of security. They will find fun. They will eat, drink, and be merry, and if the home team wins—then all the more so. A mix of class reunion, beer garden, and all-you-can-eat smorgasbord, football functions more as cultural experience than sport for many fans. The action in the parking lot entices as much as the action on the field. Football unites people in a society that divides them.

Neighbors don't worship the same god, vote for the same candidates, or even speak the same language. They cheer for the same team.

Football brings us together.

Racism pushes Americans apart.

Wallace Triplett, a talented halfback from suburban Philadelphia, earned a scholarship sight unseen to the University of Miami based on his reputation on the football field. When the prized recruit informed the school that he didn't possess the skin color they so prized in their athletes, the school rescinded the offer.[5] The African-American running back opted to stay closer to home by matriculating at Penn State in 1945. But destiny called him back to confront his former suitors.

The Nittany Lions' 1946 schedule placed them in the Orange Bowl on the last game of the season to take on the Miami Hurricanes. State law prohibited interracial athletic competition on Florida fields. The Nittany Lions would have to play without their two African-American players, or not play at all.

"Well, we had a team meeting, and it surprised the heck out of me," Triplett recalled. "The coaches said, well, we ought to play, and the players said, no, we play together, we'll stay together. The captains spoke—one was from western Pennsylvania and one from New York—they were [World War II] veterans, and they said, this stuff has got to stop. I was proud of them. So the team voted. It wasn't unanimous, but after the captains spoke, guys raised their hands slowly. It was one of the high points of my life."[6] Penn State, which refused to take the field in Miami, won anyhow.

A few years later, the San Francisco Dons' stand against racism cost them bowl game profits, a national championship, and, ultimately, their program. The 1951 team boasted three future Pro Football Hall of Famers and a 9-0 record. But the Catholic school balked at sending their team to a lucrative postseason game if it meant leaving their African-American players in San Francisco. So they never got invited while a team they defeated did. The school jettisoned their financially struggling football program immediately after its perfect season.[7]

As athletic fields acted as a melting pot in the North, they weakened the stridency of segregation in the South. Chester Pierce, later the president of the American Board of Psychiatry and Neurology and the namesake of a mountain in Antarctica, became the first African American to play against a white school in the South when the students of the University of Virginia voted to allow the Harvard tackle on their gridiron. The most tone-deaf segregationists could hear the future when the student crowd in Charlottesville awarded Pierce a standing ovation. The Orange, Sugar, and Cotton Bowls all permitted integrated teams in their contests by the mid-1950s.[8]

Racial snobbery isn't very football. African-American players were present at the creation of the NFL. It's appropriate that America's first football star was a First American. The legendary Jim Thorpe, so fast that he once returned his own punt for a touchdown, served as the NFL's first commissioner.[9] Fritz Pollard, the first African American "All American," who as a player led the Akron Pros to the NFL championship in the league's inaugural 1920 season, became the league's first black head coach the following year. Long before that, in 1904, the precursor to the University of Massachusetts named Matthew Washington Bullock its football coach, the first African American to lead a predominantly white school. In contrast, the National Basketball Association saw its first African American head coach in 1966 and Major League Baseball waited until 1975 for a black manager. Football's attraction transcended race, and franchises fielded lily-white teams at the risk of their records.

The NFL stepped off on the right foot. It unquestionably stumbled. "When he formed the Redskins in the '30s, [George Preston] Marshall, an avowed racist who never changed his views, drew the color line and, in league councils, forced his fellow owners, especially [Chicago's George] Halas and Pittsburgh's Art Rooney, to not hire black players," Jeff Davis writes in his biography of longtime NFL commissioner Pete Rozelle. Leaving aside the dubious proposition that a neophyte owner "forced" other powerful men to comply with his demands for racial exclusionism, Marshall definitely spearheaded the de facto ban on African Americans that governed the Depression-era NFL. In 1962, Marshall quipped to an inquiring reporter: "We'll start signing Negroes when the Harlem Globetrotters sign whites."[10]

Ironically, a quarter century later, a quarterback out of Grambling, Al Williams's Arizona Outlaws teammate Doug Williams, won a Super Bowl with the Redskins by establishing his bona fides as a quarterback instead of a "black quarterback." A quarter century after that, a charismatic African American quarterback revitalized the franchise and captivated a city. When Robert Griffin III explained that he would rather be judged by his character than his color, a race-obsessed reporter questioned his blackness. "Is he a brother, or is he a cornball brother?" asked the talking head. "I keep hearing these things.... We all know he has a white fiancée. There was all this talk about he's a Republican."[11]

What a long, strange trip it's been from Bobby Mitchell, a Redskins halfback and receiver in the 1960s, compelled by a prejudiced owner to stand at attention to "Dixie" shortly after integrating the Redskins, to Robert Griffin III, forced to endure questions of his racial authenticity by a prejudiced scribe.[12]

Decades before Americans integrated Topeka schools, a Woolworth's lunch counter in Greensboro, or the seats at the front of Montgomery buses, they integrated the country's playing fields. Blacks and whites played together in the NFL, in the Ivy League, and on the sandlot.

The game forced people from different backgrounds to cooperate and compete. It humbled notions of superiority and crumbled walls of separatism. On the field, and in the grandstand, one glimpses America.

Football brings us together.

Hurricane Katrina tore New Orleans apart.

The 2005 storm killed more than 1,800 people and destroyed $100 million worth of property along the Gulf Coast. Levees burst. Streets became rivers, awash in sewage, debris, and bodies. Cars lay on their roofs and under homes lifted off their foundations. Survivors clung to rooftops and took shelter under overpasses. Villains fired on relief helicopters and looted unprotected homes and businesses. Satellites conveyed images of lawlessness and helplessness to the world. New Orleans, synonymous with French Quarter fun and Mardi Gras decadence, now evoked *Mad Max* meets *Lord of the Flies* inside of *Escape from New York*. A year later, half the city's inhabitants hadn't returned.[13]

Like the city they represented, the Saints appeared down-and-out. Prior to their 2009 Super Bowl run, they had won two playoff games in their forty-two previous seasons. No NFL franchise symbolized losing quite like the Aints, cheered by faces hidden underneath brown paper bags. The notion that a barely six-foot quarterback recovering from a torn labrum and rotator cuff damage would rescue the franchise seemed as unlikely as the city staging a comeback. After Drew Brees glimpsed the torn-up city on a free-agency visit, he made a decision: "I felt it was my calling that God was leading me here for a reason to help make a difference."[14]

Winning their first thirteen games of the 2009 season, the franchise's rebound inspired a similar one among its long-suffering fans. A winning spirit captured a city on a losing streak. The Superdome, which had sheltered those battered by the storm, now served as the focal point for the city's redemption. "Having them play in the Dome really just symbolizes how you can recover," Dr. Kevin Stevens, the city's health director, observed. "Just because you're down, you don't have to stay down; it doesn't mean that you can't rebuild."[15] Winning two playoff games in the same Superdome that some feared would be totaled by Katrina, New Orleans entered the Super Bowl as underdogs to Peyton Manning's Indianapolis Colts. Coach Sean Payton ordered a dramatic onside kick to start the second half. New Orleans recovered. The city and the team never looked back.

New Orleans isn't the only city to rise from the gridiron. When the San Francisco 49ers won their first Super Bowl after the 1981 season, the Bay Area had experienced more than a decade of Altamont, Zodiac and Zebra Killings, Black Panther ambushes, Jonestown, the shocking murders of City Supervisor Harvey Milk and Mayor George Moscone, the attempted assassination of President Gerald Ford, AIDS, and the taking of Patty Hearst and the leaving of sanity. San Francisco needed a pick-me-up, and it came in the form of The Catch, a throwaway toss by Joe Montana that receiver Dwight Clark somehow snatched from its intended trajectory in the last minute of an NFC Championship game against the Dallas Cowboys. "Cities, like people, have souls," David Talbot said of The Catch. "And they can be broken by terrible events, but they can also be healed. It was just a game. It was just one catch. But sometimes that's enough."[16]

Football, possessing the power to make, also wields the power to break. Ripping the Colts from Baltimore in 1984, or the Browns from Cleveland in 1996, were moves as heartless as ripping the heart out of those cities.

The Barry Levinson documentary *The Band That Wouldn't Die* captures the collective heartbreak. The Baltimore Colts Marching Band persevering when two different incarnations of their football team didn't, and "Loudy" Loudenslager, a fan who had missed one game since 1947, plaintively showing up at Baltimore's Memorial Stadium on the opening day of the 1984 season, both evince what the sport means to a community's spirit. Band president John Ziemann explained, "When the team left, it was hard. The sun came up the next day. Nobody died. Commerce in Baltimore was moving. But a big part of our heart was taken. A big part was trucked out to Indianapolis."[17]

Hall of Famer Lou Groza commented that Art Modell taking the Browns from Cleveland was "like some man walking off with your wife."[18] Cleveland Brown, whose son, father, and grandfather shared the name, defiantly countered that his Cleveland Browns would remain in Ohio no matter what Art Modell did with his Cleveland Browns.[19]

Prefacing "Steelers," "Packers," or "Cowboys" with geographic affiliations seems redundant. It would be easier for the steel industry to leave Pittsburgh, as events have shown, than for the Steelers to leave Pittsburgh. "When Buffalo went to the Super Bowl back in the '90s, the city was alive," former Pro Bowl nose guard Fred Smerlas recalls. "If the Buffalo Bills left Buffalo, no one would know Buffalo is there." Smerlas cringes at the notion of football leaving struggling Buffalo as it left Baltimore, Cleveland, Los Angeles, and points beyond. "Football started in the core of towns like Buffalo, Cleveland, Pittsburgh," he explains. "Blue collar guys played football to get out of the steel mills and to get out of the factories. That's how the outlet was. A lot of those people still remain and their mindset is, 'Football is beautiful. It's the best.'"[20]

The home of the Saints, once also rumored as a prime locale for relocation, concurs. "I know it sounds cheesy, but they have shown us the power of teamwork," a New Orleans newcomer observed. "It's not about electing the right mayor or finding a recovery czar. After the storm we were looking for that one person to lead us out of this and we haven't found that one person. That's why when the Saints have that team mojo going you can see how they work together. There's no savior coming here, we have to work together and not fight with each other. The Saints have inspired that in us."[21]

Football brings us together.

Politics tears us apart.

It increasingly dictates what news networks we watch, what religious services we attend, what stars we admire, and even who we date. Civility almost demands not discussing it in mixed company, lest a shouting match erupt. Thanksgiving dinner conversations with extended family get too dramatic if we don't hold our tongues as we feed our faces.

On Thanksgiving, when politics divides dining rooms, football unites living rooms. Our at-each-other's-throats political leaders come together on football, too—football and kissing babies.

If horse racing is the sport of kings, football is the sport of presidents. "If ever a sport offered inducements to the man of executive ability, to the man who can plan, foresee, and manage," Walter Camp observed in the 1890s, "it is certainly the modern American football."[22] Time has vindicated the clockmaker's observation. Long before Barack Obama made headlines in 2013 by worrying about the dangers faced by an imaginary son on a theoretical gridiron, and long after Theodore Roosevelt summoned the sport's leading figures to the White House, America's political leaders have demonstrated a strange compulsion to intrude on the playing field.[23]

Woodrow Wilson helped coach both Wesleyan and Princeton in the nineteenth century. As a Princeton professor, the future president took the affirmative in an 1894 debate considering the question, "Ought Football to be Encouraged?" Wilson declared, "I believe it develops more moral qualities than any other game of athletics." The bespectacled, lemon-lipped academic held that football, like other sports, fosters "precision," "decision," "presence of mind," and "endurance." But it does more. "This game produces two other qualities not common to all athletics, that of co-operation, or action with others, and self-subordination."[24] After Theodore Roosevelt, as president of the United States, pushed football reform in 1905, Woodrow Wilson, president of Princeton University, did likewise in 1909. Wilson responded to his inclusion in a Yale-Harvard football reform effort by finding the proposed plan "too restrictive in scope."[25] When Princeton's president suggested the universities make the game more "attractive" in addition to curbing injuries, Yale President Arthur Hadley wrote to Wilson that his more ambitious proposal was "outside the sphere of action" for Yale and wrote to Walter Camp that he might be better off excluding Princeton's busybody president from their scheme.[26] A failed meddler in a boys' game, Wilson eventually turned his attention from the Ivy League to the League of Nations.

Herbert Hoover, team manager for Stanford, collected $30,000 in gate receipts at the inaugural Stanford-Cal "Big Game" delayed for lack of a ball. The haul necessitated hiring two carriages and half a dozen players-turned-guards to transport the silver dollars.[27] Harvard's freshman team cut Franklin Roosevelt, relegating the future president to captain the worst of the intramural squads.[28] Harvard man John Kennedy had better luck, making junior varsity. Though he didn't distinguish himself on the gridiron at Soldiers Field Road as his younger brother Teddy would do, John Kennedy became the most famous touch football player in history. His impact on the professional game could have been more profound. The commander in chief nearly reoriented future football history when he lobbied friend Vince Lombardi to drop the Packers for West Point.[29] Has a Navy man ever suggested anything so treasonous yet patriotic?

Dwight Eisenhower went to West Point with dreams of beating Navy, not Nazis. "Football was the number one priority in his life, and he was going to do everything in his power to be on the varsity squad for the first game of the season against the Stevens Institute of Technology on October 5." So the scrawny Kansan hit the gym hard before he hit other players hard as an undersized linebacker who played bigger than his body. Ike effectively ended his football career at Army by playing Ahab to Jim Thorpe's Moby Dick. Stalking Thorpe to knock the Carlisle Indian School star out of the game, Eisenhower instead knocked his knee out of place.[30]

Ronald Reagan, who played football for Eureka College and provided radio play-by-play for University of Iowa games, made a more permanent impression on the culture of the sport by playing that idealized version of George Gipp in 1940's *Knute Rockne: All American* remembered in chapter six. George W. Bush showed himself an enthusiast for the game not only by serving as a Yale cheerleader but by landing in jail on a 1967 disorderly conduct charge after tearing down a goalpost in Princeton, New Jersey, after a decisive Bulldogs' win.[31] Folklore holds that Richard Nixon, who struggled for a roster spot at Whittier College "but was too light and uncoordinated" to play much, later suggested a doomed reverse to former Whittier Coach George Allen when he led the Redskins during an ill-fated playoff game against the 49ers.[32] The greatest player among the presidents, though not the greatest president among the players, was Gerald Ford. The center and linebacker on two University of Michigan national championship teams later found himself accused of playing football without a helmet for too long by President Lyndon Johnson.[33]

The Oval Office outlier, in this as in so many ways, was Calvin Coolidge. Running back Red Grange, the NFL's first superstar, visited the thirtieth president during a road trip to the capital. The Galloping Ghost's home-state senator introduced him to the president as a member of the Chicago Bears. The tight-lipped Yankee replied, "Nice to meet you, young man. I've always liked animal acts."[34]

Calvin Coolidge aside, the American obsession is the presidential obsession. Why do leaders follow football? Football punishes shirkers and rewards hard workers. It involves strategy, risk-taking, sacrifice, and valor. Preparation matters more here than in other sports. Though many of the fourteen Marine Corps Leadership Traits have as much to do with football as a tea party does, several of the virtues desired of a Marine— dependability, unselfishness, endurance, decisiveness, courage, judgment, bearing—overlap with the virtues desired in a football leader. The ultimate team sport paradoxically cultivates individual leadership. One man can undermine a squad. One man can uplift it.

A bitter election pitted Richard Nixon against John F. Kennedy, a philosophy of government separated Ronald Reagan from Woodrow Wilson, a style of leadership differentiated Theodore Roosevelt from Gerald Ford. A boys' game unites them all.

Football brings us together.

War tears nations apart.

This applies even to nations at war a half a world away witnessing combat only through television. Pat Tillman turned down a fortune to fight for his country. The Arizona Cardinals offered the strong safety, who had set a team record for tackles in 2000, $3.6 million over three years following the 2001 season. Tillman signed instead with the army for three years at a starting annual salary of $18,000. After the September 11, 2001, attacks, Tillman heard a calling more meaningful than the coach's whistle. The Arizona Cardinal eventually became an Army Ranger. His enlistment brought him to Mesopotamia, where he fought in Operation Iraqi Freedom's initial invasion, and to Afghanistan, where friendly fire killed him.

Posthumously mocked as a "sap" by cartoonist Ted Rall, Tillman strangely emerged from death as both hero and villain. "Never mind the fine print," Rall's cartoon imagines Tillman telling a military recruiter. "Will I get to kill Arabs?"[35] A graduate student ridiculed Tillman as "a real Rambo" and an "idiot" who "got what was coming to him" in the University of Massachusetts-Amherst campus newspaper.[36] The fringe commentary spoke more forcefully about the bitter divisions within America than it did about a man whose sacrifice of a few million dollars now appears as a pittance compared to the ultimate price he paid.

It's a bizarro America in which a figure as heroic as Pat Tillman would be considered controversial. Stranger still to the past may be an America where a Pat Tillman would be considered unusual. The latter, rather than the former, assuredly describes a more widespread phenomenon. Americans, let alone the pampered subgroup of professional athletes, don't bear war's burdens equally.

Eighty years before Tillman played in the Rose Bowl, John Beckett, a tackle who occasionally impersonated a halfback, did. He led the 1917 Oregon Webfoots—the squad not yet having evolved into Ducks—to a New Year's Day victory over Penn. The following year, Beckett made history by returning to the Rose Bowl as his team's captain. But the Oregon team was no longer his team. John Beckett's new football club, the Mare Island Marines, defeated the Camp Lewis Army squad 19–7 in 1918's Rose Bowl. Beckett prophetically recalled that "this would be the last battle that we would fight in the name of sports."[37] Though Beckett returned home to stay with his new team, the United States Marine Corps, over the next half century, nearly half of the players in the 1918 Mare Island-Camp Lewis Rose Bowl died fighting wars far from Pasadena.[38]

The Great War had changed everything, and squads across America disbanded as their players joined the service. The entire varsity football rosters of Yale, Princeton, and Harvard signed up for service, with the latter school witnessing an exodus of every varsity letterman from Cambridge to the local military recruiter's office.[39] Percy Haughton, Bill Reid's replacement who allegedly motivated Harvard to beat Yale in 1908 by strangling a live bulldog dead in the locker room, resigned along with his assistants to fight humans overseas.[40]

By World War II, when the professional game began challenging the collegiate one's predominance, football players again responded to the call to serve. In the months following the Japanese attack upon Pearl Harbor, the National Football League experienced a departure of a third of its players to the armed forces.[41] The shortage forced rival franchises to unite. The Pittsburgh Steelers and Philadelphia Eagles, for instance, merged into the Steagles for 1943. The Cleveland Rams skipped the season entirely. Football's loss was America's gain.

Overseas, the athletes who had disappeared from the playing field reappeared on the battlefield. Their commanding officers, including former football players Admiral Chester Nimitz, and Generals George C. Marshall, Omar Bradley, Joseph Stilwell, and, of course, Dwight Eisenhower, directed the war in which so many famous football players played foot soldier. "Before the war ended in final victory after the dropping of the atomic bomb on two Japanese cities in August 1945," Robert Peterson writes in *Pigskin: The Early Years of Pro Football*, "a total of 638 active NFL players had gone into the armed forces. Sixty-nine had been decorated, and twenty-one had been killed in action or died while training."[42] The list of veterans of both the NFL and World War II includes Hall of Famers Otto Graham, Norm Van Brocklin, Tom Landry, and Art Donovan.

In May 1942, with the country at war, Chicago Cardinals Head Coach Jimmy Conzelman became a voice in demand to articulate the role of sports in preparing for war. "Football has been under fire because it involves body contact and it teaches violence. It was considered useless, even dangerous. But that's all over now. The bleeding hearts haven't the courtesy to apologize to us, but they're coming around and asking our help in the national emergency. Why?" Conzelman, who had played alongside George Halas on the Great Lakes Navy team that defeated the defending Rose Bowl champion Mare Island Marines in the 1919 New Year's Day game, understood both football and the military. "Football is the number one medium for attuning a man to body contact and violent physical shock," he pointed out to a radio audience. "It teaches that after all there isn't anything so terrifying about a punch in the puss."[43]

The post–Civil War substitute for combat had come full circle as a civilian training ground for battle. Football, a game of discipline, sacrifice, aggression, teamwork, strategy, and physical courage, prepared boys for the tasks of manhood. No less a military mind, and football fan, as Douglas MacArthur said as much: "Upon the fields of friendly strife are sown the seeds that upon other fields, on other days, will bear the fruits of victory."[44]

Careers delayed and careers interrupted, careers ended and careers never begun, the NFL was once a league of Pat Tillmans.

Football brings us together.

Tearing down the goalposts would tear America apart.

Football is what our leaders follow. It's the training ground for the military's training grounds. It's the melting pot within the melting pot. It provided a meritocracy when America didn't. It's the national religion. Almost two-thirds of Americans watch the Sunday sport; just two-fifths attend Sunday services.[45] It's what communities rally around.

The Super Bowl vies with soccer's Champions League finals for the largest global viewing audience. This speaks volumes about the game's relationship to its homeland and the world beyond. Whereas the Champions League ultimate match attracts a sizable audience everywhere but North America, the Super Bowl's audience watches from almost nowhere else.[46] Put another way, in spite of the rest of the world's indifference, football generates a huge "global" audience because of the intense attachment within the United States. Unlike Superman, Hollywood, or Coca Cola, football is not for export. It plays in Peoria but not in Paris, Prague, or Perth. Made in America, the sport stays in America. Football provides a cultural marker that separates the United States from the rest of the world.

The game so winds through our national DNA that even critics of America interchange their criticisms of the country with its sport: "The symbols, rituals, and meanings inherent in the game resulted in a clear definition of the United States as an aggressive, commercial, patriarchal culture ready to promote its ideas on the world stage."[47] Did America define football or did football define America?

Roaming the streets of a foreign country carrying a pigskin announces one's Americanism as surely as donning a ten-gallon hat, bolo tie, and snakeskin boots does. Football, like capitalism or the First Amendment, helps compose the American identity. It's who we are. Abolish football, or marginalize it like boxing, and America becomes less American.

Football brings us together.

CHAPTER TEN

IT'S OKAY TO WATCH

Football is better played than watched and better watched than described. Whereas literary treatments capture the magic of boxing, baseball, and even golf, football loses something in translation. The action, the violence, and the strategy don't lend themselves to printed pages the way they do to television screens. Even an aging Red Grange surprised a journalist by his partiality to baseball books.[1]

Rare on the thin shelf of football literature, Frederick Exley's novelized memoir *A Fan's Notes* has earned its real estate. Exley, as the title instructs, is a fan. His football obsession, like John Giacoppe's, stems from his father, who dies "at forty, which never obviates the stuff of myths."[2] Exley can't measure up to his star-athlete dad's legend. Impotent in the duties of manhood, Exley lives vicariously through Frank Gifford, whom he encounters at school as the University of Southern California's big man on campus and then back home as a celebrity running back for the New York Giants. "No doubt he came to represent to me the realization of life's large promises," the zero explains of number sixteen.[3] Exley lives for Sunday. The other six days he preoccupies himself with slow suicide. In life, as in Yankee Stadium, Frederick Exley behaves as the spectator.

Our protagonist drinks early and often. He can't stay in a job or stay out of a mental institution. He sponges off friends, family, and remote acquaintances. He ditches his kids and wife for booze. When a friend tells Exley that he didn't know he was married, Exley explains that his problem was that he didn't know it, either.[4] He tells terrible lies and thinks terrible thoughts. When he's not passive-aggressive he's aggressive-aggressive, dishing out insults so imaginative that they stupefy before they hurt ("Tell that witch you're married to that she ought to douche out her rancid soul."[5]). One runs from a character like Frederick Exley in life. One can't help but chase after him in print. *A Fan's Notes* is a beautiful book about an ugly subject.

Football, in which powerful men sacrifice to achieve common goals through planned action, becomes the passion of this passionless, irresolute, anti-social loser:

> Why did football bring me so to life? I can't say precisely. Part of it was my feeling that football was an island of directness in a world of circumspection. In football a man was asked to do a difficult and brutal job, and he either did it or got out. There was nothing rhetorical or vague about it; I chose to believe that it was not unlike the jobs which all men, in some sunnier past, had been called upon to do. It smacked of something old, something traditional, something unclouded by legerdemain and subterfuge. It had that kind of power over me, drawing me back with the force of something known, scarcely remembered, elusive as integrity—perhaps it was no more than the force of a forgotten childhood. Whatever it was, I gave myself up to the Giants utterly. The recompense I gained was the feeling of being alive.[6]

The bystander in the bleachers serves as a conspicuous metaphor for the indolent, undirected existence lived by him. The reader wishes to jump in the text and drag Exley out of the seats and onto the field. Damn it, play, man! Alas, forcing watchers to participate doesn't make them doers. It only confirms their passivity.

Many were the sins of Frederick Exley. It's a strange moral universe in which not incontinence, familial abandonment, or ingratitude but loving football ranks as a man's cardinal sin. For people who have convinced themselves that football kills players hit by hit by hit, fans rank as loathsome as the masses in ancient Rome who watched gladiators die. From this perspective, Exley's moral failings aren't a contrast to the glory of the gridiron; his enjoyment of football as a spectator is part and parcel, indeed, the worst part, of his general moral failing. Given that nearly two-thirds of Americans share in his not-so-guilty pleasure, Exley, for once, finds his Sunday sin normal, pedestrian, milquetoast even.[7]

Football, as we have been reminded elsewhere, isn't for everyone. But it is for a lot of people. Can two-thirds of America really be in such grievous moral error? The very popularity of football affirms for preachy critics their status as members of the enlightened few leading the benighted many toward the glow of truth. They know better, and are better, than the rest of us. They offer to rub their virtue on the vulgar, but the ingrates rebuff their generosity. The unctuous often confuse their condescension for charity and their aesthetic preferences for ethical insights.

The crusader crusades above all else for the acknowledgment that his personal taste reflects a profound moral choice rather than his personal taste. Like all do-gooders, he wants to bring about, even more than the good he ostensibly works for, the perception that he does good. So he necessarily makes a spectacle of foreswearing the role of spectator. He must be seen not seeing football.

"This fall, for the first time I can remember, I won't be watching football," Patrick Hruby writes. "Slowly, over time, I've found myself worrying more and enjoying football less; recently, I've come to feel that seeing people ruin themselves for entertainment's sake—so my Saturdays and Sundays are a little more fun—isn't just sordid. It's ghoulish."[8]

"Why are we letting children play this game?" asks Kevin Lincoln in an article entitled "Is Watching Football Unethical?" Making a case for the complicity of fans, Lincoln maintains: "Football might be among the greatest ethical quandaries of the 21st century. Here we are, worshipping a sport that destroys brains because of a fundamental flaw in the nature of the game."[9]

Charles Pierce writes that he can no longer tune in to football without his conscience lecturing him. "We ought not to allow people to be destroyed—either all at once, or one concussion at a time—for our amusement," lectures Pierce. "Doing so makes us amoral. Hell, it makes us vampires."[10]

There would be nothing unusual if these sentiments aired during a National Public Radio discussion or appeared in a *New Yorker* piece. But they emanated from sports writers in sports sections and on sports sites. When football's natural amen corner becomes its heckling peanut gallery, it's later than you think.

It probably felt that way for Frank Gifford in the fall of 1960. Averaging just three yards a carry, the halfback suffered through his first season since 1954 without earning an All-Pro nod. His number-one fan drank his way through the fall with "a terrible sense of foreboding."[11] The football hero, like his barstool worshipper, had lost a step, and in the unforgiving, Darwinian world of professional football, brutal punishment awaits those guilty of on-the-job aging. Frederick Exley's nervous dread came to fruition in Yankee Stadium in late November. In the fourth quarter,

> I watched Bednarik all the way, thinking that at any second Gifford would turn back and see him, whispering, 'Watch it, Frank. Watch it, Frank.' Then, quite suddenly, I knew it was going to happen; and accepting, with the fatalistic horror of a man anchored by fear to a curb and watching a tractor trailer bear down on a blind man, I stood breathlessly and waited. Gifford never saw him, and Bednarik did his job well.

Dropping his shoulder ever so slightly, so that it would meet Gifford in the region of the neck and chest, he ran into him without breaking his furious stride, *thwaaahhhp*, taking Gifford's legs out from under him, sending the ball careening wildly into the air, and bringing him to the soft green turf with a sickening thud. In a way it was beautiful to behold. For what seemed an eternity both Gifford and the ball had seemed to float, weightless, above the field, as if they were performing for the crowd on the trampoline. About five minutes later, after unsuccessfully trying to revive him, they lifted him onto a stretcher, looking, from where we sat high up in the mezzanine, like a small, broken, blue-and-silver mannikin, and carried him out of the stadium.[12]

The hit foreshadowed a decade of brutal beatings for pigskin players. Concussions came back into focus because of the wallop that knocked Frank Gifford out of competition for nearly two years. The sporting goods industry noticed, too. The leading helmet manufacturer, for instance, marketed special "concussion kits"—pads buffering the head in the suspension helmet's webbing from its hard plastic shell—in these years.[13] The Wisconsin Interscholastic Athletic Association, a coaches group reported in 1961, restricted athletes who had sustained concussions from participation in contact sports.[14] In the wake of the surge in catastrophic injuries that peaked with thirty-six contact deaths in 1968, Penn State President Eric Walker told his head coach, "Joe, if you don't do something about the injuries, soccer will be our national sport in ten years."[15] A decade later, a doctor proclaimed: "We've got a crisis of broken bodies. If we don't do something about it, we're going to wake up in five or ten years and there won't be any football."[16] Lawsuits then, as they do now, threatened the game. *Sports Illustrated*'s John Underwood asked in 1979, "If the cost of indemnifying a high school sport against the threat of litigation eliminates that sport, what happens to college sport? And, down the line, to pro sport?"[17] The same question might be asked today, only in reverse.

Like the athletes who play it, football exhibits an incredible resilience. The cover of John Underwood's 1979 book wasn't the first place where football's critics placed a flag over the pigskin and pronounced *The Death of an American Game.*

During the 1890s, Alabama, Georgetown, and Columbia banned football, Harvard and Yale briefly ceased their rivalry due to unnecessary roughness, and both houses of the Georgia legislature passed a bill outlawing the sport after a University of Georgia fullback suffered a fatal head injury.[18] Only the intercession of the fullback's mother stopped the governor from signing the legislation.[19]

In 1909, four seasons after Bill Reid's reforms, New York City and Washington, D.C., prohibited the game from their public schools.[20] That same year, Confederate cavalryman John Singleton Mosby dubbed Archer Christian's death "murder" and football a "barbarous amusement." He counseled the University of Virginia's president that he "might as well have a bull ring or a circus attached to the University: a man ought not to go to college to learn to be a circus rider or prize fighter."[21] In 1939, University of Chicago president Robert Maynard Hutchins echoed Mosby's criticisms and abolished a football program that had won two national championships with Amos Alonzo Stagg at its helm. Hutchins didn't inspire any college presidents to follow his lead. His forfeiture of the field did entice George Halas to appropriate the University of Chicago's stretched "C" insignia and its Monsters of the Midway moniker for the Windy City's NFL team.[22]

The War on Football is perpetual. It didn't start in 2013 or 1979 or 1905 or 1894. It won't end the day after tomorrow. Football's opposition fights ultimately for unconditional surrender. Piecemeal reforms don't satiate. They encourage calls for more. The latest NFL rules alteration, a fifteen-yard penalty for running backs lowering their heads in anticipation of contact in the open field, leaves those ostensibly protected feeling decidedly unprotected. Matt Forte, Arian Foster, Chris Johnson, and Ray Rice, among other NFL backs, have expressed displeasure.[23] "If I'm a running back and I'm running into a linebacker," all-time rushing leader Emmitt Smith asked, "you're telling me I have to keep my head up so he can take my chin off? You've absolutely lost your mind."[24] It wouldn't be the first time a rule designed to protect players endangered them—or failed to keep critics at bay. As the deaths attributable to contact dropped from more than twenty-five a year in the late 1960s to fewer than four a year during the last decade, the decibel level of the football-hating chorus rose.[25] It is irrational to believe that a rational correlation exists between the dangers *of* football and the dangers *to* football. A safer sport doesn't make the sport safe from its enemies.

The self-appointed safety inspectors don't stop at football. Concussion crusaders seek to eliminate heading in soccer, head-first baseball slides, ice hockey checks, and helmetless skiers.[26] Stopping football won't stop them. They'll soon spoil another game's fun, and then another's. We'll still have marbles. Will we still have men?

Football will change as it has always changed, though never enough to appease its critics. "Being bound by no traditions, and having seen no play, the American took the English rules as a starting point," Walter Camp recalled, "and almost immediately proceeded to add and subtract, according to what seemed his pressing needs."[27] Change remains an inherent component of *this* game. So does violence. Critics should reconcile themselves with the latter reality; purists, with the former.

Theodore Roosevelt tackled both radical idealists and cynical critics during his political career. In one of his most famous addresses, the president castigated the man with the muck rake whose eyes, fixated on the dirt, stubbornly refuse to glance away toward the heavens.[28] A few years later, as an active ex-president, Roosevelt, in Paris after his African safari, lamented second-guessers to praise "the man in the arena" who puts forth the effort whether in victory or defeat.[29] TR appreciated, and embodied, the doer.

So when, as a Harvard freshman, he watched his Yale counterpart Walter Camp play in 1876, Roosevelt left history a curious image of himself clapping while other men acted.[30] TR as spectator just doesn't mesh with the rugged mystique. Sidelined often, the resilient TR would from that day forward voluntarily stand on the sidelines almost never.

Every Superman grows out of a prepubescent weakling. Feeling small offers the greatest inducement to getting strong. A nearsighted, asthmatic child, Roosevelt willed himself to vigorous health. If any man had reason to pull an Exley, Theodore Roosevelt did. On Valentine's Day 1884, his wife died in the same house where his mother had passed away just hours earlier. Instead of folding, Roosevelt upped the ante. He boxed tougher fighters, chased cattle in the Badlands, charged Kettle Hill with his Rough Riders, hunted big game in Africa, delivered a ninety-minute speech with a wannabe assassin's bullet in his chest, and contracted malaria exploring South America's River of Doubt. His exuberant example imparted the lesson to his children that a life so preoccupied with existence that it neglected living wasn't one worth leading. Theodore Roosevelt and Frederick Exley, two diehard football fans, proved opposites in every other way.

"At thirteen," A Fan's Notes complains, "I was already having my abilities unfavorably compared with those of my father."[31] Theodore Roosevelt's eldest son could have empathized. A cross-eyed, asthmatic weakling with a speech impediment, Ted didn't resemble the robust dad in front of him. He broke down at the age of ten under the weight of expectations.[32] Eventually, he opted to live up to the ideal placed before him rather than shrink from it. Football provided a means to do this. As a sophomore at Groton School, young Ted broke his collar bone and damaged a tooth blocking and tackling bigger boys.[33] "I hereby grant you unconditional permission to play on the third Eleven," his father wrote the following season. "Now do not break your neck unless you esteem it really necessary. About arms and legs I am less particular, although on the whole I prefer that even they should be kept reasonably whole."[34]

On Ted's fields of friendly strife he indeed sewed victories on other fields. Gassed and shot during the Great War, Ted emerged with a chest full of medals and a heel without any feeling. As a fiftysomething general during World War II, the worn-down warrior took a mortar fragment to the face that left two teeth broken.[35] When General Omar Bradley informed senior field and flag officers that they would have ringside seats for the greatest fight in history, Ted exclaimed, "Ringside, hell! We'll be in the arena!"[36] Ted begged his way into the most famous battle of the twentieth century. He landed with his son on Utah Beach on June 6, 1944—the only father-son duo to do so. In the initial wave, Ted was the lone general to storm the beach—as much as a man with a cane storms anything—and the oldest Allied soldier to fight. His biographer noted that "no man who saw him that morning could forget the spectacle." The general's beleaguered body couldn't conceal a lively spirit. Nonchalantly limping tall amid flying bullets and bombs, Ted, if in the cartoonish fashion of his father, set an example of physical daring on June 6, 1944, that emboldened frightened soldiers.[37] Courage is contagious.

Like brother Quentin in World War I, Ted never made it home from Europe. Nearly four decades before Theodore Roosevelt's eldest son died peacefully in his tent the month after D-Day, headlines boldly announced a cut, not requiring stitches, suffered by Ted during freshman football practice at Harvard.[38] The massive coverage of something so minor necessarily, and perhaps by design, stoked hysteria over the violence of football, then under attack by Harvard's president, the *Nation* magazine, and other loud voices. In retrospect, the disproportionate attention inadvertently underscored the degree to which sports serve as a refuge from, and preparation for, the dangers that surround. Bloodier boo-boos await once the games end.

TR understood and imparted the paternal wisdom that football played as a great but mere game and, like so much worthy childhood leisure, must eventually yield to the grown-up ways for which it prepares. "I am delighted to have you play football," the father explained to a banged-up son wanting a parental imprimatur for play. "I believe in rough, manly sports. But I do not believe in them if they degenerate into the sole end of any one's existence. I don't want you to sacrifice standing well in your studies to any over-athleticism; and, above all, I need hardly tell you that character counts for a great deal more than either intellect or body in winning success in life. Athletic proficiency is a mighty good servant, and like so many other good servants, a mighty bad master."[39]

What's a gash above the eye to a football player? For Harvard freshman Teddy Roosevelt, it inoculated against the intimidation of future blows, habituated to physical bravery, and reminded that life offers a spectrum of sensation. If the size of one's arms provided the measure of manhood, the future Medal of Honor winner would have never stacked up. Not the weight a man can press above his chest, but what's in his chest, matters here. Theodore Roosevelt Jr., who left pieces of his person in various locales on the European continent and irrigated the Harvard practice field with drops of blood, was a man in full if ever there was one.

Monomania over what football does to the body overlooks what it does to the soul. Worse fates befall men than concussions. Physically maturing as the soul stunts surely ranks as one. Saving our boys from every scrape will produce, in C.S. Lewis' phrase, "men without chests"— slaves to the intellect or appetite devoid of courage, honor, heart, nobility, fight. We don't easily identify this modern mutation because the deformity comes in behavior and not appearance. The barrel-chested president knew the dangers of such men before Lewis articulated such a concern.[40] That's why he wanted his boys to play football. That's why he loved the game. That's why he fought to save it. His son's transformation from weakling to hero vindicates that decision.

Football is good for you. Play. Watch. Cheer.

Football brings a divided America together. It channels the natural aggression of testosterone-filled teenagers in a positive direction. It does so now more safely than ever. Improvements in rules, equipment, and instruction have reduced deaths from contact by 84 percent since the late 1960s.[41] Skiing, skateboarding, and cycling prove far deadlier than the gridiron.[42] Elite players live longer than their male counterparts. Heart disease, cancer, and suicide strike down retired NFL players at rates far below the national average.[43] The former pros are also far more likely to possess health insurance, own a home, boast a college degree, and earn a high income than the average American.[44]

If watching football afflicts one with guilt, then the conscience rather than the game may need recalibration. It's good to admire the great. Behaving atrociously, as every child, starlet, and mass murderer knows, remains the easiest route to attention. Notoriety by way of achieving excellence remains the road less traveled. Every night, dozens of television channels fixate upon the mundane affairs of mediocre people mugging for attention through misbehavior. The reality television broadcast during autumn Sabbaths showcases models of strength, endurance, toughness, and tenacity. Be cheerful that we cheer excellence.

Not everyone is. They crusade to take not just the fun out of a game but the entire game away. Who wants to confiscate the pigskin from John Giacoppe that he once tossed to his dad or the one he now uses to play catch with his hometown friends? What member of the fun police wants to tell Cam that he can't? Who is brave enough to inform Jessica Cabrera to her face that the gridiron is no place for a lady? Don't like football? Don't play. Don't watch. But don't tell other people they can't play or watch. Football is America's game, and playing and watching remains millions of Americans' idea of the pursuit of happiness. Move on to the next witch hunt.

Football works as a metaphor for not just Frederick Exley's life. Players get knocked down and they either stand up or stay on the dirt. Teams lose. Then they choose—regroup to fight another day or fold. Perseverance makes the impossible possible. Players succeed by transcending pain rather than brooding in it. Game day results come through hard work during practice and the offseason. No team can show up unprepared and expect victory. Competitors aren't social atoms but a part of something greater. Rules limit conduct; consequences await transgressors. Authorities—coaches, captains, referees—foster obedience, listening, learning, humility, and discipline. Players must endure short-term pains for long-term payoffs. The game rewards aggression, not lethargy; competitiveness, not surrender; fight, not flight. Everyone has a crucial role even if some of them go unheralded. Lessons abound.

One gleans that Frederick Exley, in the phlegmatic fashion character-istic of him, grasped but did not implement the lessons offered by his obsession. The night Chuck Bednarik knocked Frank Gifford out of consciousness and out of football, Exley picked a fistfight, only to suffer a beat down not altogether unlike his hero's. In the book's climactic moment, he explains the frustration that made him brawl in the streets: "I fought because I understood, and could not bear to understand, that it was my destiny—unlike that of my father, whose fate it was to hear the roar of the crowd—to sit in the stands with most men and acclaim others. It was my fate, my destiny, my end, to be a fan."[45]

It's okay to watch. It's better to play.

Football is good for you. Being a wuss isn't.

NOTES

Introduction

1. Quoted in John Nichols, "War Is a Lie," the *Nation*, November 23, 2010, http://www.thenation.com/blog/156585/war-lie, accessed on April 3, 2013.

2. Speech given by Malcolm Gladwell at the University of Pennsylvania, Philadelphia, Pennsylvania, February 14, 2013, available on YouTube, "Malcolm Gladwell at University of Pennsylvania 2/14/2013," http://www.youtube.com/watch?v=EWaPXzTDEDw, accessed on April 8, 2013.

3. Michael Ryan, "School Board Axes Dodgeball Games from Curriculum," WindhamPatch, March 21, 2013, http://windham. patch.com/articles/school-board-axes-dodgeball-games-from-curriculum, accessed on April 4, 2013; Alex Lippa, "Windham School Officials Drop Dodgeball," *Eagle-Tribune*, March 27, 2013, http://www.eagletribune.com/latestnews/x1121363328/Windham-school-officials-drop-dodgeball, accessed on April 4, 2013; Dan

Harris, "Tag Banned as Schools Fear Lunchtime Accidents," ABC News, October 26, 2006, http://abcnews.go.com/WNT/story?id=2606557, accessed on April 4, 2013.

4.   Franklin Foer and Chris Hughes, "Barack Obama Is Not Pleased," *New Republic*, January 27, 2013, http://www.newrepublic.com/article/112190/obama-interview-2013-sit-down-president#, accessed on February 1, 2013.

5.   Gavon Laessig, "A User's Guide to Smoking Pot with Barack Obama," BuzzFeed, May 25, 2012, http://www.buzzfeed.com/gavon/a-users-guide-to-smoking-pot-with-barack-obama, accessed on April 1, 2013.

6.   "Childhood Obesity Facts," Centers for Disease Control and Prevention, http://www.cdc.gov/healthyyouth/obesity/facts.htm, accessed on April 3, 2013.

7.   Associated Press, "Report Says 75 Percent of Young Americans Unfit for Military Service," Fox News, November 5, 2009, http://www.foxnews.com/politics/2009/11/05/new-report-says-percent-young-americans-unfit-military-service/, accessed on April 8, 2013.

8.   Quoted in James Dao, "Making Soldiers Fit to Fight, without the Situps," *New York Times*, August 30, 2010, http://www.nytimes.com/2010/08/31/us/31soldier.html, accessed on April 8, 2013.

9.   "Unmarried Childbearing," Centers for Disease Control and Prevention, http://www.cdc.gov/nchs/fastats/unmarry.htm, accessed on April 3, 2013.

10. Alan Schwarz and Sarah Cohen, "A.D.H.D. Seen in 11% of U.S. Children as Diagnoses Rise," *New York Times*, March 31, 2013, http://www.nytimes.com/2013/04/01/health/more-diagnoses-of-hyperactivity-causing-concern.html?_r=0, accessed on April 3, 2013.

Chapter 1

1.   Phone interview of Paul Butler on October 9, 2012.

2.   "School Board Meeting," City of Dover, NH, website, October 1, 2012, http://dovernh.pegcentral.com/player.php?video=d7d5e73daf11014891835a6274f5463b, accessed on November 28, 2012.

3.   Ibid.

4. Associated Press, "NH School Board Member Proposes Football Ban," *Boston Globe*, October 3, 2012, http://www.boston.com/news/local/new-hampshire/2012/10/03/school-board-member-proposes-football-ban/gaDcJthjBREm5pN0RBryYI/story.html, accessed on November 28, 2012.

5. John Doyle, "Dover Football Ban Proposal Surprises Some," *Foster's Daily Democrat*, October 3, 2012, http://www.fosters.com/apps/pbcs.dll/article?AID=/20121003/GJSPORTS_01/710039885/0, accessed on November 28, 2012.

6. Editorial, "Athlete Safety Is Job #1," *Foster's Daily Democrat*, October 6, 2012, http://www.fosters.com/apps/pbcs.dll/article?AID=/20121006/GJOPINION_01/121009693/0/SEARCH, accessed on November 28, 2012.

7. Phone interview of Paul Butler on October 9, 2012.

8. Quoted in Jeff Korbelik, "Lincoln Attorney to Appear on 'Pawn Stars' Monday," *Journal Star*, February 24, 2012, http://journalstar.com/entertainment/small-screen/television-and-radio/lincoln-attorney-to-appear-on-pawn-stars-monday/article_ca6c0174-97ff-5ff8-b03c-61b6ca3f5ce4.html, accessed on January 22, 2013.

9. Ronald A. Smith, ed., *Big Time Football at Harvard, 1905: The Diary of Coach Bill Reid* (Urbana: University of Illinois Press, 1994), 52, 60.

10. Quoted in John Sayle Watterson, *College Football: History, Spectacle, Controversy* (Baltimore: Johns Hopkins University Press, 2000), 45.

11. Ken Reed, "It's Time to Ban High School Football," *Chicago Tribune*, August 29, 2012, http://articles.chicagotribune.com/2012-08-29/news/ct-perspec-0829-football-20120829_1_brain-trauma-high-school-football-brain-injury-research-institute, accessed on October 30, 2012.

12. John Kass, "The Bone-Shattering Truth: U.S. Football Is Doomed," *Chicago Tribune*, May 4, 2012, http://articles.chicagotribune.com/2012-05-04/news/ct-met-kass-0504-20120504_1_apparent-suicide-dave-duerson-head-injury, accessed on October 30, 2012.

13. Quoted in Christopher Nowinski, *Head Games: Football's Concussion Crisis from the NFL to the Youth Leagues* (East Bridgewater, MA: Drummond, 2007), 77–78.

14. Quoted in John J. Miller, *The Big Scrum: How Teddy Roosevelt Saved Football* (New York: Harper Collins, 2011), 17.

15. Jen Floyd Engel, "Is Playing Football the New Smoking?" Fox Sports, May 4, 2012, http://msn.foxsports.com/nfl/story/Junior-Seau-Dave-Duerson-death-suggests-football-toll-on-health-may-be-worse-than-we-thought-050312, accessed on January 4, 2013.

16. George F. Will, "Football's Problem with Danger on the Field Isn't Going Away," *Washington Post*, August 3, 2012, http://articles.washingtonpost.com/2012-08-03/opinions/35491867_1_cte-brain-tissue-brain-trauma, accessed on December 5, 2012.

17. "Smoking & Tobacco Use," Centers for Disease Control and Prevention, http://www.cdc.gov/tobacco/data_statistics/fact_sheets/fast_facts/, accessed on January 30, 2013.

18. "Trends in Tobacco Use," American Lung Association, July 2011, http://www.lung.org/finding-cures/our-research/trend-reports/Tobacco-Trend-Report.pdf, accessed on February 25, 2013.

19. Bill Gorman, "No Surprise: 64% of Americans Watch NFL Football; 73% of Men, 55% of Women," TV by the Numbers, October 14, 2011, tvbythenumbers.zap2it.com/2011/10/14/no-surprise-64-americans-watch-nfl-football-73-of-men-55-of-women/107308/, accessed on February 25, 2013.

20. Glenn Blain, "'I Want to Protect the Children': Politicians Push to Ban Tackle in Youth Football Leagues," *New York Daily News*, February 9, 2013, http://www.nydailynews.com/new-york/politicians-push-ban-youth-football-leagues-article-1.1259327, accessed on March 28, 2013. Quote therein.

21. John Keilman, "State Lawmaker Wants to Limit Tackling during High School Football Practice," *Chicago Tribune*, February 11, 2013, http://articles.chicagotribune.com/2013-02-11/news/ct-met-football-concussions-20130212_1_high-school-football-practice-state-lawmaker-brain-damage, accessed on March 28, 2013.

22. "Football: State Rep. Files Bill to Limit Full-Contact Football Practices to Once per Week," *Cypress Creek Mirror*, February 2, 2013, http://www.yourhoustonnews.com/cypresscreek/news/football-state-rep-files-bill-to-limit-full-contact-football/article_36b586ce-6d68-11e2-a7d9-001a4bcf887a.html, accessed on March 28, 2013.

23. For a sense of *SNF*'s ratings dominance, see "'Sunday Night Football' on NBC Is, Once Again, Primetime Television's No. 1 Show," The Futon Critic, January 3, 2013, http://www.thefutoncritic.com/ratings/2013/01/03/sunday-night-football-on-nbc-is-once-again-primetime-televisions-no-1-show-887202/20130103nbc03/, accessed on February 25, 2013.

24. "Football Is America's Favorite Sport as Lead over Baseball Continues to Grow," Harris Interactive, January 25, 2012, http://www.harrisinteractive.com/NewsRoom/HarrisPolls/tabid/447/mid/1508/articleId/950/ctl/ReadCustom%20Default/Default.aspx, accessed on September 7, 2012.

25. Lisa DeMoraes, "As Super Bowl Ad Prices Rise, Some Decide to Release Commercials before Big Game," *Washington Post*, January 31, 2013, http://articles.washingtonpost.com/2013-01-31/entertainment/36659645_1_super-bowl-ad-ad-time-new-ad, accessed on February 25, 2013.

26. Wayne G. McDonnell Jr., "Disappointing Television Ratings Are a Legitimate Concern for Major League Baseball," *Forbes*, October 27, 2012, http://www.forbes.com/sites/waynemcdonnell/2012/10/27/disappointing-television-ratings-are-a-legitimate-concern-for-major-league-baseball/, accessed on January 5, 2013; Michael Hiestand, "Fox's NFL a Hit Sunday, Not Its World Series Rating," *USA Today*, October 29, 2012, http://www.usatoday.com/story/sports/2012/10/29/nfl-world-series-san-francisco-giants-tv-ratings-dallas-cowboys-fox-nbc-cbs/1666397/, accessed on June 3, 2013; Bill Gorman, "NFL on Fox Posts Highest Rating since 1995 & Ties 2010 as Most Watched Season Ever," TV by the Numbers, January 4, 2012, http://tvbythenumbers.zap2it.com/2012/01/04/nfl-on-fox-

posts-highest-rating-since-1995-ties-2010-as-most-watched-season-ever/115332/, accessed on June 3, 2013.

27. Zack Kelberman, "Adrian Peterson Not a Fan of New Helmet Rule," Helmet2Helmet, April 11, 2013, http://helmet2helmet. com/2013/04/11/adrian-peterson-not-a-fan-of-new-helmet-rule/, accessed on April 12, 2013.

28. Quoted in Clark Judge, "Ravens' Pollard: NFL Really Does Stand for Not for Long," CBS Sports, January 25, 2013, http://www. cbssports.com/nfl/blog/clark-judge/21613854/ravens-pollard-nfl-really-does-stand-for-not-for-long, accessed on January 29, 2013. Pollard joined the Tennessee Titans after his postseason release from the Ravens.

29. Judy Battista, "Saints Coach Is Suspended for a Year over Bounties," *New York Times*, March 21, 2012, http://www.nytimes. com/2012/03/22/sports/football/nfl-delivers-harsh-punishment-to-saints-over-bounty-program.html, accessed on March 4, 2013; Nate Davis, "Saints' Vilma Suspended One Year for Role in Bounty Program," The Huddle, *USA Today*, May 2, 2012, http://content. usatoday.com/communities/thehuddle/post/2012/05/saints-jonathan-vilma-suspended-one-year-for-role-in-bounty-program/1, accessed on March 4, 2013.

30. Mark Fainaru-Wada, Jim Avila, and Steve Fainaru, "Doctors: Junior Seau's Brain Had CTE," ESPN, January 11, 2013, http:// espn.go.com/espn/otl/story/_/id/8830344/study-junior-seau-brain-shows-chronic-brain-damage-found-other-nfl-football-players, accessed on March 4, 2013.

31. Interview of Scott Lazo in Southbridge, Massachusetts, on December 9, 2012.

32. Ken Belson, "A 5-Concussion Pee Wee Game Leads to Penalties for the Adults," *New York Times*, October 23, 2012, http://www. nytimes.com/2012/10/23/sports/football/pee-wee-football-game-with-concussions-brings-penalties-for-adults.html, accessed on March 4, 2013.

33. Interview of Scott Lazo in Southbridge, Massachusetts, on December 9, 2012.

34. "Tantasqua Pop Warner Statement," October 22, 2012, http://www.tantasquapopwarner.com/docs/pub/TPWPressStatement.pdf, accessed on December 10, 2012.

35. Brian Lee, "Pop Warner Suspends Southbridge, Tantasqua Coaches after Player Injuries," *Worcester Telegram & Gazette*, October 21, 2012, http://www.telegram.com/article/20121021/NEWS/121029983/1116, accessed on October 25, 2012.

36. Interview of Scott Lazo in Southbridge, Massachusetts, on December 9, 2012.

37. Belson, "A 5-Concussion Pee Wee Game"; Gary Mihoces, "Pop Warner Investigates, Suspends Coaches," *USA Today*, October 24, 2012, http://www.usatoday.com/story/sports/2012/10/24/pop-warner-coach-suspensions/1655795/, accessed on March 4, 2013.

38. Interview of Jared in Arlington, Massachusetts, on October 21, 2012.

39. Interview of Cam in Arlington, Massachusetts, on October 21, 2012.

40. Chris English, "CR Board Member Calls for Banning HS Football," phillyBurbs.com, June 11, 2012, http://www.phillyburbs.com/news/local/courier_times_news/cr-board-member-calls-for-banning-hs-football/article_4dbb7595-770a-589f-bf45-797606569742.html, accessed on January 4, 2013.

41. Larry Robbins, "Let's Ban Tackle Football under Age 18," RealClearSports, December 6, 2012, http://www.realclearsports.com/articles/2012/12/06/lets_ban_tackle_football_until_age_18_97818.html, accessed on January 4, 2013.

42. Robert Cantu and Mark Hyman, *Concussions and Our Kids: America's Leading Expert on How to Protect Young Athletes and Keep Sports Safe* (Boston: Houghton Mifflin Harcourt, 2012), 144–48.

43. "Are You Smarter than a Fifth Grader?" Massachusetts Observer, October 25, 2012, http://massachusettsobserver.blogspot.com/2012/10/are-you-smarter-than-fifth-grader.html, accessed on October 25, 2012.

44. For an age group breakdown of football participants, see Frederick O. Mueller and Bob Colgate, "Annual Survey of Football Injury Research, 1931–2012," American Football Coaches Association, National Collegiate Athletic Association, and National Federation of State High School Associations, February 2013, 3.

45. Interview of Brendan in Arlington, Massachusetts, on October 21, 2012.

46. Interview of Jack in Arlington, Massachusetts, on October 21, 2012.

47. Interview of Cam in Arlington, Massachusetts, on October 21, 2012.

48. Interview of Scott Lazo in Southbridge, Massachusetts, on December 9, 2012.

49. Walter Camp, "1918" (Walter Chauncey Camp Papers, Yale University, Box 32), 2.

50. Interview of Brandon Bergstrom in Arlington, Massachusetts, on October 21, 2012.

51. Ray W. Daniel, Steven Rowson, and Stefan M. Duma, "Head Impact Exposure in Youth Football," *Annals of Biomedical Engineering*, April 2012, 977–79.

52. I observed Arlington's practice on October 17, 2012.

53. Quoted in Lars Anderson, *Carlisle vs. Army: Jim Thorpe, Dwight Eisenhower, Pop Warner, and the Forgotten Story of Football's Greatest Battle* (New York: Random House, 2007), 4–5.

54. Interview of Scott Lazo in Southbridge, Massachusetts, on December 9, 2012.

55. Anderson, *Carlisle vs. Army*, 149–52, 169–70, 176–78.

56. Gerald R. Gems, *For Pride, Profit, and Patriarchy: Football and the Incorporation of American Cultural Values* (Lanham, MD: Scarecrow Press, 2000), 155.

57. Morris A. Bealle, *The History of Football at Harvard: 1874–1948* (Washington, D.C.: Columbia, 1948), 146–47; David M. Nelson, *The Anatomy of a Game: Football, the Rules, and the Men Who Made the Game* (Newark, DE: University of Delaware Press, 1994), 155; Gems, *For Pride, Profit, and Patriarchy*, 120–21.

58. Interview of Brandon Bergstrom in Arlington, Massachusetts, on October 21, 2012.

Chapter 2

1. Interview with Briannah Gallo in Tewksbury, Massachusetts, on January 15, 2013.

2. Mallika Marar et al., "Epidemiology of Concussions among United States High School Athletes in 20 Sports," *American Journal of Sports Medicine*, April 3, 2012, 749; National Federation of State High School Associations, *2011–12 High School Athletics Participation Survey* (Indianapolis: National Federation of State High School Associations, 2012), 52.

3. Leah J. Frommer et al., "Sex Differences in Concussion Symptoms of High School Athletes," *Journal of Athletic Training*, February 2011, 79.

4. Marar et al., "Epidemiology of Concussions," 749–51.

5. Kimberly G. Harmon et al., "American Medical Society for Sports Medicine Position Statement: Concussion in Sport," *British Journal of Sports Medicine*, January 1, 2013, 18; Robert Cantu and Mark Hyman, *Concussions and Our Kids: America's Leading Expert on How to Protect Young Athletes and Keep Sports Safe* (Boston: Houghton Mifflin Harcourt, 2012), 112; Andrew E. Lincoln et al., "Trends in Concussion Incidence in High School Sports," *American Journal of Sports Medicine*, May 2011, 962; for an alternative explanation for why girls suffer from a higher rate than boys, see Marar et al., "Epidemiology of Concussions," 754.

6. Interviews of Jen Pirog in Tewksbury, Massachusetts on January 15, 2013, and January 27, 2013.

7.   Interview of Danielle Resha in Tewksbury, Massachusetts, on January 15, 2013.

8.   Interview of Jessica Cabrera in Tewksbury, Massachusetts, on January 15, 2013; phone interview of Jessica Cabrera on January 31, 2013.

9.   Interview of Danielle Resha in Tewksbury, Massachusetts, on January 15, 2013.

10. Interview of Jen Pirog in Tewksbury, Massachusetts, on January 15, 2013.

11. Interview of Briannah Gallo in Tewksbury, Massachusetts, on January 15, 2013.

12. Phone interview of Jessica Cabrera on January 31, 2013.

13. Paul R. McCrory and Samuel F. Berkovic, "Concussion: The History of Clinical and Pathological Concepts and Misconceptions," *Neurology*, December 2001, 2284.

14. "Complete List of ImPACT® Users," Impact.com, http://impacttest.com/clients/page/all, accessed on January 31, 2013.

15. Mark R. Lovell et al., "Recovery from Mild Concussion in High School Athletes," *Journal of Neuropsychology*, February 2003, 301, 300, 297.

16. Micky Collins, Jamie Stump, and Mark R. Lovell, "New Developments in the Management of Sports Concussions," *Current Opinion in Orthopedics*, April 2004, 105.

17. Mark Lovell, Micky Collins, and James Bradley, "Return to Play Following Sports-Related Concussion," *Clinics in Sports Medicine*, July 2004, 439.

18. Mark R. Lovell et al., "Grade 1 or 'Ding' Concussions in High School Athletes," *American Journal of Sports Medicine*, Jan–Feb 2004, 47–54.

19. Brian Lau et al., "Neurocognitive and Symptom Predictors of Recovery in High School Athletes," *Clinical Journal of Sports Medicine*, May 2009, 216–21.

20. Steven P. Broglio et al., "Test-Retest Reliability of Computerized Concussion Assessment Programs," *Journal of Athletic Training*, Oct–Dec 2007, 509.

21. Lester B. Mayers and Thomas S. Redick, "Clinical Utility of ImPACT Assessment for Postconcussion Return-to-Play Counseling: Psychometric Issues," *Journal of Clinical and Experimental Neuropsychology*, March 2012, 240.

22. Christopher Randolph, "Baseline Neuropsychological Testing in Managing Sport-Related Concussion: Does It Modify Risk?" *Current Sports Medicine Reports*, Jan–Feb 2011, 21–26.

23. Dirk Knudsen, "Baseline Concussion Testing Questioned; but Who Is behind This," ImPACT.com, June 12, 2011, http://impacttest. com/news/detail/485, accessed on February 11, 2013.

24. Philip Schatz et al., "Sensitivity and Specificity of the ImPACT Test Battery for Concussion in Athletes," *Clinical Neuropsychology*, January 2006, 3, 7.

25. Dick's Sporting Goods advertisement, "What You Need to Play," available on YouTube, "Dick's Sporting Goods—What You Need to Play," http://www.youtube.com/watch?v=GOJKhGKvGcs, accessed on March 3, 2013.

26. Email from Frank Ferrelli to author, January 26, 2013.

27. "ImPACT® Pricing," Impact.com, http://www.impacttest.com/ purchase/price, accessed on January 29, 2013; "Overview and Features of the ImPACT® Test," Impact.com, http://impacttest.com/ about/background, accessed on January 29, 2013.

28. Cantu and Hyman, *Concussions and Our Kids*, 56.

29. "Who Needs NeuroSafe: Athletes and Head Injuries," www. neurosafe.com/whoneeds.html, accessed on January 25, 2013.

30. Visit the Force Field FF Headbands website at, http://www. forcefieldheadbands.com/, accessed on January 25, 2013; Committee on Commerce, Science, and Transportation, "Concussions and the Marketing of Sports Equipment," October 19, 2011 (Washington, D.C.: U.S. Government Printing Office, 2012), 73–74.

31. Committee on Commerce, Science, and Transportation, "Concussions and the Marketing of Sports Equipment," 19–22.

32. Phone interview of Briannah Gallo on February 27, 2013.

33. "No KO," www.noknockout.com, accessed on January 25, 2013.

34. "Concussion Prevention," Guardian Mouthguards website, http://www.guardianmouthguards.com/pages/concussion-prevention, accessed on January 25, 2013.

35. Julie Deardorff, "FTC Cracks Down on Anti-Concussion Claims," *Chicago Tribune*, September 6, 2012, http://articles.chicagotribune.com/2012-09-06/health/ct-met-mouthguard-concussions-20120906 _1_ftc-cracks-brain-pad-brain-protection, accessed on January 25, 2013; visit the Brain Pad website at, http://www.brainpads.com/, accessed on January 25, 2013.

36. Daniel H. Daneshvar et al., "Helmets and Mouth Guards: The Role of Personal Equipment in Preventing Sport-Related Concussions," *Clinics in Sports Medicine*, January 2011, 154–55, 157.

37. Committee on Commerce, Science, and Transportation, "Concussions and the Marketing of Sports Equipment," 31.

38. Cantu and Hyman, *Concussions and Our Kids*, 25.

39. *Small Potatoes: Who Killed the USFL?* (ESPN Films, 2009); "NFL Grants Nearly $1 Million to Concussion Research," CBS New York, December 21, 2010, http://newyork.cbslocal.com/2010/12/21/nfl-grants-nearly-1-million-to-concussion-research/, accessed on February 7, 2013.

40. Alan Schwarz, "New Advice by N.F.L. in Handling Concussions," *New York Times*, August 21, 2007, http://www.nytimes.com/2007/08/21/sports/football/21concussions.html, accessed on February 8, 2013.

41. Cantu and Hyman, *Concussions and Our Kids*, 25.

42. "NFL Grants Nearly $1 Million to Concussion Research."

43. "NATA Foundation Announces Endowment Effort to Support Concussion Research," National Athletic Trainers' Association, July 7, 2009, http://www.nata.org/NR081109b, accessed on March 3, 2013.

44. Associated Press, "NFL Pledges $30 Million for Medical Research," Fox News, September 5, 2012, http://www.foxnews.com/sports/2012/09/05/nfl-pledges-30-million-for-medical-research483500/, accessed on February 26, 2013.

45. Kay Lazar, "Harvard to Lead $100m Study of NFL Players," *Boston Globe*, January 29, 2013, http://www.bostonglobe.com/metro/2013/01/29/nfl-players-union-and-harvard-team-landmark-study-football-injuries-and-illness/YTbnGypzJXb1VkZSr1hbdP/story.html, accessed on February 7, 2013.

46. Steve Fainaru and Mark Fainaru-Wada, "Researchers Consulted with Law Firms," ESPN, April 6, 2013, http://espn.go.com/espn/otl/story/_/id/9135869/two-prominent-concussion-researchers-including-nfl-adviser-served-paid-consultants-law-firms-suing-nfl-behalf-players, accessed on April 29, 2013.

47. Cantu and Hyman, *Concussions and Our Kids*, 103.

48. Ibid., 111.

49. Committee on Commerce, Science, and Transportation, "Concussions and the Marketing of Sports Equipment," 30.

50. Lester B. Mayers and Thomas S. Redick, "Clinical Utility of ImPACT Assessment for Postconcussion Return-to-Play Counseling: Psychometric Issues," *Journal of Clinical and Experimental Neuropsychology*, no. 3 (2012), 240.

51. Lincoln et al., "Trends in Concussion Incidence in High School Sports," 958.

52. Schatz et al., "Sensitivity and Specificity of the ImPACT Test Battery for Concussion in Athletes," 95.

53. Harmon et al., "American Medical Society for Sports Medicine Position Statement: Concussion in Sport," 18.

54. "Concussion Watch," PBS, http://www.pbs.org/wgbh/pages/frontline/concussion-watch/, accessed on May 3, 2013.

55. Marar et al., "Epidemiology of Concussions," 749.

56. Michael W. Collins et al., "Relationship between Concussion and Neuropsychological Performance in College Football Players,"

Journal of the American Medical Association, September 8, 1999, 966.

57. Phone interview of Briannah Gallo on February 27, 2013.
58. Cantu and Hyman, *Concussions and Our Kids*, 48.
59. Elliot J. Pellman et al., "Concussion in Professional Football: Reconstruction of Game Impacts and Injuries," *Neurosurgery*, October 2003, 810.
60. Steven P. Broglio et al., "The Biomechanical Properties of Concussions in High School Football," *Medicine & Science in Sports & Exercise*, November 2010, http://www.ncbi.nlm.nih.gov/pmc/articles/PMC2943536/, accessed on April 18, 2013.
61. Marar et al.,"Epidemiology of Concussions," 747.
62. Frommer et al., "Sex Differences in Concussion Symptoms of High School Athletes," 76.
63. Ray W. Daniel, Steven Rowson, and Stefan M. Duma, "Head Impact Exposure in Youth Football," *Annals of Biomedical Engineering*, April 2012, 976.
64. Harmon et al., "American Medical Society for Sports Medicine Position Statement: Concussion in Sport," 15.
65. Kevin P. Kaut et al., "Reports of Head Injury and Symptom Knowledge among College Athletes: Implications for Assessment and Educational Intervention," *Clinical Journal of Sports Medicine*, July 2003, 213–21.
66. Chris Nowinski, "Hit Parade: The Future of the Sports Concussion Crisis," *Cerebrum*, February 1, 2013, https://www.dana.org/news/cerebrum/detail.aspx?id=40424, accessed on April 7, 2013.

Chapter 3

1. Elizabeth Merrill, "NFL Replacements Part of History," ESPN, June 9, 2011, http://sports.espn.go.com/nfl/news/story?id=6642330, accessed on February 19, 2013; Mark Craig, "The 1987 NFL Strike: Picking at an Old Scab," *StarTribune*, June 28, 2011, http://www.startribune.com/sports/vikings/124627618.html, accessed on February 19, 2013.
2. Phone interview of Al Williams on February 18, 2013.

3. Merrill, "NFL Replacements Part of History."

4. William C. Rhoden, "Gatineau and Jets Skirmish on the Line," *New York Times*, October 2, 1987, http://www.nytimes. com/1987/10/02/sports/gastineau-and-jets-skirmish-on-line.html, accessed on February 19, 2013.

5. Craig, "The 1987 NFL Strike: Picking at an Old Scab."

6. Phone interview of Al Williams on February 18, 2013.

7. Chris Jenkins, "Re-Play It Again," *U-T San Diego*, December 16, 2007, http://www.utsandiego.com/uniontrib/20071216/news_lz1s16sptshed.html, accessed on February 19, 2013.

8. Phone interview of Al Williams on February 18, 2013.

9. "Country Comparison: GDP (Purchasing Power Parity)," Central Intelligence Agency, https://www.cia.gov/library/publications/the-world-factbook/rankorder/2001rank.html, accessed on March 3, 2013.

10. United States District Court Eastern District of Pennsylvania, "In Re National Football League Players' Concussion Injury Litigation: Plaintiffs' Amended Master Administrative Long-Form Complaint," July 17, 2012, 10.

11. "Mr. Smith Goes to Washington," *Sports Illustrated*, February 12, 2000, http://sportsillustrated.cnn.com/football/nfl/news/2000/02/12/smith_redskins/, accessed on March 5, 2013.

12. *Small Potatoes: Who Killed the USFL?* (ESPN Films, 2009).

13. Nathan Fenno and Luke Rosiak, "NFL Concussion Lawsuits," *Washington Times*, June 21, 2012, http://www.washingtontimes. com/footballinjuries/, accessed on April 5, 2013.

14. Phone interview of Al Williams on February 18, 2013.

15. For information on these players, consult the database constructed by Fenno and Rosiak, "NFL Concussion Lawsuits," accessed on February 20, 2013.

16. Nathan Fenno, "Pat White Return to the NFL Would Set Troubling Precedent," *Washington Times*, April 3, 2013, http://www. washingtontimes.com/news/2013/apr/3/fenno-pat-white-return-nfl-would-set-troubling-pre/?page=all#pagebreak, accessed on April 5, 2013. Quotes therein.

17. *Jerry Maguire* (TriStar Pictures, 1996).

18. "The Snake Gets Set to Strike Again," *Sports Illustrated*, September 19, 1977, 1.

19. Phone interview of Curtis Worrell on March 5, 2013.

20. "Rush to Glory," *Sports Illustrated*, December 17, 1984, 1; "One Happy Camper," *Sports Illustrated*, August 12, 1991, 1.

21. United States District Court Eastern District of Pennsylvania, "In Re National Football League Players' Concussion Injury Litigation," 78.

22. Robert Cantu and Mark Hyman, *Concussions and Our Kids: America's Leading Expert on How to Protect Young Athletes and Keep Sports Safe* (Boston: Houghton Mifflin Harcourt, 2012), 148.

23. United States District Court Eastern District of Pennsylvania, "In Re National Football League Players' Concussion Injury Litigation," 1–2.

24. Ibid., 32–44.

25. Ibid., 12–13, 16.

26. Micky Collins et al., "Examining Concussion Rates and Return to Play in High School Football Players Wearing New Helmet Technology: A Three-Year Prospective Cohort Study," *Neurosurgery*, February 2006, 275–86.

27. United States District Court Eastern District of Pennsylvania, "In Re National Football League Players' Concussion Injury Litigation," 1.

28. Charles Chandler, "Ex-Players Say NFL Neglects Retirees," InsuranceNewsNet, January 16, 2006, http://insurancenewsnet. com/article.aspx?a=top_lh&id=56338#.UW2m4r8mQ5Q, accessed on April 16, 2013.

29. About a quarter (996) of the litigants launched their NFL careers in the 1980s. Fenno and Rosiak, "NFL Concussion Lawsuits," accessed on April 5, 2013.

30. Chris Colston, "NFL Retirees Feel Forgotten as Fight for Benefits Rages," *USA Today*, July 13, 2007, http://usatoday30.usatoday.

com/sports/football/nfl/2007-07-08-sw-retirees_N.htm, accessed February 21, 2013.

31. David Halberstam, "Deion, We Hardly Knew Ye," ESPN, May 15, 2001, http://espn.go.com/page2/s/halberstam/010515.html, accessed on February 19, 2013.

32. Akbar Gbajabiamila, "Concussion Lawsuits against the NFL Shouldn't Be for Everyone," NFL, http://m.nfl.com/news/0ap1000000137991/concussion-lawsuits-against-nfl-shouldnt-be-for-everyone/, accessed on March 3, 2013.

33. United States District Court Eastern District of Pennsylvania, "In Re National Football League Players' Concussion Injury Litigation," 6.

34. Ken Belson, "Concussion Liability Costs May Rise, and Not Just for N.F.L.," *New York Times*, December 10, 2012, http://www.nytimes.com/2012/12/11/sports/football/insurance-liability-in-nfl-concussion-suits-may-have-costly-consequences.html, accessed on February 20, 2013.

35. John Underwood, "An Unfolding Tragedy," *Sports Illustrated*, August 14, 1978, http://sportsillustrated.cnn.com/vault/article/magazine/MAG1093971/4/index.htm, accessed on April 5, 2013.

36. Christopher Nowinski, *Head Games: Football's Concussion Crisis from the NFL to the Youth Leagues* (East Bridgewater, MA: Drummond, 2007), 116.

37. Underwood, "An Unfolding Tragedy," accessed on April 5, 2013.

38. For a sense of the lack of choice in helmets, see "Virginia Tech Helmet Ratings," Virginia Tech, Wake Forest University School of Biomedical Engineering and Sciences, http://www.sbes.vt.edu/nid, accessed on April 5, 2013.

39. Phone interview of Curtis Worrell on March 5, 2013.

40. Ibid.

41. Phone interview of Paul Butler on October 9, 2012.

42. Email from Chris Bowler to author, February 20, 2013.

Chapter 4

1. Letter from J. W. H. Pollard to Walter Camp, September 18, 1908 (Walter Chauncey Camp Papers, Yale University, Box 20).

2. Quoted in John J. Miller, *The Big Scrum: How Teddy Roosevelt Saved Football* (New York: Harper Collins, 2011), 74.

3. Walter Camp, "Open Letters," *The Century*, February 1894, 633 (Walter Chauncey Camp Papers, Yale University, Box 32).

4. David M. Nelson, *The Anatomy of a Game: Football, the Rules, and the Men Who Made the Game* (Newark, DE: University of Delaware Press, 1994), 45–46, 49–51; Parke H. Davis, *Football: The American Intercollegiate Game* (New York: Charles Scribner's Sons, 1911), 24; John Sayle Watterson, *College Football: History, Spectacle, Controversy* (Baltimore: Johns Hopkins University Press, 2000), 19–21; Mark F. Bernstein, *Football: The Ivy League Origins of an American Obsession* (Philadelphia: University of Pennsylvania Press, 2001), 13, 18–21.

5. Nelson, *The Anatomy of a Game*, 42.

6. Ibid., 58.

7. Letter from A. A. Stagg to Walter Camp, October 17, 1902 (Walter Chauncey Camp Papers, Yale University, Box 23). In this missive, Stagg tells his former coach: "I have noticed that Harvard is playing a man named King at center and I am told by a University of Indiana graduate who played on the same team with him that this man King played for four years on the University of Indiana team."

8. For the text of Princeton's 1871 rules, see Davis, *Football*, 51–52, 55; Bernstein, *Football*, 6–8.

9. Draft: Walter Camp, "Physical Culture, 1903" (Walter Chauncey Camp Papers, Yale University, Box 32).

10. Bernstein, *Football*, 8.

11. Nelson, *The Anatomy of a Game*, 32.

12. J. T. Wheelwright, "A Football Game Thirty Years Ago," *Harvard Graduates' Magazine*, March 1905, 423–25; Bernstein, *Football*, 9–10; Davis, *Football*, 62–65.

13. Walter Camp, "A Historic Game of Football," *The Youth's Companion*, November 29, 1900, 625–26 (Walter Chauncey Camp Papers, Yale University, Box 32).

14. Nelson, *The Anatomy of a Game*, 62.

15. Davis, *Football*, 92. The football historian explains: "It originated in the humorous proclivities of a player at Princeton who in 1889 raised an enormous crop of hair merely as an act of horse-play. Playing a spectacular game against Harvard, his flaunting, flopping locks were taken seriously by the spectators, and thus this comedian unconsciously set a fashion that the next year swept the country and raged for four years."

16. Nelson, *The Anatomy of a Game*, 65.

17. Walter Camp, "1918" (Walter Chauncey Camp Papers, Yale University, Box 32). Rather than the creator of the Daily Dozen, Camp, according to David. M. Nelson, had cribbed the name as well as the routine from others. Nelson, *The Anatomy of a Game*, 170.

18. For a version of George Carlin's routine, see "Baseball and Football," available on the Baseball Almanac website, http://www. baseball-almanac.com/humor7.shtml, accessed February 1, 2013.

19. Robert M. Gorman and David Weeks, *Death at the Ballpark: A Comprehensive Study of Game-Related Fatalities, 1862–2007* (Jefferson, NC: McFarland, 2009), 21.

20. "Appendix One: Casualties in College Football," in Watterson, *College Football*, 401.

21. Robert E. Coughlin, "Fatalities in Athletic Games and Deaths of Athletes," *New York Medical Journal*, June 23, 1917, 1204.

22. For statistics on baseball's 1905–1906 body count, see Gorman and Weeks, *Death at the Ballpark*, 5; for statistics on football's 1905–1906 body count, see Watterson, *College Football*, 401.

23. Gorman and Weeks, *Death at the Ballpark*, 57.

24. Ibid., 31.

25. Ibid., 24.

26. Ibid., 45.

27. Letter from Theodore Roosevelt to Walter Camp, March 11, 1895 (Walter Chauncey Camp Papers, Yale University, Box 21).

28. For an excellent account of the evolution of the rules of college football, see Nelson, *The Anatomy of a Game*, 433–90.

29. Robert W. Peterson, *Pigskin: The Early Years of Pro Football* (New York: Oxford University Press, 1997), 17.

30. "Football Reform by Abolition," the *Nation*, November 30, 1905, 437–38.

31. Charles Eliot, "The Evils of Football," *Harvard Graduates' Magazine*, March 1905, 383–87 (Records of the President of Harvard University: Charles W. Eliot, Harvard University Archives, Box 220).

32. Thorstein Veblen, *The Theory of the Leisure Class: An Economic Study of Institutions* (1899; repr., New York: MacMillan, 1912), 261.

33. "Congressman Landis Sees One Game and Says Football Is 'Bum Sport,'" *Salt Lake City Herald*, October 15, 1905, 1.

34. "Football Reform by Abolition," 437; "Favor Revision of the Rules," *New York Times*, November 27, 1905, 5.

35. Letter from Theodore Roosevelt to Walter Camp, March 11, 1895 (Walter Chauncey Camp Papers, Yale University, Box 21).

36. Letter from Theodore Roosevelt to Walter Camp, October 2, 1905 (Walter Chauncey Camp Papers, Yale University, Box 21).

37. Miller, *The Big Scrum*, 1–12.

38. Letter from Theodore Roosevelt to Kermit Roosevelt, October 9, 1905 (Theodore Roosevelt Papers, Library of Congress, Reel 339).

39. Grant Teaff in "Foreword," in Frederick O. Mueller and Robert C. Cantu, *Football Fatalities and Catastrophic Injuries, 1931–2008* (Durham: Carolina Academic Press, 2011), xxi; John Underwood, *The Death of an American Game: The Crisis in Football* (Boston: Little Brown, 1979), 19, 115; Christopher Nowinski, *Head Games: Football's Concussion Crisis from the NFL to the Youth Leagues* (East Bridgewater, MA: Drummond, 2007), 101.

40. Miller, *The Big Scrum*, 186–90; Bernstein, *Football*, 79–80.

41. Statement from Walter Camp et al., October 9, 1905 (Walter Chauncey Camp Papers, Yale University, Box 21).

42. Ronald A. Smith, ed., *Big Time Football at Harvard, 1905: The Diary of Coach Bill Reid* (Urbana: University of Illinois Press, 1994), 92.

43. Ibid., 42–51.

44. Ibid., 175, 302–3.

45. Ibid., 2–11.

46. Ibid., 26, 135, 148, 259, 300.

47. Letter from Theodore Roosevelt to Theodore Roosevelt Jr., November 15, 1903 (Theodore Roosevelt Jr. Papers, Library of Congress, Box 7).

48. "Teddy Roosevelt Jr. Is Hurt on Football Field," *Salt Lake City Herald*, October 15, 1905, 4.

49. Letter from Theodore Roosevelt to Walter Camp, November 24, 1905 (Walter Chauncey Camp Papers, Yale University, Box 21).

50. Letter from Walter Camp to Theodore Roosevelt, October 13, 1905 (Walter Chauncey Camp Papers, Yale University, Box 21).

51. Pete Iorizzo, "Casting Shadow over Football," *Times Union*, May 22, 2012, http://www.timesunion.com/default/article/Casting-shadow-over-football-3578165.php, accessed on March 2, 2013; Frank J. R. Mitchell, *Annual Circular Letters of the Seventy Active Chapters of the Phi Delta Theta Fraternity* (Evanston, IL: Bowman, 1906), 219; "Union Football Player Dies after NYU Game," *New York Tribune*, November 26, 1905, 1.

52. Iorizzo, "Casting Shadow over Football."

53. "Union Football Player Dies after NYU Game," 1.

54. Ibid.

55. Ibid.

56. "Football Player Killed," *New York Times*, November 26, 1905, 1.

57. Christopher Klein, "How Teddy Roosevelt Saved Football," History.com, September 6, 2012, http://www.history.com/news/how-teddy-roosevelt-saved-football, accessed on March 13, 2013.

58. Carol A. Barr, "Collegiate Sport," in Lisa Masteralexis, Carol A. Barr, and Mary Hums, eds., *Principles and Practices of Sports Management: Fourth Edition* (Burlington, MA: Jones & Bartlett, 2011), 165.

59. "Football Player Killed," 1.

60. "Union Football Player Dies after NYU Game," 1.

61. Ibid.

62. "Football Player Killed," 1.

63. Ibid.; "Rib Driven into Heart," *New York Times*, November 26, 1905, 1; "Another Football Player Dies," *New York Times*, November 29, 1905, 10.

64. "Half Back's Spine Injured," *New York Times*, November 27, 1905, 1.

65. "Hurley Badly Injured," *New York Times*, November 24, 1905, 7; "Harvard's Captain Leaves Hospital," *New York Times*, December 2, 1905, 7.

66. Smith, ed., *Big Time Football at Harvard, 1905*, 306–8.

67. "Hurley Badly Injured," 7.

68. Smith, ed., *Big Time Football at Harvard, 1905*, 309n, 310n, 312, 319.

69. "The Football Situation," *Harvard Graduates' Magazine*, March 1906, 493–95.

70. Smith, ed., *Big Time Football at Harvard, 1905*, 189–90.

71. "The Football Situation," 493.

72. Smith, ed., *Big Time Football at Harvard, 1905*, 314n.

73. Nelson, *The Anatomy of a Game*, 99–100; Watterson, *College Football*, 71–72; Bernstein, *Football*, 81–82; Smith, ed., *Big Time Football at Harvard, 1905*, 318.

74. Letter from Charles Eliot to A. M. Forester, November 23, 1905 (Records of the President of Harvard University: Charles W. Eliot, Harvard University Archives, Box 194).

75. "Harvard's Tackle Gives Up Football," *New York Times*, December 5, 1905, 11; "Brill Assails Football," *New York Times*, December 11, 1905, 8.

76. Smith, ed., *Big Time Football at Harvard, 1905*, 82, 173, 229.
77. Ibid., 82–83.
78. Ibid., 300–1.
79. Ibid., 291.
80. Ibid., 150, 174, 229.
81. "Army and Navy Play Annual Game To-day," *New York Times*, December 2, 1905, 7; "Navy Has $6,000 to Wager," *New York Times*, December 1, 1905, 10.
82. "Football Conference at the White House," *New York Times*, December 5, 1905, 11.
83. "Won't Discuss Conference," *New York Times*, December 6, 1905, 8.
84. H. F. Manchester, "Reveals How College Football Was Saved in 1905," *Boston Herald*, October 17, 1926, 7.
85. Ibid.; Smith, ed., *Big Time Football at Harvard, 1905*, 317n.
86. Smith, ed., *Big Time Football at Harvard, 1905*, 36.
87. Ibid., 317n; Gerald R. Gems, *For Pride, Profit, and Patriarchy: Football and the Incorporation of American Cultural Values* (Lanham, MD: Scarecrow Press, 2000), 83; Miller, *The Big Scrum*, 196–97.
88. Davis, *Football*, 110–11; Gems, *For Pride, Profit, and Patriarchy*, 157–58; Miller, *The Big Scrum*, 201; "Want College League for Entire Country," *New York Times*, December 31, 1905, 8; "Test Football Rules by Actual Play," *New York Times*, January 14, 1906, 11.
89. Nelson, *The Anatomy of a Game*, 106; Smith, ed., *Big Time Football at Harvard, 1905*, 33–35; Ronald A. Smith, "Harvard and Columbia and a Reconsideration of the 1905–06 Football Crisis," *Journal of Sport History*, Winter 1981, 7–8.
90. Scott A. McQuilkin and Ronald A. Smith, "The Rise and Fall of the Flying Wedge: Football's Most Controversial Play," *Journal of Sport History*, Spring 1993, 57–64.
91. Smith, ed., *Big Time Football at Harvard, 1905*, 34.

92. "Football Is Prohibited by Harvard Overseers," *New York Times*, January 16, 1906, 8; "No Harvard Football for at Least a Year," *New York Times*, February 9, 1906, 6; Smith, "Harvard and Columbia and a Reconsideration of the 1905–06 Football Crisis," 5–15.

93. Bernstein, *Football*, 81; Smith, ed., *Big Time Football at Harvard, 1905*, 265–66; Gems, *For Pride, Profit, and Patriarchy*, 95; Smith, "Harvard and Columbia and a Reconsideration of the 1905–06 Football Crisis," 11–12.

94. Smith, ed., *Big Time Football at Harvard, 1905*, 271–72; Smith, "Harvard and Columbia and a Reconsideration of the 1905–06 Football Crisis," 12; Manchester, "Reveals How College Football Was Saved in 1905," 7.

95. Manchester, "Reveals How College Football Was Saved in 1905," 7.

96. Ibid.

97. "Football Player Killed," 1.

98. "Half Back Moore Buried," *New York Times*, November 29, 1905, 10; "Moore's Death Accidental," *New York Times*, December 5, 1905, 11.

99. "Abolition of Football or Immediate Reforms," *New York Times*, November 28, 1905, 11.

100. Quoted in "Football Is Abolished by Columbia Committee," *New York Times*, November 29, 1905, 1; "President Eliot Won't Act," *New York Times*, November 27, 1905, 2.

101. "Football Reformation Begins Here This Week," *New York Times*, December 7, 1905, 7; "Football Conference to Convene To-day," *New York Times*, December 8, 1905, 9.

102. Henry Beach Needham, "The College Athlete: How Commercialism Is Making Him a Professional," *McClure's*, June 1905, 117–19; Bernstein, *Football*, 78–79.

103. "Columbia Bars Football," *New York Tribune*, November 29, 1905, 1–2.

104. "Football Is Doomed, Says Mr. Wheeler," *New York Times*, September 28, 1906, 10.

105. Letter from David Starr Jordan to Walter Camp, December 15, 1904 (Walter Chauncey Camp Papers, Yale University, Box 15).

106. Letter from David Starr Jordan to Walter Camp, January 20, 1908 (Walter Chauncey Camp Papers, Yale University, Box 15); Letter from David Starr Jordan to Charles R. Van Hise, January 3, 1911 (Walter Chauncey Camp Papers, Yale University, Box 15).

107. Smith, "Harvard and Columbia and a Reconsideration of the 1905–06 Football Crisis," 8–9, 17n.

108. "Want New Rules Committee," *New York Times*, December 8, 1905, 9.

109. "Football Coalition Is Finally Restored," *New York Times*, January 13, 1906, 7.

110. Smith, "Harvard and Columbia and a Reconsideration of the 1905–06 Football Crisis," 14.

111. Bernstein, *Football*, 81–82; Gems, *For Pride, Profit, and Patriarchy*, 83; Smith, ed., *Big Time Football at Harvard, 1905*, 317n.

112. Letter from Theodore Roosevelt to Walter Camp, December 11, 1905 (Walter Chauncey Camp Papers, Yale University, Box 21).

113. Watterson, *College Football*, 83.

114. Manchester, "Reveals How College Football Was Saved in 1905," 7.

115. For a list of the reforms requested by the special committee of the Athletic Association of Harvard Graduates, see "The Football Situation," 486–88. For a rundown of the post-1905 rules changes, see Nelson, *The Anatomy of a Game*, 123–24.

116. "Football Rules Made at Last," *Salt Lake Herald*, April 2, 1906, 7; Nelson, *The Anatomy of a Game*, 181.

117. John R. Searle, *The Construction of Social Reality* (New York: Free Press, 1995), 27–29.

118. Davis, *Football*, 114.

119. Smith, ed., *Big Time Football at Harvard, 1905*, 323–39.

Chapter 5

1. Ray Schmidt, "What Reforms?" *College Football Historical Society*, May 1995, 4; "Seventeen Hurt in Football Game," *New York Times*, October 11, 1908, 1.

2. "Dies of Injuries in Football Game," *New York Times*, November 15, 1909, 4.

3. John Sayle Watterson, *College Football: History, Spectacle, Controversy* (Baltimore: Johns Hopkins University Press, 2000), 112–13; "Dies of Injuries in Football Game," 4.

4. "Cadet Byrne Dead; No Army-Navy Game," *New York Times*, November 1, 1909, 1.

5. "Wilson's Long Fight for Life Is Ended," *New York Times*, April 10, 1910, 9.

6. "Football in 1909 Caused 26 Deaths," *New York Times*, November 21, 1909, 9; Watterson, *College Football*, 401.

7. John S. Watterson, "The Gridiron Crisis of 1905: Was It Really a Crisis?" *Journal of Sport History*, Summer 2000, 297.

8. Walter Camp, "Football of the Week," *Harper's Weekly*, October 21, 1905, 1520.

9. Joe Lapointe, "Football Helmets as Weapons.... Time to Ban the Kickoff?" *Huffington Post*, October 19, 2010, http://www.huffingtonpost.com/joe-lapointe/football-helmets-as-weapo_b_768004.html, accessed on February 14, 2013.

10. Associated Press, "Study: Concussions Down Slightly," ESPN, August 7, 2012, http://espn.go.com/nfl/story/_/id/8244809/study-says-new-rule-reduced-concussions-kickoffs, accessed on May 8, 2013.

11. Frederick O. Mueller and Robert C. Cantu, *Football Fatalities and Catastrophic Injuries, 1931–2008* (Durham: Carolina Academic Press, 2011), 20, 35, 52–53, 74, 92–93, 115, 116, 140, 166–67, 178, 204.

12. Robert W. Edgren, "R. Edgren's Column," *Evening Journal*, November 27, 1905, 12.

13. "Road Deaths a Global 'Epidemic' on Par with Diseases, Says New Report," AOL Autos, May 4, 2012, http://autos.aol.com/article/road-deaths-a-global-epidemic-on-par-with-diseases-says-new-r/, accessed on February 25, 2013.

14. "Traffic Safety Facts: Bicyclists and Other Cyclists," NHTSA, Washington, D.C., June 2012, 1.

15. "Accidents in North American Mountaineering 2007," http://c535846.r46.cf2.rackcdn.com/anam_2007.pdf, accessed on February 14, 2013.

16. Associated Press, "Virginia Hunting Deaths Up in 2008–09, to Nine Total," *Virginian-Pilot*, January 8, 2009, http://hamptonroads.com/2009/01/virginia-hunting-deaths-200809-nine-total, accessed on February 14, 2013. The piece noted that the statistics did not include the drowning of two duck hunters, bringing the total hunting deaths to eleven.

17. "Unintentional Drowning: Get the Facts," Centers for Disease Control and Prevention, http://www.cdc.gov/homeandrecreational safety/water-safety/waterinjuries-factsheet.html, accessed on February 14, 2013.

18. Melissa Abbey and Steve Almasy, "Jockey Dies after Fall at California Track," CNN, July 7, 2012, http://www.cnn.com/2012/07/06/us/california-jockey-death/index.html, accessed on January 16, 2013.

19. Teresa Waters, "2011 Skateboarding Fatalities," Skaters for Public Skateparks, January 30, 2012, http://www.skatepark.org/park-development/2012/01/2011-skateboarding-fatalities/#activity, accessed on January 19, 2013.

20. "Amusement Ride-Related Injuries and Deaths in the United States: 2005 Update," Consumer Product Safety Commission, September 7, 2005, 6–9, 11–12.

21. "Facts about Skiing/Snowboarding Safety," National Ski Areas Association, October 1, 2012, http://www.nsaa.org/media/68045/NSAA-Facts-About-Skiing-Snowboarding-Safety-10-1-12.pdf, accessed on January 16, 2013.

22. Rachel George, "Caleb Moore Dies after Injuries in X Games Crash," *USA Today*, January 31, 2013, http://www.usatoday.com/story/sports/olympics/2013/01/31/caleb-moore-dies-after-injuries-x-games-crash-snowmobile/1880587/, accessed on February 24, 2013.

23. Carolyn Jones, "Alcatraz Triathlon Competitor Dies," *San Francisco Chronicle*, March 3, 2013, http://www.sfgate.com/bayarea/article/Alcatraz-triathlon-competitor-dies-4324933.php, accessed on March 4, 2013.

24. Katie Kindelan and Aaron Katersky, "Westminster Dog Show: Competitor's Death Leaves Owner, Handler Suspicious," ABC News, February 28, 2013, http://abcnews.go.com/US/westminster-dog-show-competitors-death-leaves-owner-handler/story?id=18620330, accessed on March 4, 2013.

25. Ben McGrath, "Does Football Have a Future?" *New Yorker*, January 31, 2011, http://www.newyorker.com/reporting/2011/01/31/110131fa_fact_mcgrath, accessed on September 7, 2012.

26. Don Van Natta Jr., "His Game, His Rules," ESPN, March 5, 2013, http://espn.go.com/espn/story/_/page/RogerGoodell/game-rules, accessed on March 6, 2013.

27. Chuck Hughes, a Detroit Lions receiver suffering from severe arteriosclerosis, fell dead of a heart attack while returning to the huddle in Tigers Stadium in 1971. Playing seemed incidental to his demise. Whether he watched or played in the game, Hughes's inherited heart condition would have killed him. But the game itself, which has crippled players, hasn't killed anyone—at least in the NFL.

28. Ibid.

29. David M. Nelson, *The Anatomy of a Game: Football, the Rules, and the Men Who Made the Game* (Newark, DE: University of Delaware Press, 1994), 344, 347, 349, 351–52, 357, 409, 440.

30. Ibid., 73, 77, 375.

31. Ibid., 21.

32. Draft: Walter Camp, "Spalding's How to Play Football," August 1903 (Walter Chauncey Camp Papers, Yale University, Box 32).

33. Frederick O. Mueller and Bob Colgate, "Annual Survey of Football Injury Research, 1931–2012," American Football Coaches Association, National Collegiate Athletic Association, and National Federation of State High School Associations, February 2013, 19–20.

34. Nelson, *The Anatomy of a Game*, 339, 344, 507–8.

35. Phone interview of Nelson Kraemer on March 4, 2013.

36. Mueller and Colgate, "Annual Survey of Football Injury Research, 1931–2012," 21–22.

37. Ibid., 19–20.

38. Christopher Randolph, "Baseline Neuropsychological Testing in Managing Sport-Related Concussion: Does It Modify Risk?" *Current Sports Medicine Reports*, Jan–Feb 2011, 22.

39. "Boy Struck by Lightning at Football Practice Dies," *Naples Daily News*, October 7, 2012, http://www.naplesnews.com/news/2012/oct/07/boy-struck-by-lightning-at-football-practice/, accessed on March 4, 2013.

40. Michael Gonchar, "If Football Is So Dangerous to Players, Should We Be Watching It?" *New York Times*, September 13, 2012, http://learning.blogs.nytimes.com/2012/09/13/if-football-is-so-dangerous-to-players-should-we-be-watching-it/, accessed on February 25, 2013; Joe Nocera, "Should Kids Play Fooball?" *New York Times*, December 14, 2012, http://www.nytimes.com/2012/12/15/opinion/should-kids-play-football.html, accessed on February 25, 2013; Kevin Cook, "Dying to Play," *New York Times*, September 11, 2012, http://www.nytimes.com/2012/09/12/opinion/head-injuries-in-football.html, accessed February 25, 2013.

41. Mueller and Colgate, "Annual Survey of Football Injury Research, 1931–2012," 21–22.

42. For an estimate of the number of Americans playing organized football, see Mueller and Colgate, "Annual Survey of Football Injury Research, 1931–2012," 3.

43. Jane McManus, "Greg McElroy Hid Concussion," ESPN, December 28, 2012, http://espn.go.com/new-york/nfl/story/_/ id/8785073/greg-mcelroy-new-york-jets-discussed-concussion-symptoms-teammates-coaches, accessed on February 25, 2013.

44. Interview of Scott Lazo in Southbridge, Massachusetts, on December 9, 2012.

45. "Concussion Watch," PBS, http://www.pbs.org/wgbh/pages/ frontline/concussion-watch/, accessed on May 2, 2013.

46. "Study: Concussions Down Slightly," ESPN, August 7, 2012, http:// espn.go.com/nfl/story/_/id/8244809/study-says-new-rule-reduced-concussions-kickoffs, accessed on May 8, 2013.

47. To gauge the variation in sports concussion estimates, see chapter two or Mallika Marar et al., "Epidemiology of Concussions among United States High School Athletes in 20 Sports," *American Journal of Sports Medicine*, April 3, 2012, 747; Leah J. Frommer et al., "Sex Differences in Concussion Symptoms of High School Athletes," *Journal of Athletic Training*, February 2011, 76; Ray W. Daniel, Steven Rowson, and Stefan M. Duma, "Head Impact Exposure in Youth Football," *Annals of Biomedical Engineering*, April 2012, 976.

48. Mueller and Cantu, *Football Fatalities and Catastrophic Injuries, 1931–2008*, 181.

49. Matt Crossman, "Ronald Rouse Remembered," *Sporting News*, http://aol.sportingnews.com/sport/story/2012-10-08/ronald-rouse-dies-enlarged-heart-hartsville-high-school-south-carolina, accessed on November 11, 2012.

50. "Pee Wee Football League Bans 300-Pound Kid for Being Too Big," CBS Sports, August 16, 2012, http://www.cbssports.com/general/ story/19809921/pee-wee-football-league-bans-300pound-kid-for-being-too-big, accessed on February 26, 2013.

51. Mueller and Colgate, "Annual Survey of Football Injury Research, 1931–2008," 15.

52. Ibid., 17; "Death of Athlete, 13, Sparks Heart-Testing Debate," NBC News, August 24, 2009, http://www.msnbc.msn.com/

id/32541015/ns/health-childrens_health/t/death-athlete-sparks-
heart-testing-debate/, accessed on January 16, 2013. While the
survey indicated a weight of 360 pounds for the player, the article
noted a weight of 383 pounds.

53. Mueller and Colgate, "Annual Survey of Football Injury Research,
     1931–2010," 17.

54. Ibid., 21–22.

55. NCHS Health E-Stat, Centers for Disease Control and Prevention,
     http://www.cdc.gov/nchs/data/hestat/obesity_child_09_10/obesity_
     child_09_10.htm, accessed on November 10, 2012.

56. *Knute Rockne, All American* (Warner Brothers, 1940).

57. Jack Cavanaugh, *The Gipper: George Gipp, Knute Rockne, and
     the Dramatic Rise of Notre Dame Football* (New York: Skyhorse
     Publishing, 2010), 14–15, 33, 61, 71, 79, 100, 119.

58. Ibid., 61.

59. *Knute Rockne, All American.*

60. Cavanaugh, *The Gipper*, 61.

61. Ibid., 115, 227.

62. *Knute Rockne, All American.*

63. Cavanaugh, *The Gipper*, 127–36.

64. Nelson, *The Anatomy of a Game*, 69–70.

65. Watterson, *College Football*, 46.

66. Henry Beach Needham, "The College Athlete: How Commercialism
     Is Making Him a Professional," *McClure's*, June 1905, 122–23.

67. Watterson, *College Football*, 47.

68. Cavanaugh, *The Gipper*, 226.

69. Watterson, *College Football*, 401. The 1909 "26" figure doesn't
     take into account quadriplegic Earl Wilson's death, which came
     several months after the football season had ended.

70. Mueller and Colgate, "Annual Survey of Football Injury Research,
     1931–2012," 19–20.

Chapter 6

1. Arthur Daley, "No Need for Cops," *New York Times*, November 25, 1960, 36.
2. Jeff Davis, *Rozelle: Czar of the NFL* (New York: McGraw-Hill, 2008), 79; Tom Callahan, *Johnny U: The Life and Times of John Unitas* (New York: Crown, 2006), 152.
3. Davis, *Rozelle*, 87; Callahan, *Johnny U*, 168.
4. Callahan, *Johnny U*, 172–73; Parke H. Davis, *Football: The American Intercollegiate Game* (New York: Charles Scribner's Sons, 1911), 112; David M. Nelson, *The Anatomy of a Game: Football, the Rules, and the Men Who Made the Game* (Newark, DE: University of Delaware Press, 1994), 120.
5. Robert L. Teague, "Gifford Suffers Deep Concussion," *New York Times*, November 21, 1960, 38.
6. "New Stadium Here Called 'Unworthy,'" *New York Times*, November 27, 1960, 5S.
7. "Gifford Determined to Continue Football Career Despite Injury," *New York Times*, November 23, 1960, 32.
8. Jack McCallum with Chuck Bednarik, *Bednarik: Last of the Sixty-Minute Men* (Englewood Cliffs, NJ: Prentice-Hall, 1977), 193–96.
9. Robert L. Teague, "Gifford Suffers Deep Concussion," *New York Times*, November 21, 1960, 38.
10. Ibid.
11. McCallum with Bednarik, *Bednarik*, 162.
12. Ibid., 51–56.
13. Louis Effrat, "Injured Gifford and Katcavage Are Lost to Giants for Remainder of Season," *New York Times*, November 22, 1960, 44.
14. "Gifford Determined to Continue Football Career Despite Injury," 32. For evidence of Bednarik's lingering bitterness over dubbing the hit "dirty," see McCallum with Bednarik, *Bednarik*, 164–65.
15. "Gifford Determined to Continue Football Career Despite Injury," 32.

16. Sheila Marikar and Mikaela Conley, "Junior Seau's Death Ruled a Suicide by San Diego County Coroner," ABC News, May 3, 2012, http://abcnews.go.com/US/junior-seaus-death-ruled-suicide-san-diego-county/story?id=16274600, accessed December 7, 2012.

17. Will Bunch, "The NFL: The No Future League," *Huffington Post*, May 3, 2012, http://www.huffingtonpost.com/will-bunch/junior-seau-dead_b_1473829.html, accessed on December 7, 2012.

18. Michael Arnold Glueck, "Suicide by Quarterback—Football Players Dying Young," Newsmax, October 3, 2006, http://archive.newsmax.com/archives/articles/2006/10/3/122610.shtml, accessed on March 6, 2013.

19. Gregg Doyel, "NFL Is Killing Its Players, and League Doesn't Care," CBS Sports, December 23, 2010, http://www.cbssports.com/nfl/story/14477196/nfl-is-killing-its-players-and-league-doesnt-care, accessed on December 7, 2012.

20. George F. Will, "Football's Problem with Danger on the Field Isn't Going Away," *Washington Post*, August 3, 2012, http://articles.washingtonpost.com/2012-08-03/opinions/35491867_1_cte-brain-tissue-brain-trauma, accessed on October 30, 2012; "Black and White and Re(a)d All Over: The Conservative Advantage in Syndicated Op-Ed Columns," Media Matters for America, http://mediamatters.org/research/oped/, accessed on December 7, 2012.

21. Dan Raley, "New NFL Goal: A Longer Life," *Seattle Post-Intelligencer*, May 8, 2008, http://www.seattlepi.com/news/article/New-NFL-goal-A-longer-life-1272886.php, accessed December 7, 2012.

22. LZ Granderson, "Reflecting on Football, Junior Seau," ESPN, May 4, 2012, http://espn.go.com/nfl/story/_/id/7886111/reflecting-football-junior-seau-death, accessed December 7, 2012.

23. Bill Utterback, "NFL Life Signals Early Death," *Chicago Tribune*, March 4, 1988, http://articles.chicagotribune.com/1988-03-04/sports/8804040445_1_life-expectancy-heart-attack-average-lifespan, accessed on December 8, 2012.

24. Ibid.

25. Phone interview of Everett Lehman on March 5, 2013.

26. Bill Barnwell, "Mere Mortals," Grantland.com, August 16, 2012, http://www.grantland.com/story/_/id/8274392/comparing-mortality-rates-football-baseball, accessed on April 29, 2013.

27. McCallum with Bednarik, *Bednarik*, 170; Jack Doyle, "Gifford For Luckies, 1961–1962," The Pop History Dig, March 29, 2010, http://www.pophistorydig.com/?tag=lucky-strike-advertising-history, accessed January 21, 2013.

28. Sherry L. Baron et al., "Body Mass Index, Playing Position, Race, and the Cardiovascular Mortality of Retired Professional Football Players," *American Journal of Cardiology*, March 15, 2012, 889–96.

29. Lee M. Nadler, "The Harvard NFLPA Program: Organization Overview," Harvard.edu, http://hms.harvard.edu/sites/default/files/assets/Harvard%20Integrated%20Program%20to%20Protect%20and%20Improve%20the%20Health%20of%20NFLPA%20Members.pdf, accessed on March 6, 2013.

30. Kay Lazar, "Harvard to Lead $100m Study of NFL Players," *Boston Globe*, January 29, 2013, http://www.bostonglobe.com/metro/2013/01/29/nfl-players-union-and-harvard-team-landmark-study-football-injuries-and-illness/YTbnGypzJXb1VkZSr1hbdP/story.html, accessed on February 7, 2013.

31. Baron et al., "Body Mass Index, Playing Position," 891.

32. Everett J. Lehman et al., "Neurodegenerative Causes of Death among Retired National Football League Players," *Neurology*, November 6, 2012, 1970–74.

33. Ibid.

34. Rodolfo Savica et al., "High School Football and Risk of Neurodegeneration: A Community Based Study," *Mayo Clinic Proceedings*, April 2012, 335–39.

35. John Lanzafame, "Seau's Legacy Should Be a Change in Concussion Management," Pro Player Insiders, May 4, 2012, http://proplayerinsiders.com/seaus-legacy-should-be-a-change-in-concussion-management/, accessed on January 22, 2013.

36. "Where Do Players Go When the Cheering Stops and the Game Leaves Them Behind?" GamesOver.org, http://www.gamesover.org/retirement/when_the_cheering_stops, accessed on January 18, 2013.

37. Sally Jenkins, "No Matter What Happens in NFL Labor Negotiations, the Players Pay the Price," *Washington Post*, February 25, 2011, http://www.washingtonpost.com/wp-dyn/content/article/2011/02/23/AR2011022305999.html, accessed on April 2, 2013; Charles P. Pierce, "It's All about Seeing Stars," *Boston Globe*, February 3, 2004, http://www.boston.com/sports/football/patriots/articles/2004/02/03/its_all_about_seeing_stars/, accessed on April 2, 2013; Jill Lieber Steeg, "Junior Seau: Song of Sorrow," *San Diego Union Tribune*, October 14, 2012, http://www.utsandiego.com/news/2012/oct/14/junior-seau-real-story/, accessed on April 26, 2013; Tony Dungy, *Quiet Strength: The Principles, Practices, & Priorities of a Winning Life* (Carol Stream, IL: Tyndale, 2007), 272; Charles P. Pierce, *Moving the Chains: Tom Brady and the Pursuit of Everything* (New York: Farrar, Strauss, and Giroux, 2006), 218.

38. Mallika Marar et al., "Epidemiology of Concussions among United States High School Athletes in 20 Sports," *American Journal of Sports Medicine*, April 3, 2012, 749.

39. Andrew Das, "The Fifth Down," *New York Times*, December 24, 2008, http://query.nytimes.com/gst/fullpage.html?res=9405E1DB153EF937A15751C1A96E9C8B63, accessed on December 22, 2012.

40. Quoted in David Leon Moore and Erik Brady, "Junior Seau's Final Days Plagued by Sleepless Nights," *USA Today*, June 2, 2012, http://usatoday30.usatoday.com/sports/football/story/2012-05-31/Junior-Seau-suicide-last-days-sleep-issues/55316506/1, accessed on December 22, 2012.

41. Steeg, "Junior Seau: Song of Sorrow," accessed on October 16, 2012.

42. Kevin M. Guskiewicz et al., "Recurrent Concussion and Risk of Depression in Retired Professional Football Players," *Medicine & Science in Sports & Exercise*, June 2007, 903.

43. "Junior Seau Reportedly Drives Car off of Cliff after Being Arrested," Sporting News NFL, October 18, 2010, http://aol.sportingnews.com/nfl/story/2010-10-18/junior-seau-reportedly-drives-car-off-of-cliff-after-being-arrested, accessed on March 6, 2013.

44. Christine M. Baugh et al., "Chronic Traumatic Encephalopathy: Neurodegeneration Following Repetitive Concussive and Subconcussive Brain Trauma," *Brain Imaging and Behavior*, June 2012, 245.

45. Steve Fainaru and Mark Fainaru-Wada, "CTE Found in Living Ex-NFL Players," ESPN, January 22, 2013, http://espn.go.com/espn/otl/story/_/id/8867972/ucla-study-finds-signs-cte-living-former-nfl-players-first-time, accessed on April 10, 2013.

46. Brandon E. Gavett, Robert A. Stern, and Ann C. McKee, "Chronic Traumatic Encephalopathy: A Potential Late Effect of Sport-Related Concussive and Subconcussive Head Trauma," *Clinics in Sports Medicine*, January 2011, 180.

47. Baugh et al., "Chronic Traumatic Encephalopathy," 251.

48. Gavett, Stern, and McKee, "Chronic Traumatic Encephalopathy," 185.

49. "Expert: Junior Seau CTE Was Not Caused by Football Concussions," Purdue University, January 11, 2013, http://www.purdue.edu/newsroom/releases/2013/Q1/expert-junior-seau-cte-was-not-caused-by-football-concussions.html, accessed on April 10, 2013. Linemen made up just five of the twelve current or former NFL players who killed themselves over the last quarter century.

50. Dave Scheiber, "The Mysterious Death of Andre Waters," *St. Petersburg Times*, December 11, 2006, http://www.sptimes.com/2006/12/11/Sports/The_mysterious_death_.shtml, accessed on December 22, 2012.

51. Becky Yerak, "Duerson Had Filed for Personal Bankruptcy," *Chicago Tribune*, February 22, 2011, http://articles.chicagotribune.com/2011-02-22/sports/ct-spt-0222-duerson-bankruptcy--20110222_1_alicia-duerson-freezer-supplier-bankruptcy-filing, accessed on December 22, 2012.

52. Alan Schwarz, "A Suicide, a Last Request, a Family's Questions," *New York Times*, February 22, 2011, http://www.nytimes.com/2011/02/23/sports/football/23duerson.html, accessed on January 30, 2013.

53. Julian Gavaghan, "Former NFL Star Kills Himself after Lifetime of Depression 'Brought on by Concussion During Career'—the Second in a Year," *Daily Mail*, April 23, 2012, http://www.dailymail.co.uk/news/article-2133869/Ray-Easterling-dead-NFL-star-kills-lifetime-depression-brought-concussion.html, accessed January 23, 2013.

54. Dave Masko, "NFL Player Michael Current Kills Self as Duerson," HULIQ.com, January 20, 2012, http://www.huliq.com/10282/nfl-player-michael-current-kills-self-duerson-concussion-suicide-remembered, accessed on January 23, 2013.

55. Jordan Steffen, "Former Bronco Mike Current Found Dead; He Faced Child-Sex Charges in Oregon," *Denver Post*, January 18, 2012, http://www.denverpost.com/commented/ci_19763224, accessed on January 18, 2013; Masko, "NFL Player Michael Current Kills Self as Duerson," accessed on January 23, 2013.

56. Quoted in Josh Katzenstein, "Father Says Ex-Lion Titus Young Has Brain Disorder, Needs Help," Detroit News, May 14, 2013, http://www.detroitnews.com/article/20130514/SPORTS0101/305140310, accessed on May 21, 2013.

57. Bob Hohler, "Researchers Urge Special Brain Autopsy of Bombing Suspect," *Boston Globe*, April 20, 2013, http://www.boston.com/sports/marathon/2013/04/20/researchers-urge-special-brain-autopsy-bombing-suspect/UoZExTff0K4olSTyIV5WGL/story.html. Quote therein, accessed on May 22, 2013.

58. Michael Craig Miller, "Testing the Brain of Tamerlan Tsarnaev," *Boston Globe*, April 27, 2013, http://www.bostonglobe.com/opinion/2013/04/26/let-study-tamerlan-tsarnaev-brain/1xZ10gotjsNqoo5YOpyqEM/story.html, accessed on May 22, 2013.

59. Evan Allen, "Psychiatrist Says Wayland's Fujita Had Explosive Impulse During Killing," *Boston Globe*, March 1, 2013, http://www.bostonglobe.com/metro/2013/03/01/nathaniel-fujita-could-not-control-his-actions-when-killed-his-girlfriend-psychiatrist-testifies/O4LnKkY785WlGtdIET6yuL/story.html, accessed on March 3, 2013.

60. Gabriel Medina, "Exgrandeliga Venezolano Enzo Hernández se Suicidó," Líder, January 13, 2013, http://www.liderendeportes.com/Noticias/Beisbol/Exgrandeliga-venezolano-Enzo-Hernandez-se-suicido.aspx, accessed on January 18, 2013; Bill Center, "Padres Insider: Gregerson Picked for WBC," *U-T San Diego*, January 14, 2013, http://www.utsandiego.com/news/2013/jan/14/padres-insider-gregerson-arbitration/?page=2#article-copy, accessed on January 18, 2013.

61. Center, "Padres Insider: Gregerson Picked for WBC," accessed on January 30, 2013; "Gregerson Answers Call from Torre to Pitch in World Baseball Classic," *U-T San Diego*, January 15, 2013, http://www.utsandiego.com/news/2013/jan/15/tp-gregerson-answers-call-from-torre-to-pitch-in/, accessed on January 30, 2013.

62. During the 2012 seasons, 1,284 players made plate appearances and 662 pitched in Major League Baseball games. Given interleague games, and the exclusion of the designated hitter in National League parks, a considerable number of the 662 pitchers overlap with the 1,284 batsmen. A few players entered games as pinch runners or replacement fielders. A total of 2,341 players entered National Football League games in 2012. The similarity in the number of suicides, and the disparity in the number of players, confirms a higher rate of suicide among baseball players than football players during the last quarter century. Player counts come courtesy of Sean Foreman of sports-reference.com.

63. Sherry L. Baron et al., "Body Mass Index, Playing Position, Race, and the Cardiovascular Mortality of Retired Professional Football Players," *American Journal of Cardiology*, March 15, 2012, 891.

64. Ibid.

65. Frank Bruni, "Pro Football's Violent Toll," *New York Times*, December 3, 2012, http://www.nytimes.com/2012/12/04/opinion/bruni-pro-footballs-violent-toll.html, accessed on April 26, 2013; "Should Football Be Fundamentally Changed to Make It Safer?" *U.S. News & World Report*, http://www.usnews.com/debate-club/should-football-be-fundamentally-changed-to-make-it-safer, accessed on April 26, 2013.

66. Phone interview of Everett Lehman on March 5, 2013.

67. McCallum with Bednarik, *Bednarik*, 209.

68. Quoted in Jarrett Bell, "Study Shows NFL Players Live Longer," *USA Today*, May 9, 2012, http://usatoday30.usatoday.com/sports/football/nfl/story/2012-05-08/Study-shows-NFL-players-live-longer/54847564/1, accessed on March 4, 2013.

Chapter 7

1. The data on Andrew Sullivan's hits and movements come from my observations of him at a St. John's practice in Shrewsbury, Massachusetts, on October 3, 2012. Quotes from coaches and other observations stem from St. John's practice that day and on October 2, 2012.

2. Steven P. Broglio et al., "The Biomechanical Properties of Concussions in High School Football," *Medicine & Science in Sports & Exercise*, November 2010, http://www.ncbi.nlm.nih.gov/pmc/articles/PMC2943536/, accessed on April 18, 2013.

3. The data on Andrew Sullivan's hits and movements come from my observations of him at a St. John's practice in Shrewsbury, Massachusetts, on October 3, 2012. Quotes from coaches and other observations stem from St. John's practice that day and on October 2, 2012.

4. Interviews of Andrew Sullivan in Shrewsbury, Massachusetts, on October 2, October 3, October 6, October 20, and October 27, 2012.

5. Email from Andrew Sullivan to author, October 18, 2012.

6.   Phone interview of St. John's athletic director Pat White on March 18, 2013; "Tuition and Fee Contract for New Students Entering Saint John's High School for the Academic Year 2012–2013," Saint John's High School, http://admissions.stjohnshigh.org/s/805/images/editor_documents/Business%20Office/tuition_and__fee_contract_2012-2013_new_student.pdf, accessed on March 18, 2013; "Former Football Players in the College Ranks (All Sports 2005–2011)," Saint John's High School, http://www.stjohnshigh.org/s/804/index.aspx?sid=804&gid=1&pgid=899, accessed on March 18, 2013.

7.   "MA's Top High Schools 2012," GoLocalWorcester, February 22, 2012, http://www.golocalworcester.com/lifestyle/mas-top-high-schools-2012-the-complete-list-of-1-to-392/, accessed on March 18, 2013.

8.   Jack Minch, "Leominster High School Teacher Arrested on Drug Charges," SentinelandEnterprise.com, April 22, 2012, http://www.sentinelandenterprise.com/police/ci_20454905/drug-charges, accessed on March 18, 2012; Quoted in Jack Minch, "Leominster High Teacher Set to Return to Court Friday to Face Drug Charges," SentinelandEnterprise.com, April 24, 2012, http://www.sentinelandenterprise.com/local/ci_20466928/leominster-high-teacher-set-return-court-friday-face, accessed on March 18, 2013.

9.   Interview of John Giacoppe in Shrewsbury, Massachusetts, on October 27, 2012.

10.   Ibid.

11.   Interview of Andrew Sullivan in Shrewsbury, Massachusetts, on October 27, 2012.

12.   Interview of John Giacoppe in Shrewsbury, Massachusetts, on October 27, 2012.

13.   Ibid.

14.   H. G. Bissinger, *Friday Night Lights: A Town, a Team, and a Dream* (1990; repr., New York: De Capo Press, 2004), 42, 45–46, 146–47.

15.   Walter Camp, *American Football: New and Enlarged Edition* (New York: Harper and Brothers, 1894), 120–22.

16. David M. Nelson, *The Anatomy of a Game: Football, the Rules, and the Men Who Made the Game* (Newark, DE: University of Delaware Press, 1994), 75, 184.

17. Camp, *American Football*, 36.

18. Conversation with Bill Sullivan in Shrewsbury, Massachusetts, on October 20, 2012.

19. Interview of Andrew Sullivan in Shrewsbury, Massachusetts, on October 27, 2012.

20. Interview of Garrett DelleChiaie in Shrewsbury, Massachusetts, on October 20, 2012.

21. Interview of Andrew Sullivan in Shrewsbury, Massachusetts, on October 27, 2012.

22. Interview of John Andreoli in Worcester, Massachusetts, on October 19, 2012.

Chapter 8

1. Friedrich Nietzsche, *Thus Spoke Zarathustra: A Book for All and None*, trans. R. J. Hollingdale (1892; repr., Middlesex, UK: Penguin Books, 1968), 91.

2. Interview of Garrett DelleChiaie in Fitchburg, Massachusetts, on December 1, 2012.

3. Frederick O. Mueller and Bob Colgate, "Annual Survey of Football Injury Research, 1931–2012," American Football Coaches Association, National Collegiate Athletic Association, and National Federation of State High School Associations, February 2013, 20–22.

4. John M. Carroll, *Red Grange and the Rise of Modern Football* (Urbana: University of Illinois Press, 1999), 192.

5. Lars Anderson, *The First Star: Red Grange and the Barnstorming Tour That Launched the NFL* (New York: Random House, 2009), 13–16; Carroll, *Red Grange and the Rise of Modern Football*, 5–6.

6. Larry Schwartz, "The Galloping Ghost Scared Opponents," ESPN, http://espn.go.com/sportscentury/features/00014213.html, accessed on March 29, 2013.

7.   Carroll, *Red Grange and the Rise of Modern Football*, 8.
8.   Anderson, *The First Star*, 10, 18.
9.   Carroll, *Red Grange and the Rise of Modern Football*, 15–19.
10. Anderson, *The First Star*, 31–32.
11. Quoted in Carroll, *Red Grange and the Rise of Modern Football*, 18.
12. Anderson, *The First Star*, 33.
13. Carroll, *Red Grange and the Rise of Modern Football*, 35.
14. Anderson, *The First Star*, 29, 34–36.
15. Ibid., 36.
16. William P. O'Hare, "Trends in the Child Population," in Mark Mather, Kelvin Pollard, and Linda Jacobsen, *Population Research Bureau Reports on America: First Results from the 2010 Census* (Washington, D.C.: Population Reference Bureau, 2011), 4.
17. Haya El Nasser and Paul Overberg, "Census Reveals Plummeting U.S. Birthrates," *USA Today*, June 24, 2011, http://usatoday30.usatoday.com/news/nation/census/2011-06-03-fewer-children-census-suburbs_n.htm, accessed on March 23, 2013.
18. John J. Miller, *The Big Scrum: How Teddy Roosevelt Saved Football* (New York: Harper Collins, 2011), 15.
19. Mueller and Colgate, "Annual Survey of Football Injury Research, 1931–2012," 20–22.
20. "Football Player Killed," *New York Times*, November 26, 1905, 1; "Rib Driven Into Heart," *New York Times*, November 26, 1905, 1; "Another Football Player Dies," *New York Times*, November 29, 1905, 10.
21. Jerry Ulmer, "Concussion Concerns Could Deliver a Blow to High School, Youth Football," *The Oregonian*, August 23, 2012, http://highschoolsports.oregonlive.com/news/article/-264138 7573131985089/concussion-concerns-could-deliver-a-blow-to-high-school-youth-football/, accessed on May 29, 2013.
22. Rick Maese, "Football Safety Concerns Affect Youth Leagues, Causing NFL to Take Notice," *Washington Post*, October 24, 2012, http://articles.washingtonpost.com/2012-10-24/

sports/35498322_1_youth-football-youth-league-roger-goodell, accessed on May 29, 2013.

23. Bob Labriola, "USA Football Is Fighting the Fight," Steelers.com, May 7, 2013, http://www.steelers.com/news/article-1/USA-Football-is-fighting-the-fight/c58f315b-8a99-493b-bee7-8830ba4091a9, accessed on May 29, 2013.

24. Ibid.; *National Federation of State High School Associations, 2010–11 High School Athletics Participation Survey* (Indianapolis: National Federation of State High School Associations, 2012), 52.

25. Quoted in Kay Hymowitz, *Manning Up: How the Rise of Women Has Turned Men into Boys* (New York: Basic Books, 2011), 74; an updated version of the original quote appears at Mark J. Perry, "The Increasing College Degree Gap: Will College Women's Centers Address 'This Gender Issue'?" Carpe Diem blog, April 11, 2010, http://mjperry.blogspot.com/2010/04/update-on-increasing-college-degree-gap.html, accessed on March 28, 2013.

26. Janice Lloyd, "Women Lag in Life-Expectancy Gains," *USA Today*, April 20, 2012, http://usatoday30.usatoday.com/news/health/story/health/story/2012-04-19/Life-expectancy-improves-slower-for-women/54419298/1, accessed on March 29, 2013.

27. "A–Z Health Topics," womenshealth.gov, http://womenshealth.gov/a-z-topics/index.html, accessed on March 28, 2013.

28. Aysegul Sahin, Joseph Song, and Bart Hobijn, "The Unemployment Gender Gap During the Current Recession," Federal Reserve Bank of New York, http://www.newyorkfed.org/research/economists/sahin/GenderGap.pdf, accessed on March 28, 2013; "Labor Force Statistics from the Current Population Survey," Bureau of Labor Statistics, March 8, 2013, http://www.bls.gov/web/empsit/cpseea10.htm, accessed on March 28, 2013.

29. "White House Forum on Women and the Economy," Whitehouse.gov, April 6, 2012, http://www.whitehouse.gov/blog/2012/04/06/white-house-forum-women-and-economy, accessed on March 28, 2013.

30. "Modern Life Rough on Men," CNN Health, August 18, 2011, http://thechart.blogs.cnn.com/2011/08/18/modern-life-rough-on-men/, accessed on March 26, 2013.

31. Shan Li, "Market Booms for Men's Cosmetics—but Don't Call It Makeup," *Los Angeles Times*, June 23, 2012, http://articles.latimes.com/2012/jun/23/business/la-fi-man-makeup-20120623, accessed on May 30, 2013.

32. HommeMystere, http://www.hommemystere.com/, accessed on May 30, 2013.

33. Kathleen Parker, *Save the Males: Why Men Matter, Why Women Should Care* (New York: Random House, 2008), ix.

34. C. S. Lewis, *The Abolition of Man: How Education Develops Man's Sense of Morality* (1943; repr., New York: MacMillan, 1986), 34–35.

35. "23 Dead in South African Rite of Passage; Police Open Murder Cases," *The Toronto Star*, May 17, 2013, http://www.thestar.com/news/world/2013/05/17/23_dead_in_south_african_rite_of_passage_police_open_murder_cases.html.

36. Quoted in Michael Largo, *Final Exits: The Illustrated Encyclopedia of How We Die* (New York: William Morrow, 2006), 153.

37. Christopher Lasch, "The Corruption of Sports," *New York Review of Books*, April 28, 1977, http://www.nybooks.com/articles/archives/1977/apr/28/the-corruption-of-sports/, accessed on March 29, 2013.

38. H. Paul Jeffers, *Theodore Roosevelt Jr.: The Life of a War Hero* (Novato, CA: Presidio Press, 2002), 72–73.

39. Harvey Mansfield, *Manliness* (New Haven: Yale University Press, 2006), 100.

40. Peggy Samuels and Harold Samuels, *Frederic Remington: A Biography* (Garden City, NY: Doubleday, 1982), 27.

41. Ibid., 12.

42. Ibid., 12, 14, 17–19.

43. Quoted in Mark F. Bernstein, *Football: The Ivy League Origins of an American Obsession* (Philadelphia: University of Pennsylvania Press, 2001), 12; John Sayle Watterson, *College Football: History, Spectacle, Controversy* (Baltimore: Johns Hopkins University Press, 2000), 24.

44. Samuels and Samuels, *Frederic Remington*, 92–93.

45. Letter from Theodore Roosevelt to Frederic Remington, October 28, 1908 (Frederic Remington Papers, Smithsonian Archives of American Art, Reel NOR 1).

46. Ibid.

47. Quoted in Bernstein, *Football*, 35.

Chapter 9

1. Interview of Keith Gilbert in Boston, Massachusetts, on November 17, 2012.

2. Interview of Stacy Osur in Boston, Massachusetts, on November 17, 2012.

3. Interview of Keith Gilbert in Boston, Massachusetts, on November 17, 2012.

4. Interview of Stacy Osur in Boston, Massachusetts, on November 17, 2012.

5. Kristen E. Holmes, "Barrier-Breaker Visits Cheltenham Alma Mater," *Inquirer*, August 15, 2011, http://articles.philly.com/2011-08-15/news/29889430_1_alma-mater-lamott-training-camp, accessed on March 9, 2013.

6. Robert W. Peterson, *Pigskin: The Early Years of Pro Football* (New York: Oxford University Press, 1997), 187.

7. Ron Fimrite, "Best Team You Never Heard Of," *Sports Illustrated*, November 12, 1990, http://sportsillustrated.cnn.com/vault/article/magazine/MAG1136230/index.htm, accessed on February 13, 2013; Jeff Davis, *Rozelle: Czar of the NFL* (New York: McGraw-Hill, 2008), 37.

8. Gerald R. Gems, *For Pride, Profit, and Patriarchy: Football and the Incorporation of American Cultural Values* (Lanham, MD: Scarecrow Press, 2000), 172.

9. Lars Anderson, *Carlisle vs. Army: Jim Thorpe, Dwight Eisenhower, Pop Warner, and the Forgotten Story of Football's Greatest Battle* (New York: Random House, 2007), 211.

10. Quoted in Davis, *Rozelle*, 9.

11. "First Take," ESPN, December 13, 2012.

12. Davis, *Rozelle*, 138.

13. Elizabeth Fussell, Narayan Sastry, and Mark VanLandingham, "Who Returned to New Orleans after Hurricane Katrina?" Population Reference Bureau, www.prb.org/Articles/2010/katrina.aspx, accessed on March 2, 2013.

14. Quoted in Jim Corbett, "Lifting Up New Orleans: City Rising in Unison with Saints," *USA Today*, January 24, 2010, http://usatoday30.usatoday.com/sports/football/nfl/saints/2010-01-21-new-orleans-cover_N.htm, accessed on February 12, 2013.

15. Quoted in Molly O'Toole, "Can the Saints Really Save New Orleans?" *Daily Beast*, February 7, 2010, http://www.thedailybeast.com/newsweek/blogs/the-human-condition/2010/02/07/can-the-saints-really-save-new-orleans-how-a-super-bowl-victory-could-enhance-the-health-of-a-city.html, accessed on February 12, 2013.

16. David Talbot, *Season of the Witch: Enchantment, Terror, and Deliverance in the City of Love* (New York: Free Press, 2012), 386.

17. *The Band That Wouldn't Die* (ESPN Films, 2009).

18. Quoted in Richard Goldstein, "Lou Groza, 76, Star Kicker for Cleveland Browns, Dies," *New York Times*, December 1, 2000, http://www.nytimes.com/2000/12/01/nyregion/lou-groza-76-star-kicker-for-cleveland-browns-dies.html, accessed on February 13, 2013.

19. Steve Rushin, "The Heart of a City," *Sports Illustrated*, December 4, 1995, http://sportsillustrated.cnn.com/vault/article/magazine/MAG1007505/index.htm, accessed on February 19, 2013.

20. Interview of Fred Smerlas in Marlboro, Massachusetts, on October 2, 2012.

21. Les Carpenter, "Behind Its Patron Saints, New Orleans Rallies," *Washington Post*, February 7, 2010, http://articles.washingtonpost.com/2010-02-07/sports/36885955_1_latoya-cantrell-new-orleans-broadmoor-improvement-association, accessed on February 13, 2013.

22. Walter Camp, *American Football: New and Enlarged Edition* (New York: Harper and Brothers, 1894), 209.

23. Franklin Foer and Chris Hughes, "Barack Obama Is Not Pleased," *New Republic*, January 27, 2013, http://www.newrepublic.com/article/112190/obama-interview-2013-sit-down-president, accessed on January 29, 2013.

24. "Football or No Football," *New York Times*, February 18, 1894, 24.

25. Letter from Woodrow Wilson to Arthur T. Hadley, January 1, 1910 (Walter Chauncey Camp Papers, Yale University, Box 11).

26. Ibid.; letter from Arthur T. Hadley to Woodrow Wilson, January 3, 1910 (Walter Chauncey Camp Papers, Yale University, Box 11); letter from Arthur T. Hadley to Walter Camp, January 4, 1910 (Walter Chauncey Camp Papers, Yale University, Box 11).

27. David M. Nelson, *The Anatomy of a Game: Football, the Rules, and the Men Who Made the Game* (Newark, DE: University of Delaware Press, 1994), 70; John Sayle Watterson, *College Football: History, Spectacle, Controversy* (Baltimore: Johns Hopkins University Press, 2000), 39.

28. Mark F. Bernstein, *Football: The Ivy League Origins of an American Obsession* (Philadelphia: University of Pennsylvania Press, 2001), 71–72.

29. David Maraniss, *When Pride Still Mattered: A Life of Vince Lombardi* (New York: Simon and Schuster, 1999), 299.

30. Anderson, *Carlisle vs. Army*, 255, 290–93, 295–310.

31. Lois Romano and George Lardner Jr., "Bush: So-So Student but a Campus Mover," *Washington Post*, July 27, 1999, http://www.washingtonpost.com/wp-srv/politics/campaigns/wh2000/stories/bush072799.htm, accessed on February 1, 2013.

32. Irvin F. Gellman, *The Contender: Richard Nixon: The Congress Years* (New York: The Free Press, 1999), 15; Brian Cronin, "Did Richard Nixon Call a Key Redskins Play?" ESPN, September 13, 2012, http://espn.go.com/blog/playbook/fandom/post/_/id/9424/presidential-orders, accessed on January 3, 2013.

33. Paul Gray, "Gerald Ford: Steady Hand for a Nation in Crisis," *Time*, December 27, 2006, http://www.time.com/time/nation/article/0,8599,1572927,00.html, accessed on February 27, 2013.

34. John M. Carroll, *Red Grange and the Rise of Modern Football* (Urbana: University of Illinois Press, 1999), 114. Another version of the story can be found in Peterson, *Pigskin*, 90.

35. Comic by Ted Rall, GoComics, May 3, 2004, http://www.gocomics.com/tedrall/2004/05/03, accessed on February 28, 2013.

36. Rene Gonzalez, "Pat Tillman Is Not a Hero: He Got What Was Coming to Him," *Daily Collegian*, May 26, 2008, http://dailycollegian.com/2008/05/26/pat-tillman-is-not-a-hero-he-got-what-was-coming-to-him/, accessed on February 28, 2013. The piece originally appeared in the *Collegian* on April 28, 2004.

37. "1918: Mare Island, 19 vs. Camp Lewis, 7," Pasadena Tournament of Roses, http://www.tournamentofroses.com/TheRoseBowlGame/History/GamesResultsRecaps/DAGameResultsRecaps/tabid/2108/Article/135932/1918-mare-island-19-vs-camp-lewis-7.aspx, accessed on February 28, 2013.

38. Gems, *For Pride, Profit, and Patriarchy*, 99.

39. Ibid., 79.

40. In a rather pathetic attempt to debunk a supposed urban legend, the *Los Angeles Times* offers as evidence against Haughton strangling the bulldog the existence of an American Society for the Prevention of Cruelty to Animals, the absence of newspaper accounts mentioning the locker room dog murder, and the story not meshing with Haughton's general character. They might as well have mentioned the lack of cell-phone video documenting the event. The story may not be true—with apologies to bulldogs, it's certainly far-fetched—but more than a century later it doesn't lend itself to

newspaper fact checkers determining its accuracy. "Did a Harvard Coach Once Strangle a Bulldog to Motivate His Team to Beat Yale?" *Los Angeles Times*, November 2, 2011, http://latimesblogs. latimes.com/sports_blog/2011/11/did-a-harvard-coach-once-strangle-a-bulldog-to-motivate-his-team-to-beat-yale.html, accessed on March 9, 2013. The piece's regard for facts comes through in this passage: "Haughton, by the way, left Harvard to enlist in the military during World War II. When he returned, he joined the business world before he was lured back to the world of coaching by Columbia, who offered him a staggering $20,000 to coach their football team in 1923." For a discussion of Haughton's, and Harvard's, response to World War I, see James R. Beniger, "Many Problems Confronted the Class of '18," *Harvard Crimson*, June 11, 1968, http://www.thecrimson.com/article/1968/6/11/many-problems-confronted-the-class-of/, accessed March 9, 2013.

41. Gems, *For Pride, Profit, and Patriarchy*, 99.

42. Peterson, *Pigskin*, 138.

43. Ibid., 139; Bill Schubert, "Jimmy Conzelman," Coffin Corner 19, no. 1 (1997), http://www.profootballresearchers.org/coffin_corner/19-01-689.pdf, accessed on March 9, 2013.

44. The quote appears in Maraniss, *When Pride Still Mattered*, 103; and Gems, *For Pride, Profit, and Patriarchy*, 80.

45. Bill Gorman, "No Surprise: 64% of Americans Watch NFL Football; 73% of Men, 55% of Women," TV by the Numbers, October 14, 2011, tvbythenumbers.zap2it.com/2011/10/14/no-surprise-64-americans-watch-nfl-football-73-of-men-55-of-women/107308/, accessed on March 9, 2013; Frank Newport, "Mississippi Maintains Hold as Most Religious U.S. State," Gallup, February 13, 2013, http://www.gallup.com/poll/160415/mississippi-maintains-hold-religious-state.aspx, accessed on March 9, 2013.

46. Dejan Kovacevic, "Not So Super on Global Stage," TribLive, January 31, 2013, http://triblive.com/sports/dejankovacevic/dejancolumns/3378911-74/super-bowl-million#axzz2JqZNM5kD, accessed on March 9, 2013.

47. Gems, *For Pride, Profit, and Patriarchy*, 7.

CHAPTER 10

1. John M. Carroll, *Red Grange and the Rise of Modern Football* (Urbana: University of Illinois Press, 1999), 208.
2. Frederick Exley, *A Fan's Notes* (1968; repr., New York: Vintage Books, 1988), 30.
3. Ibid., 70.
4. Ibid., 20.
5. Ibid., 343.
6. Ibid., 8.
7. "America's Sport—a Majority of Americans Watch NFL Football," Harris Interactive, October 14, 2011, http://www.harrisinteractive. com/vault/HI-Harris-Poll-Adweek-Football-2011-10-14.pdf, accessed on March 20, 2013.
8. Patrick Hruby, "Game Over," Sports on Earth, August 29, 2012, http://www.sportsonearth.com/article/37580666, accessed on March 5, 2013.
9. Kevin Lincoln, "Is Watching Football Unethical?" BuzzFeed, May 3, 2012, http://www.buzzfeed.com/ktlincoln/is-watching-football-ethical, accessed on March 6, 2013.
10. Charles P. Pierce, "American Ghouls," Grantland, April 30, 2012, http://www.grantland.com/story/_/id/7871507/metta-world-peace-ray-easterling-our-appetite-sanctioned-violence, accessed on March 5, 2013.
11. Exley, *A Fan's Notes*, 337.
12. Ibid., 347.
13. Phone interview of Curtis Worrell on March 5, 2013.
14. Frederick O. Mueller and Robert C. Cantu, *Football Fatalities and Catastrophic Injuries, 1931–2008* (Durham: Carolina Academic Press, 2011), 50.
15. Quoted in John Underwood, *The Death of an American Game: The Crisis in Football* (Boston: Little Brown, 1979), 20.
16. Quoted in ibid., 180.
17. Quoted in ibid., 16.

18. John Sayle Watterson, *College Football: History, Spectacle, Controversy* (Baltimore: Johns Hopkins University Press, 2000), 36–38; Mark F. Bernstein, *Football: The Ivy League Origins of an American Obsession* (Philadelphia: University of Pennsylvania Press, 2001), 58–59; "Football's Origin at Alabama," *Crimson Tide*, http://www.rolltide.com/trads/football-origin.html, accessed on April 6, 2013.

19. "Von Gammon," GeorgiaInfo, http://georgiainfo.galileo.usg.edu/vongammon.htm, accessed on March 13, 2013.

20. "No More Football for New York Boys," *New York Times*, November 19, 1909, 1; Bernstein, *Football*, 89.

21. Letter from John Singleton Mosby to Eppa Hunton, November 18, 1909, see the University of Virginia Library website, http://explore.lib.virginia.edu/exhibits/show/hoos/athletics/archer-christian, accessed on March 19, 2013.

22. Harry S. Ashmore, *Unseasonable Truths: The Life of Robert Maynard Hutchins* (Boston: Little Brown, 1989), 200–2; William H. McNeill, *Hutchins' University: A Memoir of the University of Chicago, 1929–1950* (Chicago: University of Chicago Press, 1991), 95–99.

23. Jim Wyatt, "Tennessee Titans' Chris Johnson among Critics of New NFL Rule," *Tennessean*, March 20, 2013, http://www.tennessean.com/article/20130320/SPORTS01/303200157/Tennessee-Titans-Chris-Johnson-among-critics-new-NFL-rule, accessed on April 5, 2013; Chris Fuhrmeister, "Arian Foster 'Not a Fan' of NFL Rule Changes," SB Nation, March 25, 2013, http://www.sbnation.com/2013/3/25/4145852/arian-foster-discussion-nfl-rule-changes, accessed on April 5, 2013; "Ray Rice: I Will Still Lower My Helmet into Defender Despite Rule Change," CBS, April 2, 2013, http://baltimore.cbslocal.com/2013/04/02/ray-rice-i-will-still-lower-my-helmet-into-defender-despite-rule-change/, accessed on April 5, 2013; James Pennington, "NFL Rule Changes: Matt Forte among

Backs Who Dislike the Change," SB Nation, March 17, 2013, http://www.sbnation.com/nfl/2013/3/17/4115706/2013-nfl-rule-changes-matt-forte, accessed on April 5, 2013.

24. Quoted in Pennington, "NFL Rule Changes: Matt Forte among Backs Who Dislike the Change," accessed on April 5, 2013.

25. Frederick O. Mueller and Bob Colgate, "Annual Survey of Football Injury Research, 1931–2012," American Football Coaches Association, National Collegiate Athletic Association, and National Federation of State High School Associations, February 2013, 19–20.

26. Robert Cantu and Mark Hyman, *Concussions and Our Kids: America's Leading Expert on How to Protect Young Athletes and Keep Sports Safe* (Boston: Houghton Mifflin Harcourt, 2012), 40, 46; Joseph Hall, "Body Checking Should Be Banned from Minor Hockey to Cut Concussions: Neurosurgeon," *The Toronto Star*, December 3, 2012, http://www.thestar.com/sports/2012/12/03/body_checking_should_be_banned_from_minor_hockey_to_cut_concussions_neurosurgeon.html, accessed on March 12, 2013; Liz Robbins, "Richardson's Accident Reignites Ski Helmet Debate," *New York Times*, March 18, 2009, http://thelede.blogs.nytimes.com/2009/03/18/richardsons-accident-reignites-ski-helmet-debate/, accessed on March 12, 2013; Cathy Bussewitz, "California Considers Mandatory Ski Helmet Laws," *USA Today*, March 15, 2010, http://usatoday30.usatoday.com/travel/destinations/ski/2010-03-15-california-ski-helmet-laws_N.htm, accessed on March 12, 2013.

27. Walter Camp, *American Football: New and Enlarged Edition* (New York: Harper & Brothers, 1894), 8.

28. Theodore Roosevelt, "The Man with the Muck Rake," PBS, April 15, 1906, http://www.pbs.org/wgbh/americanexperience/features/primary-resources/tr-muckrake/, accessed on March 21, 2013.

29. Theodore Roosevelt, "The Man in the Arena," TheodoreRoosevelt.com, April 23, 1910, http://www.theodore-roosevelt.com/images/research/speeches/maninthearena.pdf, accessed on March 21, 2013.

30. John J. Miller, *The Big Scrum: How Teddy Roosevelt Saved Football* (New York: Harper Collins, 2011), 1–12.

31. Exley, *A Fan's Notes*, 205.

32. H. Paul Jeffers, *Theodore Roosevelt Jr.: The Life of a War Hero* (Novato, CA: Presidio Press, 2002), 20; Edward J. Renehan, *The Lion's Pride: Theodore Roosevelt and His Family in Peace and War* (New York: Oxford University Press, 1998), 67.

33. Letter from Theodore Roosevelt to Endicott Peabody, January 4, 1902 (Theodore Roosevelt Papers, Library of Congress, Box 328).

34. Letter from Theodore Roosevelt to Theodore Roosevelt Jr., October 31, 1902 (Theodore Roosevelt Jr. Papers, Library of Congress, Box 7).

35. Renehan, *The Lion's Pride*, 200, 204–6, 234.

36. Ibid., 236.

37. Jeffers, *Theodore Roosevelt Jr.*, 241–53; Renehan, *The Lion's Pride*, 237–40.

38. "Teddy Roosevelt Jr. Is Hurt on Football Field," *Salt Lake City Herald*, October 15, 1905, 4.

39. Letter from Theodore Roosevelt to Theodore Roosevelt Jr., October 4, 1903 (Theodore Roosevelt Jr. Papers, Library of Congress, Box 7).

40. C. S. Lewis, *The Abolition of Man: How Education Develops Man's Sense of Morality* (1943; repr., New York: MacMillan, 1986), 35.

41. Mueller and Colgate, "Annual Survey of Football Injury Research, 1931–2012," 19–20.

42. "Traffic Safety Facts: Bicyclists and Other Cyclists," NHTSA, Washington, D.C., June 2012, 1; Teresa Waters, "2011 Skateboarding Fatalities," Skaters for Public Skateparks, January 30, 2012, http://www.skatepark.org/park-development/2012/01/2011-skateboarding-fatalities/#activity, accessed on January 19, 2013; "Facts about Skiing/Snowboarding Safety," National Ski Areas Association, October 1, 2012, http://www.nsaa.org/media/68045/NSAA-Facts-About-Skiing-Snowboarding-Safety-10-1-12.pdf, accessed on January 16, 2013.

43. Sherry L. Baron et al., "Body Mass Index, Playing Position, Race, and the Cardiovascular Mortality of Retired Professional Football Players," *American Journal of Cardiology*, March 15, 2012, 891.

44. David R. Weir, James S. Jackson, and Amanda Sonnega, "National Football League Player Care Foundation: Study of Retired NFL Players," University of Michigan Institute for Social Research, September 10, 2009, 1–37. The success of football players predates million-dollar salaries and even the NFL. A historian who pulled a sample of players from the 1930s and 1950s found that slightly more than half of NFL players from the former decade, and slightly less than half from the latter one, landed white-collar professional jobs after their athletic careers had ended. Robert W. Peterson, *Pigskin: The Early Years of Pro Football* (New York: Oxford University Press, 1997), 211–12. For an anecdotal take on the achievements of early-era college players, see Parke H. Davis, *Football: The American Intercollegiate Game* (New York: Charles Scribner's Sons, 1911), 118.

45. Exley, *A Fan's Notes*, 357.

INDEX